Lopsided Schools

Case Method Briefings

Gerard Giordano

ROWMAN & LITTLEFIELD EDUCATION
A division of
ROWMAN & LITTLEFIELD PUBLISHERS, INC.
Lanham • New York • Toronto • Plymouth, UK

Published by Rowman & Littlefield Education
A division of Rowman & Littlefield Publishers, Inc.
A wholly owned subsidiary of The Rowman & Littlefield Publishing Group, Inc.
4501 Forbes Boulevard, Suite 200, Lanham, Maryland 20706
http://www.rowmaneducation.com

Estover Road, Plymouth PL6 7PY, United Kingdom

British Library Cataloguing in Publication Information Available

Library of Congress Cataloging-in-Publication Data

Giordano, Gerard.
Lopsided schools : case method briefings / Gerard Giordano.
p. cm.
Includes bibliographical references.
ISBN 978-1-60709-786-0 (cloth : alk. paper)—ISBN 978-1-60709-787-7 (pbk. : alk. paper)—ISBN 978-1-60709-788-4 (electronic)
1. Case method. 2. Education—United States. I. Title.
LB1029.C37G57 2010
371.39—dc22
2010032475

∞™ The paper used in this publication meets the minimum requirements of American National Standard for Information Sciences—Permanence of Paper for Printed Library Materials, ANSI/NISO Z39.48-1992.

Printed in the United States of America

This book, which is based on classroom dialogues with my students, is dedicated to them.

Contents

Tables

Preface: Lopsided Schools

The mast of a lopsided ship . . . leans over.

—"Modern Methods in Navigation," 1876

Critics suspected that problems had made the schools lopsided. They initially looked for causes in buildings, playgrounds, and equipment. However, they eventually examined teaching, textbooks, curricula, testing, organizational policies, budgets, auxiliary personnel, principals, instructors, and even students.

Although they were upset by problems, the critics were upset with educators for tolerating them. Some of them alleged that the educators could not solve the problems because they were unaware of their genuine causes. They accused them of failing to recognize the impact of cerebral dominance, kinesthetic learning activities, or prowess at scanning documents.

In addition to offering explanations for school problems, the critics offered advice. Some of them insisted that students trace words in the air; others insisted that they use computers to communicate. They threatened those who did not comply.

Critics disconcerted educators when they identified problems, proposed unusual explanations, gave controversial advice, or threatened to punish them. They also disconcerted them with questions.

Should children learn speed reading? Should they concentrate on vocational activities? Should principals train their successors? Should superintendents motivate teachers with bonuses? Should employers hire the graduates with the highest scores on standardized tests? Should politicians assume greater responsibility for schooling? Should journalists investigate whether or not schools were lopsided?

This book uses the case method to examine school critics. It looks at them from World War I to the present. It highlights the problems that they identified, the solutions that they proposed, the threats that they made, and the changes that they provoked.

Acknowledgment

This book is part of a series that was conceived by my remarkable editor, Tom Koerner.

Introduction: Are Philosophy, Zen, Cycles, and the Case Method Related?

> All this time [that my son has been sitting behind me on my motorcycle] he's been staring into my back.
>
> —Robert Pirsig, 1974

Robert Pirsig studied ancient Greek philosophy at the University of Chicago. He also studied Zen philosophy at Banaras Hindu University. Guided by the professors at these institutions, he contemplated problems posed by Western and Eastern intellectuals.

Pirsig examined the origin of perception, the characteristics of ethical behavior, and the meaning of human endeavor. However, he was particularly fascinated by another problem—the nature of quality. He made this topic the focal point of his intellectual and emotional life.

ZEN AND THE ART OF MOTORCYCLE MAINTENANCE

Pirsig wrote a peculiar book during the early 1970s. The book was distinctive because of its title, *Zen and the Art of Motorcycle Maintenance: An Inquiry into Values*. However, it had other distinctive features (Pirsig, 1974).

Pirsig's book stood out because of the topics that it covered. It recapitulated his philosophical speculations. It also recounted his unsettling relationship with a didactic professor, his nervous breakdown, and his commitment in a mental health facility.

Editors at over one hundred publishing houses reviewed and rejected Pirsig's manuscript. They predicted that readers would have little interest in his autobiography. They added that they would have even less interest in his philosophical ruminations.

A contrarian editor finally agreed to publish the book. He told Pirsig that he would pay him three thousand dollars in advance. He added that he should not expect additional royalties.

After the book was published, it created a sensation. It sold over four million copies.

THE MESSAGE

Readers relished Pirsig's book. They were impressed by the candid and sensitive manner in which it recounted his nervous breakdown and eventual recovery.

The editors who had rejected it were sure that Pirsig had made a rhetorical error by combining philosophical discourse with autobiography. However, readers judged that the philosophical speculations enriched the personal recollections.

Within the philosophical passages, Pirsig noted his early conviction that a chasm separated the ancient Greek and Zen philosophers. He had been confident that this chasm could not be bridged. However, he later changed his opinion.

THE METAPHOR

Pirsig described his thoughts during a motorcycle trip. He was upset because he had abandoned his university studies; he worried that he might never reach the stage of enlightenment that he would have achieved had he completed them.

Pirsig also described the ways in which he identified, prioritized, and solved maintenance problems on the trip. He gradually realized that he could use these quotidian tasks to acquire the wisdom that he would have gained by listening to philosophy professors.

Pirsig was excited by his life-altering insight. Meanwhile, his son, who had been sharing his vehicle, was exasperated and unhappy. During a roadside stop, the son insisted that they end their trip.

After the argument had passed, the son reconciled with his father. Although he climbed back onto the motorcycle and continued the journey, he did something unexpected: he removed his helmet and stood up on the rear pegs.

Ignoring the protestations of his father, the son rode helmetless and upright. After a while, he leaned forward and explained that this new position enabled him for the first time to taste the air and see the road.

THE CASE METHOD

Pirsig did not supply readers with answers; he instead indicated how they could locate them. He advised them that they could locate them with the help of Western guides, with the assistance of Eastern guides, or without the assistance of any guides.

Although the case method does not duplicate the advice in *Zen and the Art of Motorcycle Maintenance*, it does have similarities. It encourages persons to take off their safety helmets, rise above their drivers, feel the wind, and enjoy unobstructed panoramas.

1

Is the Case Method Unique?

> We construct a narrative for ourselves, and that's the thread that we follow from one day to the next.
>
> —Paul Auster, 2005

The case method can be applied to the schools; it can be used to analyze the narratives that educators and their critics created about them.

INVESTIGATING COLLEGE STUDENTS

Researchers wished to gather information about students. However, they had to take preliminary steps. For example, they had to designate the students on whom they would focus.

The researchers who were professors realized that the college students on their campuses would be convenient research subjects. Nonetheless, they still had to decide whether they would gather information about them from records, interviews, written surveys, or other sources.

Researchers had to make still more decisions. They had to decide how to organize their information. Some of them turned to their institutions to solve this problem. They used structured college experiences as guides for sorting information. They created guides from the sciences, the liberal arts, the creative arts, religion, careers, ethics, and civics (Astin, 1977, 1993; Levine & Cureton, 1998; Hu, Scheuch, Schwartz, Gayles, & Li, 2008; Pascarella & Terenzini, 1991).

Journalists Become Opponents

Researchers were exhilarated when they designed, conducted, and compiled investigations about college students. However, they became upset after they realized that few persons shared their excitement. They were especially annoyed at journalists.

Although the journalists wanted information, they showed little interest in what the researchers offered them. They explained that it simply was not stimulating.

The journalists recommended that researchers change their investigative techniques. They proposed that they use different sorts of questions; they suggested that they ask students about the respective amounts of time that they spent studying and partying.

The journalists had another suggestion. They recommended that the researchers gather information about the students who left their campuses each spring, journeyed to warm beaches, consumed alcohol, and created public disturbances (Deas & Clark, 2009; Franek, 2008; Mattila, Apostolopoulos, Sonmez, Yu, & Sasidharan, 2001).

Unable to get the information that they wanted from educational researchers, the journalists gathered it themselves. Because their perspectives diverged from those of the researchers, the substance of their reports differed. Even their writing styles differed.

More Opponents

Some academicians agreed with the journalists who ignored or challenged educational researchers. They accused the researchers of gathering ambiguous information and then interjecting their own biases into it.

Academic opponents gave advice about ways that educational researchers could eliminate biases. They suggested that they allow students to identify important issues and then make these into the bases for survey and interview questions (Grigsby, 2009; Miller, 2005; Nathan, 2005).

The opponents even illustrated the procedures that they had in mind. They personally asked students about the ways in which college experiences influenced their political values. They asked them whether they had opportunities to develop conservative or liberal views (Bérubé, 2006; Giroux, 2007; Horowitz, 2007; O'Neil, 2008; Shapiro, 2004).

The opponents had more advice for the educational researchers. Some of them suggested that they examine the ways in which college experiences influenced minority groups. They again demonstrated how to acquire information. They personally gathered it from minority students at colleges that had distinct sizes, locations, methods of funding, and academic programs (Moore, 2006; Renn, 2004).

Some opponents examined the ways in which minority students influenced other students on college campuses. They studied the influence of students from racial and ethnic minority groups; they also studied the influence of lesbian, gay, bisexual, and transgender students (Baez, Howd, & Pepper, 2007; Dilley, 2002; Sanlo, Rankin, & Schoenberg, 2002; Shand-Tucci, 2003).

Opponents of tradition-minded researchers asked college students about topics that they felt had been overlooked. They asked them about alcohol, drugs, classmates, friends, sexual partners, roommates, fraternity brothers, sorority sisters, and teammates (Bogle, 2008; DeSantis, 2007; Freitas, 2008; Nuwer, 1999; Seaman, 2005). They even asked them about emotional issues such as loneliness and fear of failure (Kadison & DiGeronimo, 2004; Vye, Scholljegerdes, & Welch, 2007).

Searching for Allies

Tradition-minded researchers were disappointed when opponents rejected, belittled, or ignored their work. Although they were accused of designing inconclusive studies, they made the same accusation against their opponents.

Tradition-minded researchers were unable to change the minds of their opponents. Wishing to strengthen their cases, they tried to persuade other groups to agree with them.

Their opponents were in the same predicament as the tradition-minded researchers. Like them, they searched for allies.

Entrepreneurs

Tradition-minded researchers and their opponents identified problems, provided advice about how to resolve them, and searched for allies. In addition to competing against each other, they competed against a third group—entrepreneurs.

Entrepreneurs used anecdotal data to gather information about college students. They then circulated it through workshops, books, and electronic media.

The entrepreneurs claimed that they had discovered solutions to the problems that college students faced. Their solutions frequently duplicated those that they already had devised for other groups.

Covey (1989) was one of the entrepreneurs who disclosed information about business leaders. He noted that they were proactive, purposeful, organized, and cooperative. He added that they promoted communication, synergy, and personal regeneration. He assured readers, viewers, and workshop participants that these seven traits not only described highly successful business leaders but also accounted for their achievements.

Inspired by the best-selling advice about business leaders, entrepreneurs resolved that they would give comparable advice about college students. They directed it at professors and university administrators (Benz, 2006; Flippo & Caverly, 2000; Martínez-Alemán & Wartman, 2008; McWhorter, 2007). They also directed it at parents (Borden, Burlinson, & Kearns, 1995; Carr, 2009; Raskin, 2006; Spohn, 2008; Woodacre & Bane, 2006).

The entrepreneurs aimed most of their advice at students. They wrote books to help with mathematics, science, English, and social studies. They tried to help them succeed in programs for nurses, psychologists, and athletes. They even designed books to help them become art historians, midwives, and cosmetologists (Freeman, 2006; Kirk, 2002; Latto & Latto, 2009; Mason-Whitehead & Mason, 2003; Scullion & Guest, 2007).

Some of the entrepreneurs realized that they might be able to help students master virtually any type of textbook, learning assignment, or assessment problem. They redrafted their specialized manuals to help students with a wide range of problems (Burns & Sinfield, 2008; Flippo & Caverly, 2000; Hansen & Hansen, 2008).

Entrepreneurs prepared products to help undergraduate students use textbooks, retain information, and take exams. After they noticed that many of them were insecure about the social and emotional issues associated with college life, they prepared materials on these topics as well (Carter, Bishop, & Kravits, 2006; Hamachek, 2007; Miller & Buchanan, 2009; Natavi Guides Company, 2005; Paulsen, 2005; Westheimer & Lehu, 2000).

Some entrepreneurs noted that students were concerned about graduate school. They adapted their undergraduate manuals for this audience (Becker, 2004; Gosling & Noordam, 2006; Jerrard & Jerrard, 1998; Johnson & Huwe, 2003; Wisker, 2008). They also adapted them for students who were fretting about specialized graduate programs, such as those in law (Burkhart & Stein, 2008; Frank, 1997; Hartwig, 2009; Houchin, 2009; Housman, 2001; Miller & Bissell, 2006; Whitebread, 1995).

Although some entrepreneurs targeted students who were enrolled in distinctive programs, others targeted those with distinctive identities. As examples, they aimed materials at students who were African American or who were lesbian, gay, bisexual, or transgender (Baez, Howd, & Pepper, 2007; Farmer, 2003; Fertman, 2009; Maranci, 2005).

Entrepreneurs developed resources for college students with peculiar learning problems. They designed them for individuals with dyslexia, attention deficit hyperactivity disorder, Asperger's syndrome, and multiple types of learning disabilities (Du Pré, Miles, & Gilroy, 2008; Hargreaves, 2008; Harpur, Lawlor, & Fitzgerald, 2004; Moody, 2007; Nadeau, 2006; Olivier & Bowler, 1996; Simpson & Spencer, 2009).

INVESTIGATING ELEMENTARY SCHOOL STUDENTS

Researchers who investigated college students were unsure about the procedure that they should follow; they needed templates to guide them. They decided to base their templates on university conventions. However, they had to defend the templates against opponents.

Opponents were concerned about bias. They suspected that the perceptions of researchers were very different from those of students. They urged them to reduce biases by interacting with students.

Like the educational researchers who investigated college students, those who investigated elementary schools had to identify the students from whom to collect information, the types of information to collect, the ways to analyze it, and the ways to report it. They needed templates to guide them.

Researchers turned to the elementary schools. They noted that the personnel in them relied on common instructional and assessment techniques. They decided that they could use these techniques as templates.

The researchers were particularly interested in standardized testing. In fact, they made it the foundation for their investigations. However, they had to justify this choice to opponents (Giordano, 2005).

Opponents

Some persons disapproved of standardized tests because they feared that they were invalid. One of the reasons they had this worry was that many of the questions on them did not resemble classroom learning tasks.

Persons also disapproved of standardized tests because they contained questions that were not sensitive to the learning styles and background experiences of minority students. They worried that the tests would penalize them (Giordano, 2005).

Opponents of standardized tests recommended that researchers find alternative techniques for assessing students. They urged them to collaborate with educators, who could help them identify techniques that were relevant to the learning within students' classrooms.

Some opponents suggested that teachers record the amounts of time that students spent reading books, solving mathematical problems, engaging in social studies, or executing scientific investigations. Others proposed that they gather samples of students' academic activities, organize them into portfolios, and substitute the portfolios for standardized tests (Giordano, 2005).

Opponents were aware that persons valued standardized tests because of their uniformity. They therefore identified alternative tasks that all of the students in a school, district, or state could employ. For example, they suggested that they respond to uniform surveys about attitudes toward school.

Searching for Allies

The researchers who viewed elementary school students from traditional academic perspectives and those who viewed them from nontraditional perspectives disagreed about numerous issues. They argued more vehemently after politicians entered the ruckus.

Politicians wanted to use students' scores on standardized tests to identify exemplary school staffs. Some of them wanted to reward them with greater control over curricula and budgets. Others proposed to reward them with job security, promotions, raises, and bonuses (Giordano, 2009).

The supporters and the opponents of standardized tests tried to enlist allies. They made appeals to persons who worked directly in the schools: they reached out to teachers, school administrators, instructional specialists, psychologists, nurses, and auxiliary personnel. They also appealed to persons who worked closely with the schools: they reached out to school board members, directors of teachers' unions, and professors of education.

The supporters and the opponents reached out to still more groups: they tried to enlist the support of journalists, employers, military leaders, medical personnel, court officials, police officers, social workers, mental health personnel, and unionized workers in noneducational fields (Giordano, 2009).

Entrepreneurs

When educational researchers investigated students in the elementary schools, they needed a template to guide them. One group relied on standardized testing. However, another group preferred a different template. Although these groups tried to design corroborative studies, they were only somewhat effective.

The entrepreneurs who managed the billion-dollar standardized testing industry also had advice about schools. They gave their advice directly to politicians; they urged them to mandate extensive standardized testing (Giordano, 2005).

The entrepreneurs also had opinions about learning materials. The amount of materials that they published is indicated by sales. Textbooks were the most profitable materials for the entrepreneurs. They generated considerable income for centuries; they still produce significant income for them today (Giordano, 2003).

Many types of teaching materials that were popular during earlier eras still remain profitable. For example, educational flash cards retain a robust market (Educational Flash Cards, 2009; Flashcard Exchange, 2009; Memorization Software Reviewed, 2009).

The entrepreneurs were aware that educators disagreed about learning materials. They counseled the politicians to resolve these disputes. They suggested that they force educators to use textbooks and even mandate the books that they could adopt (Giordano, 2003).

PROFESSORS USE THE CASE METHOD

Researchers, critics, and entrepreneurs relied on templates to examine the schools. These templates were similar to narratives: they specified characters, situations, plots, and morals. The narratives can be examined with the case method.

Professors in education experimented with the case method. They hoped that it would enable learners to solve problems within and beyond their college classrooms. They were inspired by their colleagues in law and business (Giordano, 2009, 2010).

Law

When law professors used the case method, they asked their students to read decisions from judges. They then required them to orally analyze the decisions during class sessions.

The law professors changed some of the ways in which they historically had conducted classes. However, they retained other practices. For example, they still required all of their students to complete comprehensive written exams. Furthermore, they made these exams the sole basis for their grades.

Business

When business professors began to use the case method, they did not duplicate all of the law school procedures. For example, they lacked materials that were comparable to judicial decisions. Therefore, they personally wrote synopses of business incidents.

The business professors used the synopses that they had written as the bases for dialogues. However, they made several other key changes in their classrooms. They formed students into teams, encouraged them to study cooperatively, and evaluated them on the basis of their group efforts.

Education

Professors in education were aware that their colleagues in law and business were pleased with the case method. However, they noted that the two groups were using distinct learning and assessment procedures. Before they could use it with their own students, they had to decide which group to follow.

The educators observed that the law professors required students to compete against each other. They contrasted them with the business professors, who encouraged students to collaborate. Because they were preparing students for jobs that were more like those in business than in law, they selected the business approach (Giordano, 2010).

ANALYZING THE ADVICE OF RESEARCHERS, CRITICS, AND ENTREPRENEURS

This book highlights information from educators and their critics. If you are reading it alone, use the activities in it to simulate the discussions that you would experience within case-based classes. If you are reading it with others, use them as the bases for actual discussions.

Activity 1.1

You might wish to analyze the ways in which members of the public responded to information about college students. You could rely on Table 1.1.

Table 1.1 lists nine types of information: that about curriculum, politics, race, sexual orientation, social organizations, sex, alcohol, fear of failure, and concern about loneliness.

Complete the table by indicating the significance that members of the general public assigned to each type of information. You can use symbols.

Use the symbol – if they viewed it as insignificant. Use the symbol ± if they displayed a mixed response to it; use the symbol + if they viewed it as significant.

Table 1.1. The Public Responds to Educational Information

Information	*Response to**	*Explanation*
Curriculum		
Politics		
Race		
Sexual Orientation		
Social Organizations		
Sex		
Alcohol		
Fear of Failure		
Loneliness		

* − Insignificant
± Mixed
+ Significant

Finally, provide explanations for your responses. You can base your responses on information from this chapter, the materials discussed within it, or other sources.

Activity 1.2

You might wish to examine the ways in which parents responded to information about college students. You could rely on Table 1.2.

Table 1.2 lists six types of information: that about curriculum, politics, society, sex, drugs/alcohol, and emotions.

Complete the table by indicating the significance that parents of college students assigned to each type of information. You can rely on symbols.

Use the symbol − if they viewed it as insignificant. Use the symbol ± if they displayed a mixed response to it; use the symbol + if they viewed it as significant. Finally, provide explanations for the symbols that you selected.

Table 1.2. Parents Respond to Educational Information

Information	*Response to**	*Explanation*
Curriculum		
Politics		
Society		
Sex		
Drugs/Alcohol		
Emotions		

* − Insignificant
± Mixed
+ Significant

Activity 1.3

You could analyze the ways in which groups responded to information about college students. You could rely on Table 1.3.

Table 1.3 lists six groups: members of the general public, college students, university administrators, researchers from academic fields other than education, journalists, and entrepreneurs.

This table identifies two types of information: that gathered by persons with traditional views of college students and that gathered by those with nontraditional views.

Complete this table by indicating the ways in which groups responded to information. You can use symbols.

Use the symbol − if they viewed it as insignificant. Use the symbol ± if they displayed a mixed response to it; use the symbol + if they

Table 1.3. Responses to Two Types of Educational Information

	*Response to**		
Group	*Traditional*	*Nontraditional*	*Explanation*
Public			
Students			
University Administrators			
Noneducation Researchers			
Journalists			
Entrepreneurs			

* − Insignificant
± Mixed
\+ Significant

viewed it as significant. Finally, explain the bases for the symbols that you selected.

Activity 1.4

You could analyze the ways in which groups responded to information about students in the elementary schools. You could rely on Table 1.4.

Table 1.4 lists five groups: teachers, principals, parents, journalists, and politicians. It also identifies two types of information: that gathered with standardized tests and that gathered without them.

Complete this table by indicating the ways in which groups responded to each type of information. You can use symbols.

Use the symbol − if they viewed information as insignificant. Use the symbol ± if they displayed a mixed response to it; use the symbol + if they viewed it as significant. Finally, provide explanations for the symbols that you selected.

Table 1.4. Responses to Two Types of Educational Information

	*Response to**		
Group	*Standardized Tests*	*Alternative Tests*	*Explanation*
Teachers			
Principals			
Parents			
Journalists			
Politicians			

* − Insignificant
± Mixed
+ Significant

Table 1.5. Responses to Advice about Standardized Tests

	*Response to**			
Group	*Proponents*	*Opponents*	*Entrepreneurs*	*Explanation*
Teachers				
Principals				
Parents				
Journalists				
Politicians				

* − Negative
± Mixed
+ Positive

Activity 1.5

You might wish to examine the ways in which groups responded to advice about standardized tests. You could rely on Table 1.5.

Table 1.5 lists five groups: teachers, principals, parents, journalists, and politicians. It also identifies advice from three sources: proponents of standardized tests, opponents of standardized tests, and entrepreneurs.

Complete this table by indicating the ways in which groups responded to advice from each source. You can rely on symbols.

Use the symbol − if they had a negative response. Use the symbol ± if they displayed a mixed response; use the symbol + if they displayed a positive response. Finally, provide explanations for the symbols that you selected.

SUMMARY

The case method can be applied to the schools. It can be used to examine information from both proponents and critics.

2

Do Teachers and Taxi Drivers Face Similar Problems?

> Twelve hours of work and I still can't sleep . . . days go on and on . . . they don't end.
>
> —Robert De Niro, as Travis Bickle in the film *Taxi Driver*, 1976 (quoted by Schrader, 1990)

Researchers were struck by the intense problems that some workers faced. They asked whether or not they arose from occupational, personal, or incidental circumstances. They asked the same questions about educators' problems.

TAXI DRIVERS AND THEIR PROBLEMS

Many taxi drivers had stark, lonely, and stressful careers. They attracted the attention of researchers, who wondered why some of them were more successful than others.

Researchers suspected that successful taxi drivers had special characteristics. To verify this hunch, they looked for obvious characteristics. Superior maneuvering skill was an obviously helpful trait; it enabled divers to steer clear of traffic and avoid collisions. Physical stamina was another obviously helpful trait; it enabled them to work longer hours and earn more fares.

In addition to discerning traits that were obviously helpful, researchers distinguished those that were relatively subtle. For example, interpersonal aptitude enabled drivers to gain tips. The ability to recognize threatening situations and the resourcefulness to escape from them also had benefits (Chinn, 2008; Gambetta & Hamill, 2005; Machin & De Souza, 2004; Peltzer & Renner, 2003).

Identifying Problems

Researchers noted that some taxi drivers could deal with situations that others could not handle. Nonetheless, they suspected that this occupation created unusual stress for all drivers. They tried to confirm their suspicion.

Some of the researchers gathered objective data. They searched employment records for quantifiable information about ailments, physical injuries, and accidents (Chen, Chang, Chang, & Christiani, 2005).

Some researchers gathered less objective types of information with surveys and interviews. Even though they personally had confidence in this information, they worried when opponents challenged its reliability and validity. Although they conceded that their information was less reliable and valid than that about injuries and accidents, they insisted that it still enabled them to form invaluable insights.

Some researchers decided that they would use both physical and behavioral types of information. They explained that this joint approach enabled them to authenticate the driver-reported information with objective information (Koichi, Masaharu, Tomoko, Shoji, & Keizo, 2000).

A group of investigators wanted to extend their investigations into a third dimension—psychological stress. They gathered information by asking drivers about the situations or routines that produced fatigue, anxiety, and tension. They then complemented it with additional information about the ways in which they dealt with their stress (Berraho et al., 2006; Dalziel & Job, 1997).

Researchers noted that taxi drivers had particular difficulty when problems were caused by factors that they could not control. They provided multiple examples: bad weather, heavy traffic, reckless motorists, construction projects, unreliable vehicles, inadequate salaries, and proximity to crime (Essenberg, 2003; Nakano et al., 1998; Peltzer, 2003).

Proposing Solutions

Researchers observed that taxi drivers regularly experienced stress. They were curious about the reason that some of them handled it well. They investigated key personality traits, such as optimistic dispositions (Dalziel & Job, 1997).

Researchers concluded that optimistic dispositions were helpful to drivers. However, they recognized that these dispositions were difficult to duplicate. They continued to look for traits that were not only helpful but also that other drivers could copy. For example, they looked at superstitions and ritualistic practices (Peltzer & Renner, 2003).

Researchers noted that stress and physical problems were interrelated. They turned their attention to solutions that would affect both types of problems.

Researchers noted that resistance to some types of physical disabilities, such as lower back ailments, was affected by the drivers' general health. However, it also was affected by medication, exercise, and adaptive equipment. They encouraged all drivers to use these interventions.

Even though they offered advice to taxi drivers, researchers conceded that it would be only somewhat effective. They explained that the degree of effectiveness depended on the characteristics of the drivers, the situations with which they had to deal, and the numerous other factors that were difficult and sometimes impossible to control.

CLINICAL THERAPISTS AND THEIR PROBLEMS

During the 1960s, some citizens rebelled against America's foreign policies. Others rebelled against its social policies. Journalists reported extensively about the protesters. They were pleased when audiences exhibited interest.

Although audiences were interested about the antiestablishmentarian protesters who came from multiple occupations, they showed more interest in certain types of workers. They were intrigued by psychologists. In fact, they were particularly fascinated by one psychologist.

A Tarnished Therapist

Timothy Leary was a professor at an elite Ivy League university. He attracted attention when he investigated the effects of psychedelic drugs on individuals with behavioral problems. He attracted more attention when he announced that he personally was consuming drugs, observing their effects, and judging their properties.

Leary detected benefits from psychedelic drugs. He expounded euphorically about the wisdom and happiness that he discovered under their influence. He then encouraged other persons, including his students, to follow his example.

Although Leary inspired some persons, he antagonized others. His opponents were pleased when he was arrested by the police and fired by his university. Nonetheless, they were upset when the arrests and dismissal increased Leary's fame and influence (Greenfield, 2006; Leary, 1990).

The counterculture enthusiasts of the 1960s and 1970s were drawn to Leary. They realized that he was an eminent scholar who could provide intellectual legitimacy to a movement that their critics viewed as shallow and hedonistic.

Journalists followed Leary because he enticed readers, listeners, and viewers. However, they portrayed him as a figure in a morality tale. They warned rebellious intellectuals to change their behaviors if they did not wish to be treated in the same fashion.

Critics of Therapists

More and more members of the public disapproved of rebellious professors. They demanded that politicians punish them and the students who sympathized with them. They were pleased when the governor of a populous state listened to them.

Governor Ronald Reagan challenged and censured the liberal professors on the California campuses. He motivated President Richard Nixon, Vice President Spiro Agnew, and numerous other politicians to copy his rhetoric and maneuvers (Perlstein, 2001, 2008).

The audiences that watched television, listened to radio, and read news reports were excited when journalists reprimanded professors and intellectuals. They particularly were captivated when they scolded therapists. Even though some journalists focused exclusively on Leary, they implicitly called attention to his profession.

Journalists reasoned that psychologists, who were supposed to help individuals with emotional problems, could not discharge these responsibilities if they were incapacitated by their own emotional problems. Simultaneously rueful and gleeful, they hoped that their readers would share their schadenfreude.

Many of the journalists used anecdotes when they castigated therapists. However, some of them did rely on systematically gathered information. They used it when they referred to rates of divorce and suicide among psychologists, psychiatrists, and mental health counselors (Chemtob, Hamada, Bauer, Torigoe, & Kinney, 1988; Correlations of Divorce Rates, 2009; S. M. Phillips, 1999).

Therapists Defend Themselves

Therapists identified the emotional issues with which they dealt in their occupations as sources of stress. They identified the ethical conflicts that they faced as still another source (Bersoff, 2008; Koocher & Keith-Spiegel, 2008; Pryzwansky & Wendt, 1999; Sperry, 2007).

The therapists reminded critics of the multiple professional challenges that they faced. They pointed out that they had to deal with the isolation within their practices. They noted that this isolation reduced the likelihood that they would turn to other therapists when they required help with their own problems.

The therapists gave another reason that they did not respond to treatments from their peers. They noted that they already were intimately familiar with those treatments. This familiarity reduced the potency of the treatments (Skorina, Bissell, & De Soto, 1990).

Some therapists faced special challenges when they internalized their clients' problems. They maintained that they then began to exhibit symptoms similar to those of clients. They noted that many neophytes exhibited this sort of stress while learning to counsel patients (Worthless, Competent, Lemonde-Terrible, 2002).

Veteran as well as novice therapists exhibited the symptoms associated with stress. The experienced therapists revealed the symptoms when they were treating clients with complex psychological problems, such as postcombat traumatic stress disorders (Figley, 2002; D. M. Johnson, 2009; Rothschild & Rand, 2006; Stamm, 1999).

When journalists alleged that therapists faced difficult challenges, the therapists agreed with them. However, they did not agree when journalists portrayed them as emotionally and professionally unstable. They objected when reporters relied on anecdotal data; they even objected when they relied on systematically gathered data.

Therapists accused the journalists of partially analyzing data. They highlighted the selective manner in which they had analyzed the data about suicides. After they personally had analyzed this information, they drew different conclusions.

When the therapists analyzed data about the frequency of suicides among their peers, they noted that many instances pertained to earlier eras. They explained that most of the therapists during those eras were men. Because suicide rates had been historically high among men, the skewed suicide rate and gender ratio in their profession may have been related. They added that the suicide rate among psychologists declined as more women entered their ranks (S. M. Phillips, 1999).

The therapists disputed other data-based allegations about suicides. They disputed the allegation that high rates demonstrated that persons were emotionally unstable. They noted that the workers in many other fields showed high rates of suicide and had not faced these accusations.

The therapists contended that a correlation between a factor and a problem did not prove that the factor had caused the problem. Although emotional factors and occupational problems were correlated, so were numerous other factors. The therapists gave examples.

The therapists noted that a disproportionately high number of suicides transpired on Wednesdays. However, they did not believe that calendars were responsible. They pointed out that Wednesday was the day on which occupational stress spiked. They judged that this spike provided a better explanation for the suicides than the day of the week on which they occurred (Kposowa & D'Auria, 2009).

Therapists challenged contentions that their suicide rates were linked to their profession or to their emotional instability. They also challenged similar contentions about their divorce rates.

Therapists did not ascribe special significance to their high divorce rates. They pointed out that similarly high rates were discernible among police officers, lawyers, members of the military, and the workers in numerous other professions. They added that divorces correlated with many factors, including age, religion, race, poverty, region of residence, alcohol consumption, and even tobacco use (Correlations of Divorce Rates, 2009).

NINETEENTH-CENTURY EDUCATORS AND THEIR PROBLEMS

Nineteenth-century critics were aware that many students were failing in school. They worried that instruction and learning materials might be responsible. Some blamed the regimented classroom practices and materials that had become increasingly popular.

Other critics focused on personnel. They worried about the ways in which teachers and school administrators were being prepared, hired, and evaluated.

Still other critics focused on factors originating outside the schools. They worried about racism, ethnic conflict, religious discrimination, poverty, nutrition, alcoholism, drug addiction, sexual abuse, juvenile delinquency, psychological illness, neighborhood violence, and difficulty communicating in English (Giordano, 2009).

Responding to Problems

Educational critics worried about the problems in the schools. They deliberated about whether they were caused by scholastic conditions, incompetent personnel, or communitywide situations.

Some educators tried to ignore their critics; others agreed to cooperate. They tried to cooperate with those who were calling for new types of instruction.

Some critics called for alternatives to regimented instructional practices; they claimed that these practices harmed students directly and indirectly. They asserted that they harmed them directly when they prevented them from completing classroom assignments. They asserted that they harmed them indirectly when the teachers who relied on them became less sensitive to their students' needs.

Critics who opposed regimentation turned to the progressive education movement for guidance. The members of this movement decried uniform textbooks, standardized tests, lockstep drills, districtwide curricula, standards-geared budgeting, and factorylike approaches to school management.

Some of the critics who opposed regimentation turned to the special education movement. Like the progressive educators, the special educators were concerned about individual learners. They initially tried to help children who were blind, deaf, hard of hearing, crippled, or mentally retarded. They eventually tried to help learners with a much wider range of disabilities, including those with moderate and even mild disabilities (Giordano, 2007).

Critics who opposed regimentation tried to get support from parents. They attracted those who shared their philosophical sentiments. However, they also attracted those who were exasperated with tradition-minded educators who could not help children.

Early Reading Materials

The early teachers prized reading textbooks. However, not all of them had these specialized materials. Those who did not have textbooks relied on materials from their community. They used the Bible, the Tanakh, the Book of Mormon, collections of sermons, prayer books, novels, or children's books.

Some teachers taught reading with transcriptions of oral language. As they discussed issues with students, they wrote the conversations onto pads or chalkboards. They then taught them to read printed copies of their remarks.

Sometimes instructors elicited oral remarks from each child, wrote them out, reproduced them with rudimentary copying machines, and assembled the pages. They then used the homemade anthologies in the same ways that other teachers used professionally published textbooks (Giordano, 2000).

The early teachers matched reading materials with suitable types of reading instruction. For example, they paired basal readers, workbooks, and traditional classroom materials with analytical strategies.

The analytical strategies focused students' attention on the roots of words, spellings, phonic generalizations, and entries in dictionaries.

Some teachers paired magazines, novels, and nontraditional classroom materials with holistic strategies. These strategies directed students to word shapes, context clues, and supplementary pictorial information (Giordano, 2000).

Kinesthetic Reading Materials

Some early reading teachers tried to help students recognize verbs. After printing verbs on flash cards, they asked students to say their names and pantomime their meanings. They asked them to repeat the pantomimes when they encountered the words on activity sheets or in books. They hoped that these gross-motor movements would simplify and accelerate learning (Giordano, 2000).

Teachers also encouraged students to learn through fine-motor movements. They promoted fine-motor movements by requiring students to write words. If their students were incapable of writing, they would personally write words and encourage the students to trace them. They were sure that written repetition was more helpful than oral repetition (Giordano, 2000).

Special Educational Materials

Even though some early teachers were using alternative types of materials and instruction, they still anticipated that only academically talented students would learn to read. They expected struggling students to drop out of school, become laborers, and devote themselves to menial tasks.

During the late 1900s, teachers began to consider learners from a new perspective. Some of them changed their views after they observed special educators helping students with disabilities. The special educators employed distinctive instructional activities. As examples, they encouraged students to stand up, get away from their desks, and make rhythmic movements (Giordano, 2007).

The special educators wished to make academic tasks less abstract for their students; they relied heavily on learning materials that the students could touch and manipulate. If they were teaching students to read about cookies, they allowed them to mix, shape, bake, and eat them as well. Teachers in regular education classrooms were intrigued; they began to adapt these activities for their own students (Giordano, 2007).

TWENTIETH-CENTURY EDUCATORS AND THEIR PROBLEMS

At the beginning of the twentieth century, educators detected improvements in the schools. They had larger budgets, better facilities, more textbooks, current technology, professional training programs, and innovative instructional strategies.

Although they detected improvements, educators were aware that many students were not making progress. They continued to search for the causes of these problems and their solutions. They were motivated by professionalism and personal commitments to students; they also were motivated by the pressure from critics.

The Fernald Method

Twentieth-century teachers were impressed by the kinesthetic instructional activities of the special educators. They hoped that they could adapt these activities for their own classrooms. They especially hoped to adapt them for reading instruction.

Grace Fernald and Helen B. Keller were two of the teachers who experimented with kinesthetic reading activities. After designing distinctive drills, they tried them out during the first quarter of the twentieth century.

Fernald and Keller directed children to manually encode words by writing them down. However, they realized that writing was not always practicable. They therefore told the children that they also could pretend that they were writing words. They explained that they could use their fingers to form them in the air.

Fernald and Keller had an additional suggestion for students: they encouraged them to say words out loud as they were writing them in the air. However, they were aware that oral reading was sometimes impracticable. Therefore, they instructed them that they also could move their lips as if they were reading orally. They hoped that these drills would enable the students to recognize words when they later encountered them in books (Fernald, 1943; Fernald & Keller, 1936).

The parents of struggling readers were impressed by the new learning activities. They insisted that teachers use them. They were pleased when some of them followed their advice. However, opponents of this approach were upset.

Opponents

Opponents were skeptical about kinesthetic learning activities. Although they conceded that students improved with the activities, they suspected that they did not improve because of them. They reasoned that the students would have made comparable progress even if their teachers, who were master instructors, had used very different sorts of activities. They demanded that Fernald and Keller articulate a convincing rationale for their activities.

Fernald and Keller were unnerved by their opponents' demands. They acknowledged their difficulties in a 1943 textbook. They stated that "perhaps we can go no further in theory than to say that . . . lip and hand" movements were critically important when learning to read (Fernald & Keller, 1943, p. 376). Worried that this explanation would not be sufficient, they turned to a friend for help.

Fernald and Keller asked Lewis Terman, who was a prominent psychologist, to write the foreword to their 1943 textbook. Aware that the two reading specialists had been badgered for failing to adduce a convincing theory of learning, Terman conceded that they did not have one. However, he claimed that they did not need one because the value of their activities was self-evident (Terman, 1943).

The Orton-Gillingham Method

Opponents challenged the reading specialists who employed kinesthetic activities. They were not impressed by their pragmatic explanations. They demanded that they provide a supportive theory.

Samuel Orton tried to help the reading specialists. Unlike Terman, he did not ignore opponents. He tried to mollify them with a neurological theory about the origins of reading problems.

Orton was convinced that effective reading required students to engage the dominant hemisphere of the brain, which was that area in which they processed language. He added that struggling readers engaged the nondominant hemisphere, which was designed to decode visual images.

Orton coined a term to describe students who tried to comprehend printed words through visual decoding—he claimed that they suffered from *strephosymbolia*. He opined that this disability, which was caused by neurological irregularities, was aggravated by inappropriate instruction.

Orton identified the reading of whole words as an example of an inappropriate instructional strategy. He contrasted it with phonics, which he viewed as an ideal strategy (Orton, 1937, 1966).

In addition to endorsing phonics, Orton recommended the use of kinesthetic activities. He reasoned that kinesthetic activities, which required learners to use multiple senses, minimized the impact of strephosymbolia.

Orton advised teachers to make students write or trace words with pencils. He told them that students who held their pencils in their right hand would engage their language hemispheres.

Orton, who was a psychologist, had never taught children to read. However, he inspired remarkable instructors such as Anna Gillingham, Bessie Stillman, Margaret Stanger, and Ellen Donohue. These teachers transformed his theoretical ruminations into structured learning activities (Gillingham & Stillman, 1997; Stanger & Donohue, 1937).

Opponents

Opponents characterized Orton's theory as extremely speculative. Orton himself conceded that "whether or not our theory is right, I do not know" (S. Orton, 1940s, as quoted by J. Orton & Money, 1966, p. 45). However, he quickly qualified this remark. He added that even wrong theories were worthwhile when they spawned effective instructional activities.

After Orton died in 1948, enthusiasts continued to repeat his theoretical speculations. However, they discovered that their opponents were equally persistent. To defend themselves, they formed a professional organization, named it after Orton, and republished his books (e.g., Orton, 1989; Slingerland, 1988).

TWENTY-FIRST-CENTURY EDUCATORS RESPOND TO PROBLEMS

Educators endorsed kinesthetic learning activities throughout the twentieth century; they continue to recommend them today. They still assure teachers, parents, and members of the public that these activities help students acquire academic skills.

Like their predecessors, the enthusiasts have been confronted by opponents. They attempted to change their minds.

Educational Kinetics

Enthusiasts maintained that the benefits of kinesthetic educational activities were evident. In fact, they contended that they were so evident that the activities should be organized into a special branch of pedagogy—educational kinetics.

The proponents of educational kinetics were confident; they also were entrepreneurial. They demonstrated their entrepreneurial aptitude when they marketed educational kinetics with a proprietary trademark, distinctive catchphrases, and supplementary learning resources (Cohen, Dennison, Dennison, & Goldsmith, 2002; Dennison, 2006; Dennison & Dennison, 1986, 1994).

The proponents of educational kinetics relied on the kinesthetic activities that had been used for decades. However, they attributed additional benefits to them. They claimed that they helped entire communities. They explained that they helped communities by reducing road rage, social intolerance, violence, and crime (Welcome to Brain Gym, 2008).

Opponents

Like earlier proponents of kinesthetic activities, the persons who endorsed educational kinetics were asked to provide a theoretical rationale. They responded that their activities were effective because they incorporated natural developmental movements. They added that these movements stimulated the neurological connections among senses, limbs, muscles, and the brain (Edu-K of South Africa, 2009).

Enthusiasts were disappointed when their rationale did not quiet opponents (e.g., Jacobson, Foxx, & Mulick, 2005b). Therefore, they adopted a rhetorical strategy that the early proponents had used to justify kinesthetic learning activities. They claimed that educational kinetics did not need a theory because it was validated by testimonials from practitioners and clients.

The enthusiasts again failed to persuade their opponents. Nonetheless, they continued to sell materials, train practitioners, organize conferences, and attract clients.

More Entrepreneurs

Many of the educational kinetics enthusiasts were business leaders. In addition to making an impression on clients, they attracted the attention of entrepreneurs. Some of the entrepreneurs joined them; others duplicated their enterprise.

Entrepreneurs wrote books about kinesthetic learning. They recommended exercises that were strikingly similar to educational kinetics. Nonetheless, they attempted to validate their exercises in a convincing fashion. They followed the example of Samuel Orton.

Entrepreneurial authors claimed that kinesthetic learning activities were supported by neurological research. They insisted that these research-based activities were essential aspects of sound curriculum and effective instruction. Some of them claimed that they represented the most effective way to educate disabled, normal, and even gifted children (Armstrong, 1998; Campbell & Campbell, 2009; Erlauer, 2003; Smilkstein, 2003; Sousa, 2001, 2003).

Authors claimed that neurologically supported kinesthetic activities could solve scholastic problems; they added that they also could solve emotional, cultural, and social problems (Gregory & Parry, 2006; Hannaford, 1995; Hardiman, 2003; James, 2007, 2009; Jensen, 2006; Promislow, 1999; Sylwester, 2003; Willis, 2007).

ANALYZING CAUSES AND CORRELATES

Observers noted that some workers experienced unusual stress. They investigated the ways in which they were affected, their coping strategies, their workplaces, and their personal characteristics.

Some observers turned their attention to teachers. They looked for the symptoms of stress; they also looked for the causes. Some of them alleged that teachers felt stress because they did not have the resources to deal with difficult problems. They recommended increased school funding.

Some observers claimed that teachers felt stress because they lacked the training and skill to manage their current resources responsibly. They were sure that they set low goals in order to reduce that stress. They advised them to raise their scholastic goals, become more attentive to individual learners, and experiment with potent types of instruction and materials.

Teachers did experiment with new instructional strategies and learning materials. Although they appeased some persons, they irritated others. The disgruntled persons demanded that they provide convincing justifications for the classroom changes they were making.

Activity 2.1

You might wish to analyze the ways in which persons responded to causes and correlates. You could use Table 2.1.

Table 2.1 identifies three topics: taxi driving, clinical therapy, and early twentieth-century teaching. It also contains an allegation about each topic.

Persons alleged that taxi drivers had to deal with debilitating stress. Provide two explanations for this allegation. One explanation should rely on cause and effect; the other should rely on correlation.

Provide explanations for the allegation that clinical therapists were emotionally unstable. Also provide them for the allegation that teachers who employed kinesthetic learning activities were extremely effective. In both cases, provide one explanation that relies on a causative factor and another that relies on a correlate.

You can complete the table with information from this chapter, the resources cited in it, or other materials. If you are reading this chapter with colleagues, you can collaborate with them.

Table 2.1. Researchers Identify Causes and Correlates

Topic	*Allegation*	*Cause*	*Correlate*
Taxi Driving	Drivers Can Be Debilitated by Stress		
Clinical Therapy	Therapists Can Be Emotionally Unstable		
Teaching	Teachers Can Be More Effective with Kinesthetic Activities		

Activity 2.2

You might wish to examine the ways in which groups viewed causes and correlates. You could use Table 2.2.

Table 2.2 lists three groups: critics, journalists, and members of the public. It also identifies three situations: taxi drivers with physical problems, clinical therapists with emotional problems, and students with reading problems.

Some researchers alleged that the drivers' problems were connected to occupational stress, the therapists' problems were connected to aberrant personalities, and the students' problems were connected to the abstraction of learning activities.

Complete the table by indicating whether groups judged allegations to involve causes or correlates. You can use abbreviations. Use the letters *CS* for causes and *CR* for correlates. As a final step, explain the bases for your selections.

Activity 2.3

You might wish to examine the ways in which groups responded to learning materials. You could use Table 2.3.

Table 2.3 lists four groups: early nineteenth-century educators, the educators who joined the progressive education movement, the initial special educators, and the educators who used kinesthetic reading activities.

This table identifies two types of classroom learning materials: typical and atypical. Typical classroom materials included basal readers, student workbooks, and the resources that were designed for school use. Atypical

Table 2.2. Specifying Causes and Correlates

Group	*Response to**			*Explanation*
	Drivers and Stress	*Therapists and Personality*	*Students and Abstract Tasks*	
Critics				
Journalists				
Public				

**CS* Cause
CR Correlate

Table 2.3. Responses to Learning Materials

Group	*Response to**		*Explanation*
	Typical Materials and Effective Reading	*Atypical Materials and Effective Reading*	
Early Educators			
Progressive Educators			
Special Educators			
Kinesthetic Educators			

**CS* Cause
CR Correlate

classroom materials included religious books, children's literature books, and resources that were not designed for school use.

Complete the table by indicating the relationships that groups ascribed between the learning materials and effective reading. You can use abbreviations. Use the letters *CS* for causes and *CR* for correlates. As a final step, explain the bases for your selections.

Activity 2.4

You might wish to examine the ways in which groups responded to learning activities. You could use Table 2.4.

Table 2.4 lists four groups: early nineteenth-century educators, the educators who joined the progressive education movement, the initial special educators, and the educators who used kinesthetic reading activities.

The table identifies two types of classroom reading activities: oral and physical. Oral reading activities included calling out the letters in printed words, calling out the names of words, and sounding out words. Physical reading activities included tracing, simulated tracing, and rhythmic body movements.

Table 2.4. Responses to Learning Activities

	*Response to**		
Group	*Oral Activities and Effective Reading*	*Physical Activities and Effective Reading*	*Explanation*
Early Educators			
Progressive Educators			
Special Educators			
Kinesthetic Educators			

**CS* Cause
CR Correlate

Complete the table by indicating the relationships that groups ascribed between activities and effective reading. You can use abbreviations. Use the letters *CS* for causes and *CR* for correlates. As a final step, explain the bases for your answers.

Activity 2.5

You might wish to examine instances in which groups were accused of confusing correlates and causes. You could use Table 2.5.

Table 2.5 lists four groups: clinical therapists, enthusiasts of the Fernald approach to remedial reading, enthusiasts of the Orton approach to remedial reading, and enthusiasts of educational kinetics.

Complete the table by identifying accusations that entailed correlates and causes. Also identify the ways in which groups responded to the accusations. You can use abbreviations.

Use the letter *A* if they altered their professional behaviors. Use the letter *C* if they made counterarguments. Use the letter *I* if they ignored their critics. Finally, explain the bases for your answers.

Table 2.5. Allegations about Causes and Correlates

Group	*Accusation*	*Response**	*Explanation*
Therapists			
Enthusiasts—Fernald			
Enthusiasts—Orton			
Enthusiasts—Educational Kinetics			

**A* Altered Behavior
C Counterarguments
I Ignored

SUMMARY

Investigators noted that taxi drivers, clinical therapists, and educators faced intense problems. They concluded that occupations, personalities, or incidental circumstances could be responsible. However, they had to deal with critics, who accused them of confusing causes and correlates.

3

Do Educators Copy Food Photographers?

> A dish needs to be fresh-looking and well-prepared to begin with, and then enhanced with a bit of oil here and a little fake steam there.
>
> —Kim Severson, 2009

Photographers, filmmakers, and journalists used persuasive techniques occasionally. Educators and their critics used them extensively.

FOOD PHOTOGRAPHERS

Although most commercial photographers use digital media currently, they relied on film during earlier eras. They recognized film's great power; they also recognized its limitations.

Portraits captured on film retained subjects' features: they retained even their unflattering features. After the photographers were unable to solve this problem, they asked artists to help them.

The artists were eager to assist. They used pencils and paints to remove troublesome features from portraits; they eliminated blemishes, curls, wrinkles, and the reflections in eyeglasses. Sometimes they made corrections on negatives; at other times they made improvements directly onto the prints (Eastman Kodak Company, 1967; Wade, 1982).

Like the photographers who captured images of persons, those who captured images of food had to deal with problems. Because some of their problems were similar to those of the portrait photographers, they tried to solve them by touching up negatives and prints.

Photographers had to deal with some problems that could not be solved with pencils and paints. They noted that many foods, which were visually enticing when they were prepared, deteriorated under hot studio lights. Vegetables wilted, meat dried out, fruit festered, and whip cream melted (Plimmer, 1988).

The photographers were particularly vexed when they tried to capture images of hot dishes. Although these dishes were surrounded by steam when they were served, they lost them rapidly. The photographers wondered how to create the illusion that they still exuded vapors.

The photographers tried to create the appearance of steam with cigarettes. For example, they hid a lit cigarette behind fried chicken, hamburgers, or mashed potatoes. Although this strategy helped, it produced fumes that were noticeably different from those naturally surrounding hot food. The photographers asked artists for suggestions.

The artists came up with a novel strategy. They lit cigarettes, inhaled the smoke, and then placed drinking straws in their mouths. Seconds before dishes were to be photographed, they exhaled the smoke in the vicinity of food (Davis, 2004).

The photographers were pleased with advice about making food appear hot. However, they had another nettlesome problem: the foods in their images did not appear moist. When they applied water to items, the drops dehydrated too quickly under their lights. They again turned to the artists.

The artists devised a simple but effective antidote for dried-out food. They used cans of aerosol hair spray to create glistening veneers on them. They sprayed sheens onto fruits, vegetables, meats, fish, and starches (Bellingham & Bybee, 2008; Carafoli & Smith, 1992; Davis, 2004; Rowse, 2007).

The photographers were delighted with the artists. Referring to them as food stylists, they regularly collaborated. In addition to depending on them to make food appear hot or succulent, they asked them to arrange lighting, position props, and enhance compositions.

When they began to employ digital media, photographers acquired powerful software. They easily could alter substantive and subtle aspects of images. However, they still relied on food stylists before, during, and after photo shoots (Bellingham & Bybee, 2008; Manna, 2005).

The filmmaker Nora Ephron did not take the contributions of food stylists for granted. When she made a movie about Julia Child, she hired a master chef to ensure that dishes were authentic. However, she also hired a food stylist to make them appear appetizing (Severson, 2009; Turan, 2009).

Like food photographers and filmmakers, restaurateurs were impressed by food stylists. They asked for advice about displaying as well as creating photographs. The stylists featured the photographs within advertisements and restaurant exhibitions. Some of them became so specialized that they focused their efforts exclusively on the designs and displays in menus (Kershaw, 2009).

FILMMAKERS

Orson Welles created several monumental films. However, he also created memorable radio programs. While adapting novels for a series of 1930s broadcasts, he decided that he would use a book by H. G. Wells. He selected *The War of the Worlds.*

Welles was highly inventive. The original novel described a Martian invasion of Victorian England. When he adapted it, he changed the period to 1938, the location to New Jersey, and the format to news bulletins. To heighten the sense of realism, he decided to present the bulletins as if they were interrupting a regularly scheduled radio show.

Welles mischievously scheduled his broadcast for Halloween eve. He assumed that listeners would use this clue, as well as the show's outlandish premise, to recognize that the news bulletins were fictitious.

Some listeners assumed that the broadcast was legitimate. Convinced that Martians were attacking New Jersey, they panicked (McBride, 2006; Rosenbaum, 2007).

Documentary Films

While listening to a 1938 broadcast, members of the audience believed that the information in it was genuine. When they contemplated absurd information in other typically factual media, they again assumed that it was genuine.

Audiences recognized that most films were fictitious. However, they distinguished them from documentary films. The name *documentary* seemed to designate a genre of media that was restricted to nonfictitious information. The formats of these films also created this impression.

The early documentary films were similar to college lectures. Narrators with sober demeanors recapitulated information about science, geography, biography, history, or current events (Aitken, 2006; Boon & Rotha, 2008; Ellis & McLane, 2005).

Mockumentary Films

Members of an audience were annoyed after they were deceived by a 1938 radio program. They accused Welles of deliberately misrepresenting the nature of that broadcast. They censured him for undermining their confidence in radio-transmitted news (Hand, 2006; Koch, 1970).

Welles did not apologize to critics. He admitted that he had used a typically factual medium in a novel fashion. However, he insisted that he had made this transposition to amuse listeners. He inspired numerous artists, including filmmakers.

Woody Allen

Some filmmakers used factual media to entertain audiences. Woody Allen provided an example in *Zelig*. This 1983 film described a character who was involved with the major historical events of the 1920s and 1930s.

Allen used technology to blend his central character's image with those of celebrities and politicians from an earlier era. Because he inserted that image onto genuine newsreels, the results were remarkably realistic (Allen et al., 2001).

When viewers saw the image of Zelig next to those of F. Scott Fitzgerald and Babe Ruth, they might have judged that the film was a genuine documentary. Their convictions might have been strengthened when Susan Sontag, Saul Bellow, and prominent intellectuals appeared in the film and provided testimonials about Zelig's authenticity. Nonetheless, they eventually should have been disconcerted.

As viewers watched newsreels about Zelig, they should have been struck by the fact that he associated with Woodrow Wilson, Calvin Coolidge, Herbert Hoover, and Adolph Hitler. Additionally, they should have noticed that he had an uncanny resemblance to Woody Allen. On the basis of these observations, they should have concluded that the newsreels, the accompanying narratives, and Zelig himself were fabricated.

Film critics were delighted by Allen's film. They recognized that *Zelig*, which pretended to be a documentary, was an ingenious comedy. Coining a phrase, they referred to it as a *mockumentary* film.

Rob Reiner

Another mockumentary film was released a year after *Zelig*. It depicted the rise and decline of a British rock group—Spinal Tap. Marti DiBergi was introduced as the person who recorded the documentary.

The film featured the reports that DiBergi had made during concert tours. It depicted his spontaneous interviews with members of the band, professional colleagues, fans, and critics (Guest, McKean, Shearer, & Reiner, 1984).

Viewers should have realized that the plot and the characters in DiBergi's film were outlandish. Additionally, they should have realized that DiBergi looked exactly like Rob Reiner.

Viewers had ample opportunities to realize that Reiner's film was not a bona fide documentary and that Spinal Tap was not a genuine band. Nonetheless, some viewers concluded that the film and the band were authentic. They even clamored for a chance to see the band perform live (De Seife, 2007).

Reiner waggishly suggested that his film, *This Is Spinal Tap*, should be recognized as a special genre of filmmaking—the *rockumentary*. He later incorporated this term into its title (Reiner et al., 2000).

Political Documentaries

Even the persons who resolved to make objective documentary films employed discretion. They employed it when they selected the topics for their films. They used it when they made decisions about sets, background music, supplementary images, questions for interviews, the portions of topics that they would cover, the date on which they would commence filming, the duration of filming, and the ways in which they would edit scenes (Hampe, 2007).

Michael Moore

The individuals who made political documentaries showed discretion while they were airing their own views. For example, Michael Moore did not attempt to conceal his personal views when he made films about gun control, American foreign policy, nationalized health care, and free market economics (Glynn, Weinstein, Weinstein, O'Hara, & Moore, 2007; Moore et al., 2004; Moore et al., 2003; Moore et al., 2010).

Viewers should have noted the differences between Moore's documentary films and those of his professional colleagues. For example, they should have been startled by the degree to which he was featured in his works. Although other filmmakers made appearances in documentaries, they typically showed themselves journeying to sites or asking questions to characters. In contrast, Moore made observations, asked questions, badgered anyone who disagreed with him, and became the de facto star of each film.

Critics

Those critics who shared Moore's political convictions insisted that his films were genuine documentaries. Those with different convictions characterized them as political advertisements.

Like critics, viewers had to decide whether to become Moore's supporters or opponents. Their political values may have influenced them when they made this decision (Hamm, 2008; Hardy & Clarke, 2004; Larner, 2006; Toplin, 2006).

Errol Morris

Critics compared Michael Moore to other persons who had made documentaries about political topics. For example, they compared him to Errol Morris.

One of Morris's films investigated the ways in which Robert McNamara had influenced the Vietnam War. Another depicted the ways in which Iraqi prisoners were treated at the Abu Ghraib military prison (Morris et al., 2008; Morris, Williams, Ahlberg, McNamara, & Glass, 2004).

Morris contended that he minimized his own voice. He did not appear in films, infrequently asked questions, and allowed characters to speak without interruption. Although he edited his characters' statements, dialogues, and conversations, he insisted that he retained their original contexts (Cunningham, 2005; Gourevitch & Morris, 2008).

Some filmmakers were impressed with Morris's assertions about the objectivity of his documentaries. Expropriating his logic, they made similar assertions about their own documentaries (Rothman, 2009; Stubbs, 2002).

Critics

Critics disagreed with the documentary filmmakers who claimed that they were objective. They contended that they interjected bias in the ways that they treated their audiences. They explained that they used their films to reassure partisans, confront antagonists, and sway independents (Austin, 2007; Cooper, 2006).

Critics discerned additional instances of filmmaker bias. For example, they observed that many of the events that they recorded did not embody genuine cinematic structure. They pointed out that the filmmakers imposed structure because they realized that audiences would not watch disorganized collections of scenes. Although this structuring introduced opportunities to create stories, it also introduced opportunities to promulgate political messages.

Critics gave an example of one documentary filmmaker who had reported about homeless persons in an abandoned Manhattan subway tube. They accused him of creating a narrative in order to elicit sympathy for homeless persons (Heumann & Murray, 2006; Singer, 2001). Critics provided numerous examples of filmmakers who had demonstrated political biases (Benson & Snee, 2008; Chanan, 2007; McEnteer, 2006; Saunders, 2007; Winston, 2000).

The debate about biased documentaries came to a climax during the 2008 Democratic presidential primary. A group of filmmakers released an unflattering film about Hillary Clinton, who was competing for the Democratic Party's nomination. Although this film might have gone unnoticed, it became highly publicized after Clinton tried to suppress it (Patterson et al., 2008).

Clinton argued that the film was not a documentary but a corporate-funded advertisement. She reasoned that it violated laws restricting political advertising. She asked the courts to prohibit its distribution.

The defenders of the movie were ready for this argument. Although they admitted that their movie contained politicized messages, they asserted that they were no more political than those in other documentary films. They asked the courts to stay out of the fray.

The courts became involved in the dispute. Siding with Clinton, they restricted viewing of the film. They later refused to relax their restrictions.

The filmmakers who created the Clinton documentary were unabashedly partisan and conservative. Nonetheless, they recruited a politically diverse entourage; they even attracted the American Civil Liberties Union. Supported by an impressive group of allies, they objected to the repressive ruling. They eventually prevailed in the Supreme Court (Liptak, 2009, 2010; Savage, 2009).

JOURNALISTS

Journalists routinely made reports about complex problems. They hoped to inform readers, listeners, and viewers; they also hoped to entice them. They searched for rhetorical strategies with which to achieve these goals.

Because they wished to provide accurate information, journalists filled their reports with statements from scientists, researchers, or professors. However, they realized that these statements did little to promote audience interest. They were forced to look for other rhetorical strategies.

Reporting about Environmental Crises

Journalists hoped to locate rhetorical devices with which to stimulate the public. When they searched for devices to raise interest in disease, disaster, and terrorism, they were extremely successful (DiMaggio, 2008; Fry, 2003; Moeller, 1999, 2009; Nacos, 2002; Norris, Kern, & Just, 2003; Tuman, 2010; Wilkins, 1987). However, they had greater difficulty with some other topics.

Journalists had difficulty creating interest in environmental issues. They initially relied on remarks from scholars. When they realized that their readers, listeners, and viewers had limited interest in these remarks, they substituted comments from popular musicians, athletes, actors, and even religious leaders (e.g., Bartholomew, 2009; Global Consumers Vote, 2007; Vergano, 2006).

Journalists were pleased with the ways that audiences responded to remarks from celebrities. Nonetheless, they hoped to find even more effective strategies. They tried linking their reports to problems with which audiences would empathize; they linked them to accounts about depleted forests, wetlands, and minerals. Although they had some luck, they continued their search.

Journalists, authors, and editors eventually discovered an ideal way to raise interest in environmental issues; they explained that catastrophes were caused by the gases that humans produced through pollution. They referred to this concept as global warming. They featured it in the headlines of reports and the titles of books (e.g., Bily, 2006; Gore, 2006; Johansen, 2006; Walker & King, 2008).

Some scientists were unenthusiastic about global warming; they questioned whether the concept accurately represented complex environmental issues (e.g., Totty, 2009). Nonetheless, they appreciated its rhetorical power.

Critics

Persons criticized the journalists who reported about environmental issues. They accused them of ignoring some of the groups that caused environmental damage. They pointed out that they concentrated on individuals who owned sports utility vehicles but ignored those who owned pets. They protested that this reporting was indefensible because the pet owners actually caused greater damage than the SUV owners (Ravilious, 2009).

Critics accused journalists of selectively presenting information about nontraditional energy sources, such as windmills. They noted that the journalists had publicized the birds killed by traditional energy sources but not those that were killed by windmills (Bryce, 2009). They also noted that they had omitted information about the emotional, psychological, and physical damage from windmill noise (Bryce, 2010).

The critics had reservations about the ways in which journalists reported about electric cars. Although the critics conceded that electric cars produced relatively little pollution while they were operating, they insisted that they produced a great deal when one calculated all of the factors involved in their creation and disposal (Healey, 2008).

The irreverent authors of *SuperFreakonomics* delighted critics when they took environmental journalists to task (e.g., Stephens, 2009). They accused them of ignoring bovine flatulence, which was a greater source of global warming than SUV exhausts (Levitt & Dubner, 2009).

Critics accused journalists of relying on biased statisticians. To validate this accusation, they asked an impartial group of analysts to examine data about climate change; however, they did not reveal the nature of these data. They noted that the uninitiated statisticians did not detect significant patterns (Borenstein, 2009).

Critics claimed that journalists had depended on unprofessional scientists. They alleged that these scientists revealed their unprofessionalism by altering and suppressing data (Ball & Johnson, 2010a; Global Warming, 2009; K. Johnson, 2009; Meagher, 2009; Revkin, 2009).

Critics reproached those journalists who collaborated with politicians. They explained that politicians could not be trusted because they inevitably had ulterior motives (Bethell, 2005; Essex & McKitrick, 2007; Lomborg, 2007; McCaffrey, 2008; Michaels, 1992; Romm, 2007; Spencer, 2008).

Critics were upset when a 2009 survey revealed that 57 percent of respondents believed that global warming had been confirmed by scientists. They felt some pleasure only because that number had eroded significantly during a three-year period (Fewer Americans, 2009).

Reporting about Economic Crises

When journalists wrote about the 2008 recession, they went to economists. They relied on them for hermetic information about subprime mortgage rates, excessive banking deregulation, and global competition (Lewis, 2009; Smick, 2008; Taylor, 2009).

The journalists anticipated that their readers, listeners, and viewers would show interest in observations from economists. When they realized that they were mistaken, they searched for a different strategy.

Thomas Friedman was a journalist who detected similarities between global warming and the 2008 recession. He also detected a common solution. He telegraphed that solution in his book's title: *Hot, Flat, and Crowded: Why We Need a Green Revolution—And How It Can Renew America* (Friedman, 2008). Some journalists agreed with Friedman's solutions for economic problems; others were skeptical. However, even the skeptics admired the way in which he had handled a vexing rhetorical problem.

Journalists continued to search for effective rhetorical strategies. Those who focused on the housing market characterized it as a bubble that had grown, stretched, and eventually burst (Bernanke Warns, 2010). Even though they were pleased with the way that the public responded to this metaphor, they searched for rhetorical strategies that were more flexible and potent.

Journalists featured rhetorical strategies in the titles of books. They laced them with emotional phrases such as *market mayhem, the age of greed, a financial epidemic, the chain of blame, the corruption-shattered financial system, the crisis of 2008, the depression ahead, depression economics, financial insanity, the credit crisis,* and *the great credit crash* (Barbera, 2009; Dent, 2009; Krugman, 2009; Lewis, 2009; Mason, 2009; Morris, 2008; Muolo & Padilla, 2008; Soros, 2008; Talbott, 2009; Vanden Heuvel, 2009).

Some journalists applied rhetorical devices to persons. They depicted bankers and financial speculators as Wall Street schemers; they depicted victims as Main Street citizens.

Journalists explained that the Wall Street schemers inflicted harm while they were pursuing bonuses. They insisted that the earning of bonuses harmed not only citizens but also national and international economies. They searched for allies.

Journalists were able to persuade some professors, workers, homeowners, and business leaders to join them (Bray, 2010; Mintzberg, 2009; Seib, 2010; Story & Dash, 2010). However, they focused their greatest effort on politicians. They urged the politicians to condemn and restrict executive bonuses (Fed Considers Sweeping, 2009; Grocer, 2010; Paletta & Hilsenrath, 2009; SEC Going to Trial, 2009; Tse, 2009).

Critics

Critics challenged the journalists who had characterized business leaders as reckless and irresponsible. They asked financial and economic experts for support.

The experts judged that the risks taken by business leaders were judicious. They explained that they seemed imprudent only after the recession had eventuated. They noted that many professional groups, including journalists, had failed to predict the recession. They added that some of them had been unable to recognize it until it had reached an advanced stage (McKinnon & Crittenden, 2010a).

Journalists insisted that business leaders were taking irresponsible risks; they demanded that federal bureaucrats use regulatory procedures to discourage them. However, critics questioned this plan. They explained that the bureaucrats, who lacked an objective method of determining financial risk, would have to rely on their personal intuitions (e.g., Kessler, 2009; Weisman, Paletta, & Sidel, 2010).

The critics identified instances in which poorly crafted regulations had been impractical and ineffective. They claimed that the Sarbanes-Oxley Act of 2002 was impractical because it required business leaders to spend an unreasonable amount of effort to comply with it; they added that it was ineffective because it did not prevent troubles from emerging in the mortgage-backed securities markets (Sarbanes-Oxley on Trial, 2009).

Critics pointed to additional instances in which poorly crafted regulations had failed to resolve fiscal problems. They complained about the federal rules that superseded state banking regulations. They claimed that these 2004 rules, which were intended to reduce high-risk lending, had not been enforced by federal regulators. As a result, they inadvertently reduced safeguards (McKinnon & Crittenden, 2010b).

Some journalists wished to create a political structure to prevent business leaders from taking excessive risks or pursuing lucrative bonuses. Nonetheless, they eventually settled for public hearings at which they had a chance to excoriate business leaders (Doyle, 2010; Ex-Fannie Mae, 2010; Financial Crisis Inquiry Commission, 2010; McKinnon & Smith, 2010).

SCHOOL PROBLEMS

The early teachers had to deal with obvious problems. Many of them suffered in buildings that had been designed as churches or synagogues rather than schools. African American teachers taught in facilities that were segregated, crowded, run-down, and unsafe.

The early teachers required facilities. The facilities needed to be spacious and safe. They needed to accommodate traditional academic curricula. They also needed to accommodate emerging curricula, such as those for vocational and physical education.

Facilities were a genuine and important problem. However, many other problems were evident.

Early Problems

The early teachers required many resources in addition to buildings. They required desks, chalkboards, textbooks, technology, recreational materials, sports gear, and vehicles in which to transport students.

Instructors needed better professional preparation. They knew little about the content that they were to teach and the pedagogy through which they were to present it.

Instructors needed effective school policies. They needed policies to define which children would be permitted to attend school, supplied with textbooks, offered meals, and admitted to specialized programs.

Instructors needed the support of key professionals. They needed the aid of doctors, dentists, optometrists, nurses, police officers, social workers, and court officials.

The early educators faced problems because of materials, personnel, curricula, school policies, and training. They protested that they could not solve these problems without additional funds. They requested them from politicians.

Later Problems

Not all citizens ascribed the same level of importance to early public education. Residents in the Northeast and the Midwest assigned a very high priority; they rapidly established numerous and excellent elementary schools, high schools, normal schools, and universities.

Residents in the South and the West assigned a lower priority to schools; they developed them at a relatively slow pace. Nonetheless, they too made progress (Giordano, 2009).

Educators were able to replace hastily constructed schoolhouses with spacious, comfortable, and safe buildings. They made sure that the new buildings had enough classrooms to group children according to ages and academic levels. They ensured that they contained libraries, laboratories, gymnasiums, art studios, recital halls, vocational workshops, kitchens, health clinics, cafeterias, playgrounds, and sports complexes (Giordano, 2009).

Educators eventually discerned improvements in facilities. Nonetheless, they continued to request money to make additional types of improvements. Although some of them directed their requests to politicians, others steered them to parents, employers, business leaders, and members of the clergy. After describing their plight to these intermediaries, they encouraged them to approach the politicians (Giordano, 2009, 2010).

SCHOOL CRITICS

Educators and critics detected problems in the schools. However, the two groups did not detect the same causes. In fact, critics judged that the educators had caused some problems by mismanaging budgets, hiring unqualified staffs, and failing to prepare students for essential careers.

After they had identified problems, critics also identified solutions. They rejected suggestions to give educators additional funding; they proposed that they use fiscal practices from business to manage their current funds more effectively. They explained that they would reward them with additional money only after they had demonstrated greater fiscal responsibility.

Critics had advice for educators about ways to help their students gain employment. They urged them to collaborate with business leaders so that their graduates would be ready for demanding jobs.

Critics also had advice for educators about ways to prepare students for the armed services. They urged them to collaborate with military leaders to ensure that their graduates were patriotic as well as academically qualified (Giordano, 2004).

The critics even had advice for school administrators about ways to manage teachers. They urged them to pay bonuses to them if their students earned high scores on standardized tests. Some of them added that the administrators should fire them when students had low scores (Giordano, 2005).

Critics claimed that money would not solve school problems. The politicians who agreed with them withheld funds. However, they also had philosophical reasons for withholding funds. Some local politicians believed that the federal government had a responsibility to supply more educational money (Giordano, 2009). They challenged those federal politicians who came up with legal reasons for disputing this responsibility (Aquila, 2008; Heise, 2007; Palestini & Palestini, 2005).

Some politicians had pragmatic reasons for withholding school funds. They judged that the needs of educators were not as great as those of other constituents. They preferred to allocate their limited revenue to the agencies that managed roads, bridges, canals, prisons, tourism, and health care.

EDUCATORS RESPOND TO CRITICS

Critics adjured educators to follow their advice. When educators declined, they asked school stakeholders to help them. They searched for rhetorical devices with which to attract them. However, they were upset when they realized that the educators were attempting to gain the support of the same groups.

Educators used rhetorical strategies to influence stakeholders' attitudes toward teacher-centered issues: raising salaries, increasing job security, reducing employee discrimination, securing retirement benefits, and unionizing the workforce. They also used them to influence their attitudes toward student-centered issues: helping children with disabilities, females, the members of racial minority groups, and students who were struggling scholastically (Giordano, 2009).

Teacher Unions

Educators began to form professional organizations during the 1800s. They were hoping that they would serve as forums for exchanging critical scholastic information.

The members of educational organizations originally allowed only males to participate. However, they were aware that women were filling more and more teaching positions; they eventually invited them to join.

The members of the National Teachers Association decided to admit women into their ranks. They made several other substantive changes. They absorbed smaller organizations, transformed their association into a labor union, and rechristened it as the National Education Association.

The members of the National Education Association claimed that teachers did not have adequate wages, job security, or pensions. They added that the majority of them had to deal with bitter, demeaning, and unconcealed discrimination. They made speeches, published editorials, and circulated data (Cohen & Scheer, 1997; Giordano, 2009; Rousmaniere, 2005).

The members of the National Education Association hoped to convince persons that teachers were treated unfairly. They also hoped to persuade them to become advocates. They urged them to pressure local, state, and federal politicians to make educational changes.

The National Education Association evolved into an organization with three million members and a multimillion-dollar budget. It used some of that budget to circulate information and change attitudes. It used another portion to unionize teachers, represent them in labor disputes, and lobby politicians.

Critics complained that the National Education Association assigned a higher priority to teachers than students (Brimelow, 2003; Lieberman, 1997; Paige, 2006). However, advocates retorted that it benefitted both groups (Hannaway & Rotherham, 2006; Kerchner, Koppich, & Weeres, 1998; Smylie & Miretzky, 2004).

Remedial Learners

When educators applied rhetorical devices to teacher-centered issues, they attracted attention. They were pleased when they elicited sympathy and money; they were upset when they elicited censure.

Educators were reproached for concentrating too intently on labor issues. Although they continued to be concerned about these issues, they did exhibit greater concern for students. Their concern was evident in the ways that they responded to the remedial learning movement.

During the early part of the twentieth century, educators had ignored children who were struggling in the schools. The parents of these children demanded that the teachers take responsibility. They were excited when they heard that novel instructional strategies and materials could help more students learn to read.

Although parents became aware of novel approaches to reading, they frequently had difficulty gaining access to them. The approaches were offered in large cities and only from entrepreneurs. Those parents who were unable to locate a nearby or affordable provider were frustrated.

Public school administrators were pressured to offer remedial instruction. However, they were concerned about its expense; those who provided it limited it to students with severe learning problems. Some parents urged educators to help students with mild or moderate problems; others urged them to help students who were learning on schedule or at advanced rates (Giordano, 2000, 2009, 2010).

School administrators were cheered by parents when they expanded remedial reading instruction. Some of them promised to institutionalize it.

The administrators added that they could help even more learners with remedial instruction in writing, mathematics, and speech. However, they needed to hire specialists and purchase materials. They urged parents to lobby politicians for the additional funds.

When they were asked to fund remedial instruction, politicians objected that the costs were excessive and the benefits meager. However, they had difficulty convincing the parents.

Learners with Disabilities

At the end of the nineteenth century, American educators turned children with disabilities away from schools. Some rejected them because of negative stereotypes. However, others rejected them because they were not sure how to help them.

Many members of the public wanted to send persons with disabilities to asylums; most educators agreed with them. Nonetheless, they had difficulty locating asylums that had the space to accommodate them; they even had difficulty locating jails or poorhouses with room (Giordano, 2007).

Parents feared that institutionalized children would lose touch with them and be treated poorly. They were excited about chances for them to receive day care in local schools.

Some persons fiercely opposed the placement of children with disabilities in the schools. They worried that they would hurt the other students, corrupt their morals, and require an excessive amount of teachers' attention. They tried to recruit sympathizers (Giordano, 2007).

The advocates for children with disabilities also tried to recruit sympathizers. They detected an opportunity to partner with the politicians who were fretting about the high cost of asylums. They persuaded them that school-based programs would be much less expensive (Giordano, 2007; Osgood, 2008; Safford & Safford, 2006; Winzer, 1993).

Their opponents had a rejoinder. Even though school care was less expensive than residential care, it still required funding. They warned parents and teachers that it would take that funding from the other sections of educational budgets.

The advocates of school-based day care had difficulty attracting allies. They realized that their plan appeased some groups but angered others. They asked educators to support it (Giordano, 2007).

More and more educators began to support special education. They supported it for different reasons. Some of them agreed with the movement's philosophical goals. Some succumbed to pressure from pro-special-education parents. Some were coerced by legislators and judges. Still others viewed this new type of education as a rhetorical device with which to steer sympathy and funding to the schools.

African American Learners

Some educators were upset about the ways in which children with disabilities were treated. Others were upset about the treatment of gay and lesbian students (Harris, 1997; Meyer, 2009). Still others were alarmed by the sustained discrimination directed at African American learners.

The early southerners had disclaimed responsibility for educating slaves. They later refused to educate the children of freed slaves. They told African American parents to take care of their own children.

Postbellum African Americans did take charge of education. They personally built schoolhouses, provided instruction, devised curricula, and collected books. They sometimes were aided by the northern teachers, who journeyed to their communities and worked elbow-to-elbow with them (Giordano, 2009).

During the first half of the twentieth century, African American educators in the South recognized that their students had greater educational opportunities. However, they realized that they had fewer opportunities than white students; they also recognized that they were restricted to segregated schools.

African American educators worried about the educational, psychological, social, and economic damages from legally segregated schools. They also worried about the consequences of the nation's many de facto segregated schools (Beckwith, 2009; Douglas, 2005; Tushnet, 1987). They turned to the courts for help.

African Americans celebrated when a 1954 Supreme Court decision barred segregation in public schools (*Brown v. Board of Education of Topeka*, 1954). They anticipated that this decision would protect their children from racial prejudice. However, they changed their minds after they observed its limited effects.

African Americans were disappointed by *Brown v. Board of Education of Topeka*; they continued to be disheartened by other court rulings. They urged politicians to enact comprehensive federal laws. Although the politicians complied, they were unable to help many students.

Disillusioned by court decisions and legislative acts, African Americans led the civil rights movement during the 1960s. However, they later acknowledged that even this movement affected too few students (Balkin & Ackerman, 2001; Clotfelter, 2004; Irons, 2002; Orfield & Eaton, 1996; Patterson, 2001; Rhode & Ogletree, 2004; Street, 2005).

African Americans realized that they would not be able to reform the schools without allies; they asked numerous groups to join them. They made special supplications to teachers.

Some teachers joined African Americans because they shared their philosophical and political goals. Some joined because of pressure from legislators and judges. Others joined because of pressure from parents. However, some joined because they detected an opportunity to use minority education as a rhetorical device. They argued that they needed larger budgets to hire personnel, purchase materials, and establish programs that would reduce discrimination.

Female Learners

The discriminatory manner in which girls and young women were treated created problems while they were in school; they contributed to the social, economic, legal, and political problems that they faced outside of school. They even contributed to their emotional problems (Ayres, 2001; Lenhart, 2004).

Women hoped to improve the schools. They began by documenting instances of gender discrimination. When they searched for instances in textbooks, they found multiple examples.

Women noted that some materials, such as social studies textbooks, omitted women. They noted that others, such as basal readers, depicted them exclusively as subordinates (Giordano, 2003).

Authors and publishers treated women inappropriately. However, other groups also were culpable. School administrators treated female students unfairly when they discouraged them from curricula that would prepare them for careers in business, law, medicine, and engineering.

School administrators advised female students to take curricula that would prepare them to work in the home. When they confronted headstrong students, they directed them to nursing, teaching, or secretarial curricula (Bank & Hall, 1997; Giordano, 2009, 2010; Miller-Bernal, 2000; Salkin, 2008).

Those women who resisted sexist advice originally faced insurmountable obstacles. When a nineteenth-century woman asked the members of the Wisconsin Bar to review her qualifications to practice law, she was turned down. After the justices of the Wisconsin Supreme Court listened to her appeal, they concurred with the Bar.

The justices wrote that the "law of nature destines and qualifies the female sex for the bearing and nurture of children" but not for practice of law. They added that law was "a profession that has essentially and habitually to do with all that is selfish and malicious, knavish and criminal, coarse and brutal, repulsive and obscene, in human life" (In the Matter of the Motion, 1875, p. 8).

The prohibitions against women lawyers eventually were removed. However, the women who attended law schools still had to deal with implicit types of discrimination in their programs (Gaber, 1998; University of Maryland Women, Leadership, & Equality Program, 2009; Weiss & Melling, 1988).

Female law students had different experiences than males. They had to deal with situations that were similar to those that they had confronted in other phases of their schooling. For example, those women who were athletes recognized that they had fewer opportunities than the male athletes (Lapchick, 1996; Lenskyj, 2003; O'Reilly & Cahn, 2007).

Girls and young women were treated differently from males when they participated in social activities. They were steered to different clubs than males. Those who ignored this advice were offered subordinate responsibilities (Brody, 2000).

Women battled against de jure discrimination. The early political reformers battled the restrictions that excluded them from voting. In fact, they made the removal of these restrictions into focal points of political campaigns (C. Adams, 2003; Mani, 2007; Mountjoy & McNeese, 2008).

During the late 1960s and the early 1970s, women acknowledged that discriminatory laws had changed during the initial wave of feminist activism. However, they identified multiple social, cultural, and economic biases that had not been codified as laws and that had endured. Referring to themselves as second-wave feminists, they continued to call for reforms.

The second-wave feminists detected biases in the schools; they detected them in learning materials, scholastic experiences, and extracurricular opportunities. Even though they eliminated some of them, they detected many more. They judged that these biases, which influenced the values and attitudes of preadult women and men, perpetuated discrimination throughout society (Gerhard, 2001; Gilmore, 2008; Nicholson, 1997; Valk, 2008). They asked educators to join them.

Some educators joined feminist reformers because they shared their philosophical and political goals. Some joined because of pressure from parents. Others joined because of the pressure from legislators and judges. Still others joined because they detected opportunities to garner attention and funds.

ANALYZING PERSUASIVE TECHNIQUES

Commercial photographers made images of food enticing. They hoped that their enhanced images would persuade consumers to purchase products.

The professionals in numerous fields recognized the power of persuasive techniques. Journalists and documentary filmmakers used them to change attitudes toward political issues. Educators used them to change attitudes toward scholastic issues.

Activity 3.1

You may wish to examine persuasive techniques. You could rely on Table 3.1.

Table 3.1 identifies groups that used persuasive techniques. It lists four groups: photographers, filmmakers, journalists, and educators.

Table 3.1. Employing Persuasive Techniques

Group	*Persuasive Technique*	*Strength*	*Weakness*	*Explanation*
Photographers				
Filmmakers				
Journalists				
Educators				

Complete this table by providing examples of the techniques on which groups relied. Also, identify strengths and weaknesses of the techniques. Finally, explain your answers.

You can complete this table with the information in this chapter, the resources cited in it, or additional resources. If you are completing it with other readers, you can collaborate with them.

Activity 3.2

You may wish to focus on the persuasive techniques that were applied to educational issues. You could rely on Table 3.2.

Table 3.2 identifies two groups: educators and their critics. It also identifies issues about which they argued. It lists five issues: materials (e.g., facilities/equipment/textbooks), personnel, curricula, scholastic policies, and educator training programs.

Complete this table by identifying the types of arguments that the groups developed. You can use abbreviations.

Use the letters *TC* if they developed teacher-centered arguments. Use the abbreviation *SC* if they developed student-centered arguments. Finally, explain the bases for your responses.

Table 3.2 Educators and Critics Employ Persuasive Techniques

	Persuasive					
Group	*Materials*	*Personnel*	*Curricula*	*Policies*	*Training*	*Rationale*
Educators						
Critics						

**TC* Teacher-Centered
SC Student-Centered

Activity 3.3

You could focus on the rhetorical devices that were applied to select educational issues. You could use Table 3.3.

Table 3.3 lists issues about which educators were concerned. It lists five issues: unionizing the teacher workforce, providing remedial help to learners, establishing programs for learners with disabilities, reducing discrimination against African Americans, and reducing discrimination against women.

Complete the table by identifying educators' persuasive techniques. Indicate whether those techniques depended on economic, philosophical, political, scholastic, social-cultural, or other types of argument.

Table 3.3. Educators Employ Persuasive Techniques

Issue	*Persuasive Technique**	*Explanation*
Teacher Unions		
Remedial Learners		
Learners with Disabilities		
African Americans		
Women		

**ECO* Economic
PHI Philosophical
POL Political
SCH Scholastic
SOC Social-Cultural
OTH Other

Table 3.4. Responses to Educators' Persuasive Techniques

	*Response to**					
Group	*Unions*	*Remedial Learners*	*Special Learners*	*African Americans*	*Women*	*Explanation*
Parents						
School Board Members						
Politicians						

*– Unsympathetic
± Moderately Sympathetic
+ Sympathetic

You can use abbreviations. Use the abbreviation *ECO* for economic arguments, *PHI* for philosophical arguments, *POL* for political arguments, *SCH* for scholastic arguments, *SOC* for social-cultural arguments, and *OTH* for other arguments. As a final step, explain your answers.

Activity 3.4

You might wish to consider the ways in which groups responded to persuasive techniques. You could rely on Table 3.4.

Table 3.4 identifies three groups: parents, the members of school boards, and politicians.

This table also identifies issues to which persuasive techniques were applied. It lists five issues: unionizing the teacher workforce, providing remedial help to learners, establishing programs for learners with disabilities, reducing discrimination against African Americans, and reducing discrimination against women.

Complete the table by indicating the ways in which groups responded to issues. You can use symbols.

Use the symbol – if they were unsympathetic. Use the symbol ± if they were moderately sympathetic and the symbol + if they were sympathetic. Finally, explain the bases for the symbols that you selected.

SUMMARY

The professionals in numerous fields devised strategies to reinforce or alter persons' dispositions. Educators and their critics relied extensively on these strategies.

4

Is Education Like Graffiti?

> Subway riders . . . find [graffiti] yet another of the awful indignities visited upon them by a city apparently out of control.
>
> —Nathan Glazer, 1987

Scholars recognized that graffiti was unconventional and controversial; nonetheless, they insisted that it was a genuine form of art. They defended unconventional and controversial initiatives in numerous other fields, including education.

GRAFFITI WRITING

Some art scholars were traditionalists; others were innovators. They feuded about the materials from which art should be created, the audiences with whom it should be shared, and the settings in which it should be displayed.

Journalists, politicians, and members of the public were concerned about the feuding factions. They worried that they would influence public art displays. They became alarmed when some of them argued that graffiti should be encouraged and protected (Urban Safaris, 2008).

Critics

The graffiti writers were controversial because they disturbed residents in their communities. They also upset the owners of the property on which they placed displays (Glazer & Lilla, 1982; GRAFFITAGE, 2008).

Graffiti writers were controversial for an additional reason: some of them were criminals. Those who belonged to street gangs used distinctive symbols to mark their territories, frighten lawful residents, provoke opponents, and drive away visitors (Kontos & Brotherton, 2008; S. A. Phillips, 1999; Rahn, 2002).

Enthusiasts recognized the graffiti writers' crimes. However, they argued that their crimes were overshadowed by their achievements.

Critics were not persuaded. They retorted that graffiti emboldened practitioners to experiment with public intoxication, disorderly conduct, trespassing, drug abuse, and felonies.

Advocates

Enthusiasts depicted the graffiti writers as a new generation of counterculture artists; they compared them to the early jazz artists. They pointed out that the musicians, who originally had been dismissed by tradition-minded critics, eventually achieved stature comparable to that of classical musicians. They added that this stature came at a price because many of their listeners lost interest as jazz became establishmentarian (Teachout, 2009).

Enthusiasts explained that artists used graffiti to express outrage at political, economic, and social injustice. They compared them to the environmental activists who glued deprecating slogans onto the bumpers of sports utility vehicles. They argued that the members of both groups committed petty crimes to achieve political goals (Ganzi Licata, 2003; Goewey, 2005).

Some enthusiasts justified graffiti with another type of argument: they claimed that restrictions against it were oppressive forms of censorship. They added that attempts to enforce the restrictions could be dangerous (Byrd, 2006).

The enthusiasts made entreaties to business leaders, building owners, government leaders, gallery owners, and museum administrators; they encouraged them to collaborate with the graffiti writers. They urged them to purchase their paint, offer commissions, arrange exhibitions, and market their works (Bamberger, 2010; Chang, 2005; K. Johnson, 2006; Record Price, 2007; Ryzik, 2010; Steinhauser, 2010).

Academic Analysis

Enthusiasts gave advice about graffiti to critics. They realized that the critics looked at graffiti from multiple and frequently incompatible perspectives. They tried to address the concerns of politicians, journalists, police officers, business leaders, professors, judges, city planners, and educators.

The enthusiasts had a difficult time changing the minds of their critics. They therefore turned to members of the public; they tried to convince them that graffiti was similar to traditional art (e.g., Naar, 2007).

Showcasing Locations

Enthusiasts identified New York City as the birthplace of artistic graffiti; they documented, wrote about, and photographed the historic sites in that community. They featured the famous displays on buildings, bridges, and tunnels (Martinez, 2006; Sutherland & Revs, 2004).

In addition to studying the graffiti on New York City's permanent structures, enthusiasts contemplated examples on subway cars. They even found extensive samples within those cars (Cooper & Chalfant, 2009; Stewart & Stewart, 2009).

Graffiti writers in numerous communities copied the New York City subway writers. Those who did not have access to subway cars decorated the cars on freight and commuter trains. The trains then became mobile exhibitions of their work (Gastman, Rowland, & Sattler, 2006).

Enthusiasts identified the styles of graffiti in American communities. They were struck by the distinctive styles in Los Angeles, San Francisco, and Miami (Gastman & Teri, 2007; Grody, 2006; Murray & Murray, 2009; Rotman, 2008).

Artistic graffiti spread to North American communities outside of the United States. It also spread to other continents (Bagshaw & Oates, 2008; Camerota, 2008; Ganz & Manco, 2004; Grévy, 2008; KET, 2007; Macdonald, 2001; Manco & Neelon, 2005; Nicholls, 2000; Rahn, 2002; Ruiz, 2009).

Creating Taxonomies

Enthusiasts had difficulty comparing the different styles of graffiti. They lacked the academic constructs that art scholars employed when they discussed the styles within traditional art. They decided to create academic constructs for graffiti.

The graffiti writers used heterogeneous lettering techniques. Moreover, some of them accompanied the lettering with idiosyncratic pictorial images. The enthusiasts created taxonomies with which to categorize the lettering and the pictorial aspects of graffiti (e.g., Gottlieb, 2008).

The enthusiasts judged that graffiti writing was a component of a broader genre—street art (Burns, 2005; Levitt, Coles, Harris, & Hoshino, 1987). Pleased with the usefulness of this academic generalization, they incorporated other generalizations into their taxonomies.

Enthusiasts sorted graffiti writers on the basis of their application techniques. They stipulated that persons who used stencils constituted a distinctive subgenre (Manco, 2002). They distinguished them from practitioners who did stencil-free painting or who used stickers (Kumar, 2006; Walde, 2007).

Some enthusiasts depicted the artists who used paints, stencils, and stickers as street artists; others depicted them as street performance artists. However, the two groups disagreed about how restrictive they should make these categories (Dixon, 2007; McEvilley, 2005; Wasik, 2006).

The enthusiasts who were professors had difficulty persuading their tradition-minded peers to support graffiti. They also had difficulty persuading police officers, judges, politicians, and some members of the public. They had difficulty because graffiti had a direct impact on their communities. They faced the type of resistance that scholars in other fields faced when they became advocates for unconventional and intrusive initiatives.

FEAR OF INFECTION

Twentieth-century Americans were concerned about illness. Although they worried about numerous types, they worried especially about those that resulted from influenza viruses. Some of them learned about the dangers of viruses from health officials, politicians, or journalists; others learned from personal experiences.

Flu—1918

American soldiers were jubilant when the World War I powers ceased fighting. Having survived the conflict, they looked forward to joining their families and communities. They assumed that they could resume their careers in industry, commerce, sales, and agriculture.

Few veterans anticipated the conditions that they would encounter. They discovered that their jobs had been taken by women, older individuals, or even persons with disabilities. Although some employers fired their wartime workforces after the conflict, they still could not accommodate the veterans because of a severe postwar recession (Giordano, 2003, 2009).

African American veterans found it particularly hard to get jobs. Many of them became so desperate that they relocated to more prosperous areas of the country. They antagonized local laborers when they agreed to work for lower wages.

The employment problems of African Americans were aggravated by racial conflicts. During the summer of 1919, bloody riots erupted throughout the United States. The journalists who chronicled this era referred to it as the red summer. Contemporaries agreed that the phrase was apt.

Americans hoped that President Woodrow Wilson would address the country's economic and racial problems. However, they were disheartened by his postwar political plans. Wilson left the United States and spent months at a conference in France. After he returned, he kept international affairs at the top of his agenda (J. M. Cooper, 2001; Hogan, 2006).

Postwar citizens were grieving over the deaths of more than one hundred thousand American soldiers. They were discouraged by insufferable racial prejudice, heart-wrenching economic problems, and an unresponsive president. They were unprepared to deal with a health crisis.

Journalists began to report about a new type of flu at the end of the war. Incorrectly assuming that it had originated in Europe, they called it the Spanish flu. Although Americans were fascinated by this name, they came to dread the disease that it represented (Cunningham, 2009; Gunn, 2008; Hays, 2005; Kolata, 1999; Phillips & Killingray, 2003).

The 1918 flu spread worldwide. It infected fifty million persons, including one out of every four Americans. It was frightening because of the speed at which it spread and its consequences.

Members of the public watched young, healthy, and robust individuals drown in their pulmonary secretions. They were startled as they realized that the number of Americans who were dying from flu exceeded the number that had perished from combat.

Polio Virus

Medical researchers recognized that illnesses upset Americans. However, they frequently could not determine whether they resulted from flus, viruses, or bacteria. They sometimes spent decades investigating their origins.

Medical researchers had detected polio in the first half of the nineteenth century. Although they could not determine its cause, they easily recognized its consequences. It annually infected, paralyzed, and killed numerous adults and children.

Journalists initially did not provide a great deal of publicity to polio. They circulated more information after Franklin Delano Roosevelt contracted it in the 1920s. They eventually transformed it into a topic about which the general public was both knowledgeable and alarmed. They then continued to report about it for decades.

Journalists noted that hundreds of thousands of Americans were contracting polio during the 1950s. They emphasized that more than fifty thousand of them died each year (Silver & Wilson, 2007; D. J. Wilson, 2005).

Medical researchers resolved that they would find a vaccine. They debated about whether they should create it from inactive or active polio viruses. They eventually tried both types.

Parents were worried when physicians first began to inject viruses into their children. Nonetheless, they were reassured by the testimonials from health officials, medical researchers, and parents of children who had been inoculated and then remained healthy. Although parents of nonvaccinated children were comforted by testimonials, they were impressed more by statistics: the number of children with polio dropped dramatically.

Journalists extolled the polio vaccines; they even extolled the medical personnel who had created them. They made researchers such as Jonas Salk and Albert Sabin into celebrities.

Journalists eventually reported that polio no longer threatened American children. Nonetheless, they underscored the peril that it still posed worldwide (Guth, 2010; Kluger, 2004; Oshinsky, 2005; Salgado, 2003).

Swine Flu—1976

Richard Nixon celebrated his presidential reelection in 1972. At that moment, he was unaware of a gathering storm. However, he should have detected clouds when his vice president, Spiro Agnew, was indicted for bribery (Witcover, 2007).

After Agnew resigned, Gerald Ford was appointed vice president. When Nixon later resigned, Ford became president. He had the opportunity to complete most of Nixon's term.

Ford had several key goals: reduce partisan feuding, advance the interests of the nation, win the confidence of voters, and compile enough achievements to win an election.

When it was time for an election, Ford struggled to win the nomination of his party; he then lost the general contest. Most analysts linked his failure to blunders. They noted that he made a particularly damaging decision while contemplating a strain of flu (Cannon, 1994; DeFrank & Ford, 2007; Mieczkowski, 2005; Werth, 2007).

A group of medical researchers had detected a pernicious type of swine flu; they concluded that it was the same type that had caused the pandemic after World War I. They advised Ford to produce a vaccine and encourage every citizen to take it.

Ford discerned benefits to the researchers' recommendations. He realized that suffering could be reduced and deaths prevented. In addition to detecting benefits for citizens, he detected personal benefits: he would convey the appearance of a decisive leader.

Ford also weighed the political risks associated with a federal vaccination campaign. He worried that he would be in trouble if persons were injected with a vaccine for an insignificant threat. Additionally, he worried that the vaccine might be unsafe (Neustadt & Fineberg, 1983; Osborn, Crosby, Millar, & Viseltear, 1977).

Ford decided that he would follow the recommendations of the researchers. He appeared on television and warned that a catastrophe was imminent. However, he assured the viewers that the government would produce and distribute enough vaccine to protect them.

Pollsters indicated that viewers reacted in different ways to the president's announcement. Trusting individuals asked health officials to vaccinate them as soon as possible; skeptics waited. Persons who were less educated tended to be trusting; those who resided in the Midwest also were more trusting. Those who were better educated and those who lived in the Northeast tended to be skeptical.

Journalists and members of the public watched for signs of a pandemic. When they did not detect them, they questioned whether the inoculations had been needed. They also asked whether they were effective and safe.

Because relatively few persons contracted swine flu, health officials could not gauge the inoculations' effectiveness. However, they did have opportunities to judge their safety: they became alarmed after hundreds of persons developed Guillain-Barré syndrome.

Although Guillain-Barré syndrome could be fatal, less than thirty persons died from it during this period. Nonetheless, it had terrifying symptoms: it caused legs, torsos, upper limbs, and faces to become weak and then numb.

Avian Flu—2003

Sometimes members of the public were impressed by the ways in which health officials responded to influenza viruses; at other times they were disappointed. They were disappointed during the Ford administration.

In 2003, health officials again gave advice about a dangerous flu. They warned that the avian flu, which was carried by birds, could create a devastating crisis. They added that they already discerned early signs of a crisis.

Health officials asked politicians to help them. They encouraged them to fund, produce, and stockpile vaccines; they also asked them to identify which groups should have priority access to them (Altshuler, 2006; M. Davis, 2005; Farndon, 2005; Greene & Moline, 2006; Mercola & Killeen, 2006; Siegel, 2006).

The 2003 epidemic did not eventuate. Nonetheless, health officials continued to issue warnings. In addition to warning about the danger from avian flu, they warned about the peril of swine flu. Journalists echoed their warnings.

Swine Flu—2009

American health officials were on the lookout for swine flu in 2009. They concluded that a strand had appeared, infected persons, and caused more than three hundred deaths by the summer. They viewed these events as harbingers of an epidemic.

American health officials joined their peers in eight other countries; they announced that they would take actions to combat a global pandemic. They hoped to vaccinate hundreds of millions of persons before flu season (CDC: U.S. Swine Flu deaths, 2009; Global Swine Flu Deaths, 2009).

American government leaders spent a billion dollars getting ready. They used most of the money to produce two hundred and fifty million doses of swine flu vaccine. Nonetheless, they reserved a portion of their funds for a campaign to persuade persons to take the vaccine.

Federal bureaucrats and health officials were distressed when they learned that only 40 percent of citizens intended to take the vaccine (Stein, 2009). However, they remained optimistic; they assumed that additional persons would respond to the federally funded information campaign (McKay, 2009).

Bureaucrats and health officials had a second reason to be optimistic. They assumed that citizens would change their minds about inoculations after they listened to reports about flu-related deaths (McKay, 2009).

The journalists were ready to assist by distributing information about deaths. They prepared to get this information from the World Health Organization and the U.S. Centers for Disease Control. However, critics challenged the credibility of the data from these organizations.

The critics asked personnel at the health organizations about their procedures for validating the causes of death among persons with flu-like symptoms. The personnel acknowledged that their data comprised deaths that were proven to be flu related as well as those that were assumed to be flu related.

Critics badgered the scientists at the World Health Organization and those at the Centers for Disease Control. They demanded that they cease releasing misleading information. They were pleased when the scientists eventually succumbed (Stobbe, 2009). Although they made the same demands of politicians, they were not able to deter them.

Politicians were not fazed by accusations that they relied on misleading information. In the fall of 2009, President Obama proclaimed that swine flu had become a national emergency. After he was challenged, he explained that he had issued the proclamation for a practical reason: he wished to enable public health providers to bypass federal regulations were a genuine health crisis to eventuate (Obama Declares, 2009).

Some of the persons who were vaccinated against swine flu reported ailments. For example, they came down with Guillain-Barré syndrome. Journalists reminded audiences that the identical syndrome had been linked to swine flu inoculations during the Ford era (Aleccia, 2009).

Although some persons accepted swine flu inoculations, many declined. Enough persons declined that the nation could have been devastated by a severe flu outbreak. However, the outbreak never transpired. In fact, the 2009–2010 flu season turned out to be unusually mild (McKay, 2010).

The swine flu warnings were alarming in the United States; they were even more frightening in some other countries. The warnings in Mexico resulted in the loss of billions of dollars from tourists.

The Mexican health officials and politicians eventually admitted that their warnings were premature. Nonetheless, they insisted that they had provided priceless opportunities to test the country's health system (Stevenson, 2010).

FEAR OF IMMUNIZATION

The federal government initiated immunization campaigns throughout the twentieth century; it continued to spearhead them during the subsequent era. Even though most Americans were relieved by these actions, some opposed them.

Opponents sometimes did not like the role that politicians played in public immunization campaigns. Suspicious that the politicians had ulterior motives for collaborating with health officials, they resisted the campaigns in which they were involved (Morone, Litman, & Robins, 2008). However, the government was prepared for their resistance.

Politicians expected all citizens to comply with immunization campaigns. They explained that essential childhood vaccinations were necessary to protect children as well as the persons with whom they came in contact. They noted that the essential vaccinations included those for polio, measles, mumps, rubella, chicken pox, diphtheria, hepatitis A, hepatitis B, pneumococcal disease, and tetanus.

Politicians hoped to frighten obstinate parents into compliance. They threatened to turn their unvaccinated children away from the schools and public day care centers (Fisher, 2006; Murkoff & Mazel, 2008; Smith, 1997).

Persons who opposed the government needed allies. They anticipated that other persons would join them if they could prove that government leaders were behaving irresponsibly. They looked for incriminating evidence.

Fluoride and Cancer

Some of the persons who opposed inoculations were anxious about major governmental health regulations. They even worried about relatively minor regulations, such as those affecting the fluoride in drinking water.

When fluoride enthusiasts were challenged by skeptics, they had a response. They were able to document the improved dental health of children and adults who consumed fluoridated water (Fluoridated Water, 2005; Water Fluoridation and Cancer, 2006).

Opponents conceded that persons who drank fluoridated water had fewer cavities. Nonetheless, they were convinced that they paid a dreadful price—cancer. They established information campaigns to highlight this danger (Armfield, 2007; Harvard Study: Strong Link, 2006; Hertsgaard & Frazer, 1999).

Vaccines and Autism

Persons with skeptical temperaments distrusted health officials. Others distrusted them because these officials collaborated with politicians. Wishing to strengthen their influence, they looked for allies; they hoped to find them among disgruntled citizens.

Some parents were upset with health officials because of the way in which they had responded to autism. The parents feared autism because of its symptoms: communication difficulties, social problems, and obsessive repetitive behaviors. They demanded that health officials find the cause of this awful syndrome.

Some parents resolved to take matters into their own hands. In fact, they believed that they already had found the basis for autism; they claimed that it was triggered by measles, mumps, and rubella vaccinations. They located parents who said that their children began to display autistic symptoms soon after receiving these vaccinations.

Persons reacted differently to allegations about a link between vaccinations and autism. Most scholars and health officials admitted that they did not have enough evidence to confirm or dispute this link. Nonetheless, the overwhelming majority dismissed the allegations (Offit, 2008; What Parents Should Know, 2009).

Parents responded cautiously. Some of them demanded additional research studies (Boushey, 2004, 2007; McCarthy, 2007, 2008; Park, 2001). Others became opponents of the vaccinations. The opponents felt vindicated after a group of scholars published a report that confirmed their suspicions (Wakefield et al., 1998).

Journalists were divided. Some of them agreed with the health officials; others sided with the parent activists. Both groups tried to influence the public (Villarosa, 2008).

Parents of children who did not have autism were conflicted. Although some of them continued to vaccinate their children, others were fearful. Their fear contributed to a noticeable decline in British and American vaccinations during the 1990s (*Lancet*'s Vaccine Retraction, 2010; Wang, 2010).

As recently as 2010, 25 percent of American parents expressed fears about vaccinations triggering autism. More than 10 percent of them admitted that they had prevented doctors from administering vaccinations to their children (Child Vaccine Safety, 2010; C. K. Johnson, 2010).

INSTRUCTION

Teachers experimented with learning activities in special education classrooms. They were impressed with the positive ways that the students responded to kinesthetic activities. They believed that they improved their dispositions, learning, and recall.

Special educators used kinesthetic activities to develop vocational and life skills. They eventually used them to develop academic skills. Some of them wondered whether they could use them for communication (Giordano, 2007).

Augmentative and Alternative Communication

Special education teachers and speech-language pathologists were concerned about nonverbal persons. They hoped that they could help individuals with apraxia—the inability to articulate words.

Teachers realized that individuals who could not articulate words still could communicate in other ways. For example, they could transmit messages by manipulating cards with words or pictures on them.

The handling of cards was a kinesthetic activity. Although persons who could complete it benefited, those who could not were frustrated.

The teachers decided to make adaptations for those who had not been successful.

The teachers arranged a display of cards and encouraged students to point at, gesture toward, or simply stare at one of them. The teachers then verbalized the item on the designated card.

Proponents

Teachers realized that communicating with cards was cumbersome. They tried to make things easier with technology. They experimented initially with mechanical devices; they progressed eventually to electric devices.

Teachers were pleased when students learned to communicate with electric learning devices. Nonetheless, they still were disappointed at those who could not communicate spontaneously.

The teachers hoped to improve their communication devices by making them more accessible and practical. They asked engineers for help.

The engineers were eager to assist. To increase accessibility, they made the devices easier to use. For example, they created portable keyboards with illustrations on the keys. The students could communicate by pressing these keys.

The engineers also increased the practicality of communication devices; they adapted them so that they synthesized speech. By pressing a key, students created the sound of a word. By pressing several keys, they could create the sounds of sentences.

Teachers and speech-language pathologists applied a cumbersome phrase to their new tools: they referred to them as *augmentative and alternative communication devices*. They eventually substituted an acronym: AAC (Beukelman, Yorkston, & Reichle, 2000; Hurtig & Downey, 2008; M. Smith, 2005).

Opponents

Opponents raised questions about augmentative and alternative communication. They noted that the price of the equipment could be thousands of dollars for a single child. They questioned whether the usefulness of the equipment justified this high price (Augmentative and Alternative Communication, 2009).

Opponents questioned the practicality of AAC devices. They noted that they were flimsy, prone to dysfunction, and difficult to service (Huer & Lloyd, 1990; Shepherd, Campbell, Renzoni, & Sloan, 2009).

Opponents identified pedagogical disadvantages. They noted that instructors had difficulty teaching students to use AAC devices in clinical or classroom settings. They added that the difficulties were compounded when they tried to help students use devices in community settings (Rackensperger, Krezman, McNaughton, Williams, & D'Silva, 2005).

Opponents even challenged the scholarly protocols on which the AAC enthusiasts relied. They complained that they used outdated and poorly designed studies. They added that many of them endorsed studies without investigating whether results could be replicated (Schlosser, 2003).

Facilitated Communication

Teachers were distressed when some students, such as those with severe mental disabilities, could not handle kinesthetic learning materials. They searched for an extraordinary technique with which to help them.

Proponents

Educators suspected that persons with severe mental disabilities would respond to kinesthetic communication activities if their teachers provided greater assistance to them. They began to experiment.

After arranging a display of picture cards, teachers encouraged students to transmit messages by pointing to them. However, the teachers gave additional assistance; they personally guided the students' hands to the cards.

The educators who held hands asserted that they did not select the cards. They explained that they were able to use subtle movements within the limbs to guide them to the destinations that the students wished to select. Insisting that they had facilitated rather than determined the selections, they referred to the process as *facilitated communication.*

Although opportunities to communicate with cards were limited, they expanded with computers. Educators could guide learners' fingers to computer keys, help press them, and then read the words that were displayed on monitors. They reported that the monitors revealed meaningful words, phrases, and sentences (Biklen, 1993; Biklen & Cardinal, 1997; Crossley, 1994; Hundal & Lukey, 2003; Twachtman-Cullen, 1997).

Persons with disabilities engaged in facilitated communication at private clinics. Relying on support from their teachers, they typed statements about the value of the technique. The owners of the clinics then published their testimonials. Although the owners and some parents were pleased, they had to deal with skeptics.

Opponents

Opponents were not impressed by testimonials from the persons who owned, managed, or worked at facilitated communication clinics. They pointed to their conflicts of interest.

The opponents also had doubts about the testimonials from parents. They observed that the parents, who were emotionally fragile, may have been biased. To illustrate the power of subconscious biases, they pointed to the unreliable testimonials that persons had provided about Ouija boards, divining rods, and other patently ineffective techniques (Jacobson, Foxx, & Mulick, 2005a; Spitz, 1997).

Opponents pointed out that facilitated communication had not been verified by impartial investigators. They were joined by numerous professionals (American Academy of Child and Adolescent Psychiatry, 1994; American Academy of Pediatrics, 1998; American Association on Mental Retardation, 1994; American Psychological Association, 1994; American Speech-Language-Hearing Association, 1995).

The enthusiasts were asked to provide a convincing theoretical rationale for facilitated communication. When they did not comply, they were bombarded with accusations. Nonetheless, they continued to publish books, run clinics, provide services, and attract clients (Facilitated Communication Institute, 2009).

ANALYZING CONTROVERSIAL ADVICE

Scholars admired graffiti writers; they highlighted their aesthetic, political, economic, and social contributions. They tried to publicize and protect them.

Critics disagreed with the enthusiasts. They pointed out that graffiti writers defaced property, committed crimes, and disturbed the lives of other residents.

The group that endorsed the graffiti writers started out small but grew larger. Some of the groups that endorsed other controversial initiatives also grew. However, some of them did not change in size. The faction that feared fluoride started out and remained small; the one that endorsed vaccinations started out and remained large. Nonetheless, all of these factions shared two traits: they tried to retain their current allies and attract new ones.

When educators endorsed controversial practices, they attempted to retain and attract sympathetic persons. They had success when persons shared their values and assumptions; they had difficulty when they did not share them.

Activity 4.1

You might wish to consider the ways in which the public responded to scholars' advice. You could rely on Table 4.1.

Table 4.1 identifies five situations: the debates about whether graffiti was art, fluoridated water caused cancer, polio vaccines were dangerous, swine flu vaccines were necessary, and bird flu vaccines were necessary.

To complete the table, give a sample of advice for each situation. Also indicate the ways in which members of the public responded to it. You can use symbols.

Use the symbol − if they were not supportive. Use the symbol ± if they were somewhat supportive and the symbol + if they were supportive. As a final step, explain your selections.

Table 4.1. The Public's Response to Scholarly Advice

Incident	*Advice*	*Response to**	*Explanation*
Graffiti and Art			
Fluoride and Cancer			
Vaccine and Polio			
Vaccine and Swine Flu			
Vaccine and Bird Flu			

*− Unsupportive
± Somewhat Supportive
+ Supportive

You can base your answers on the information in this chapter, the materials that are referenced in it, or additional materials. If you are completing this activity with other readers, you can collaborate.

Activity 4.2

You might wish to consider the ways in which groups responded to highly controversial advice. You could use Table 4.2.

Table 4.2 lists five groups: parents of children with autism, parents of children who were at risk for autism, educators, public health officials, and politicians.

Complete this table by indicating the ways in which the groups responded to the controversial warnings about a link between autism and vaccinations. You can use symbols.

Table 4.2. Responses to Allegations That Vaccines Cause Autism

Group	*Response**	*Explanation*
Parents—Children with Autism		
Parents—Children at Risk		
Educators		
Public Health Officials		
Politicians		

*– Unsupportive
± Somewhat Supportive
+ Supportive

Use the symbol − if they were not supportive. Use the symbol ± if they were somewhat supportive and the symbol + if they were supportive. As a final step, explain the bases for the symbols that you selected.

Activity 4.3

You may wish to consider the ways in which groups responded to scholarly and populist advice. You could use Table 4.3.

Table 4.3 lists seven groups: parents of children with autism, parents of children who were at risk for autism, special education teachers, regular education teachers, school administrators, public health officials, and politicians.

This table identifies advice. It lists four instances: the advice to use vaccines, avoid vaccines, use facilitated communication, and avoid facilitated communication.

Complete the table by indicating the ways in which groups responded. You can use symbols.

Use the symbol − if they were not supportive. Use the symbol ± if they were somewhat supportive and the symbol + if they were supportive. Finally, explain the bases for the symbols that you selected.

Activity 4.4

You may wish to consider the ways in which groups responded to advice about instruction. You could use Table 4.4.

Table 4.4 lists five groups: parents of children who had communication problems, parents of children who did not have communication problems, special education teachers, regular education teachers, and school administrators.

This table identifies kinesthetic instructional activities. It list two types: augmentative/alternative communication and facilitated communication.

Complete the table by indicating the ways in which groups responded. You can use symbols.

Use the symbol − if they were not supportive. Use the symbol ± if they were somewhat supportive and the symbol + if they were supportive. As a final step, explain the bases for the symbols that you selected.

SUMMARY

Scholars gave advice to numerous groups. They were pleased when they listened to them; they were chagrined when they ignored them.

Table 4.3. Responses to Advice from Scholars and Populists

	*Response to**				
Group	*Use Vaccines*	*Avoid Vaccines*	*Use Facilitated Communication*	*Avoid Facilitated Communication*	*Explanation*
Parents—Children with Autism					
Parents—Children at Risk					
Teachers—Special Education					

Teachers— Regular Education					
School Administrators					
Health Officials					
Politicians					

*− Unsupportive
± Somewhat Supportive
+ Supportive

Table 4.4. Responses to Advice about Kinesthetic Instruction

	*Response to**		
Group	*AAC*	*Facilitated Communication*	*Rationale*
Parents—Children with Communication Problems			
Parents—Children without Communication Problems			
Teachers—Special Education			
Teachers—Regular Education			
School Administrators			

*– Unsupportive
± Somewhat Supportive
+ Supportive

5

Do Athletes Become the Best Coaches?

Athletics is peppered with former stars.

—Katherine Merry, 2009

Some athletes believed that they were ready to serve as leaders. They maintained that they had been prepared by their experiences as players. Others claimed that they had been prepared by university training programs. They argued about the merits of the two approaches. Persons in many fields, including education, joined the debate.

COACHES

American sports enthusiasts would have little difficulty recognizing Phil Jackson, Jimmy Johnson, Beverly Ann Kearney, Tommy Lasorda, Vince Lombardi, Frank Robinson, Vivian Stringer, Pat Summitt, Marian Washington, and Mary Wise. They would recognize them as players, coaches, or authorities on sports leadership.

Practitioners Provide Advice

The owners of professional teams wanted to recruit superior coaches. Many of them identified playing experience as a critical factor for candidates. They hoped that the former athletes could transform their player achievements into coaching achievements (Gogol, 2002; Halberstam, 2005; Hawkes & Seggar, 2000).

Publishers were eager to disseminate advice from coaches. They realized that their reputations would validate their advice. They published books by high-profile coaches such as Yogi Berra, Paul "Bear" Bryant, Lou Holtz, Tom Landry, Vivian Stringer, and Pat Summitt (Berra & Kaplan, 2008; Bryant & Underwood, 2007; Holtz, 2006; Landry & Lewis, 1990; Stringer & Tucker, 2008; Summitt & Jenkins, 1998).

Although coaches with storied accomplishments gave advice, even those who had failed gave it. Coach Homer Rice, who had won only twelve football games in four coaching seasons, repeatedly gave advice to aspiring leaders (Rice, 1973, 2000, 2004; Rice & Moore, 1985).

Professors Provide Advice

Professors gave advice to sports leaders within university programs. They promised to prepare them for positions in schools, colleges, and professional sports.

The professors identified the traits of sports leaders and devised academic programs to develop them. They wrote books to complement their academic programs (Cassidy, Jones, & Potrac, 2004; Cluck, 2001; Curran, Newhan, & Lopez, 2007; Herbst & Howe, 2007; National Soccer Coaches Association of America, 2004).

The professors searched for information about leadership in various training programs. They then transferred it to sports leadership. They realized that the fields of management and business administration contained invaluable information (Foster, Greyser, & Walsh, 2006; Watt, 2003).

The professors were sure that leaders needed information about marketing. They demonstrated ways that they could market their sports to athletes, viewers, and sponsors (Davis, 2008; Fullerton, 2007; Rein, Kotler, & Shields, 2006; Silk, Andrews, & Cole, 2005; Wakefield, 2007).

Professors advised aspiring sports leaders about finance (Andreff & Szymanski, 2006; DeMause & Cagan, 2008; Fizel, 2006; Masterman, 2007). They urged them to study the fiscal problems associated with professional, collegiate, and Olympic teams (Bowen & Levin, 2003; Brownell, 2008; Hogshead-Makar & Zimbalist, 2007; Krüger & Murray, 2003; Krzyzewski & Spatola, 2009; Porto, 2003; Staudohar & Mangan, 1991; Torr, 2003).

Professors even urged candidates to acquire specialized information about sports law and sports psychology (Dosil, 2006; Epstein, 2003; Gardner & Moore, 2006; D. Greene, 2001; Jarvis, 1999; Silva, Metzler, & Lerner, 2007; Tenenbaum & Eklund, 2007; Thorpe, 2009; G. M. Wong, 2002).

MILITARY PILOTS

Some persons who were interested in sports leaders turned to practitioners for advice; others turned to college professors. Persons in numerous fields, including the military, asked the same groups for help about leadership.

During World War I, personnel officers had to deal with the millions of young men who had enlisted or been inducted. They needed a way to identify the types of vocational responsibilities for which they were qualified (Giordano, 2003).

The officers assigned some soldiers to jobs that were similar to those that they had as civilians. They were able to find corresponding jobs for butchers, bakers, cooks, welders, carpenters, accountants, shoe repairmen, truck drivers, and mechanics.

Although the officers assigned some soldiers to jobs with which they were familiar, they assigned others to eccentric wartime occupations. They gave them novel responsibilities on dreadnought ships, armored vehicles, mobile artillery, observation balloons, submarines, and airplanes (Giordano, 2005).

The officers anticipated that wartime technology would be critical for victory. They were concerned particularly about aviation. They asked the instructors at flight schools for advice about the best persons to serve as pilots. The instructors were confident that they could help; they organized boards to observe, interview, and evaluate candidates (Giordano, 2005).

Professors Provide Advice

The officers accepted the advice of the flight school instructors. However, they still wanted to confirm that their advice was sound. When they compared the number of persons who were admitted to flight schools with the number who graduated, they noted that 96 percent of the students were successful. They wondered whether they could do better.

The officers asked professors to help them identify persons with piloting aptitude. They asked them to devise a screening procedure that was straightforward, easily scored, readily interpreted, reliable, and accurate.

The professors created a set of tests. Because they already had consulted with the flight school trainers, they were confident that they would endorse this new battery (Giordano, 2005).

Opponents Respond

The piloting battery measured multiple skills. It assessed visual acuity, auditory acuity, ability to maintain equilibrium, perception of tilt, perception of depth, reaction to swaying, and athleticism. It included two affective components—stability of emotions and interest in athletics. It also included a cognitive component—mental alertness.

The professors initially allowed the flight school trainers to suggest the tasks for their battery. For example, they acceded to them when they insisted that an equilibrium test was indispensable. However, they later had reservations.

After conducting experiments, the professors concluded that the equilibrium test was a poor predictor of piloting. They even had a better option—a test of emotional stability.

The flight school instructors protested when professors recommended changes to the original battery. Most of their fellow officers sided with them. They eventually recommended the elimination of the piloting aptitude battery; they then recommended the elimination of all other professor-developed tests (Giordano, 2005).

BUSINESS LEADERS

Employers needed persons to fill leadership positions. Although they promoted some current workers, they also selected persons from outside of their firms.

Employers sometimes selected persons with college degrees in the humanities or sciences to serve as managers and executives. They then provided them with training. At other times, they hired business school graduates, whom they assumed already had appropriate training.

Professors Provide Advice

By the end of the twentieth century, professors were educating workers within special business schools. Wishing to make sure that graduates met the expectations of employers, they provided them with comprehensive coursework.

The professors taught undergraduate students about accounting, business law, economics, entrepreneurial ventures, finance, logistics, management, computerized information systems, marketing, and real estate (Schlessinger & Karp, 1995; Shoup, 2005).

The professors also offered courses to graduate students. For example, they provided them with courses that would lead to doctoral degrees. Persons who aspired to jobs with highly specialized responsibilities detected value in certain doctoral degrees, such as those in economics. Nonetheless, most of them concluded that these degrees were better for academicians than business leaders.

Aspiring business leaders and employers judged that doctoral programs had limited usefulness for them. They were intrigued by another type of program—the master of business administration (MBA). They made an impression on university administrators, who asked students and employers about the features of the programs that they valued.

Students indicated that they prized programs with practical features. They valued programs in which they had opportunities to progress rapidly. They also valued chances to take coursework on weekends, during summers, or through computerized modules that they could complete while they retained their current employment.

Students gave a high priority to the reputations of schools. They explained that those reputations created opportunities for them to meet business leaders, secure jobs, and earn competitive salaries (Dick, 2009; Garone, 2009; Middleton, 2009).

Some universities were lauded for superlative business programs. The faculty at those institutions used their reputations to attract the attention of students and employers. Prospective students and employers had little difficulty identifying the most prominent leadership programs in the United States. They readily recognized Carnegie Mellon University; Columbia University; Harvard University; Indiana University; Massachusetts Institute of Technology; New York University; Northwestern University; Stanford University; University of California, Berkeley; University of Chicago; University of Michigan, Ann Arbor; University of North Carolina, Chapel Hill; University of Pennsylvania; University of Southern California; University of Texas, Austin; and the University of Virginia (Middleton, 2009).

Prospective students and employers were able to identify prominent business training programs in Europe. The programs included IE, IESE, and ESADE in Spain. They encompassed IMD in Switzerland, INSEAD in France, and the Copenhagen Business School in Denmark. They included the Cranfield School of Management, the Durham Business School, and the University of Oxford in Great Britain (Middleton, 2009).

After they recognized that MBA degrees were valued, university personnel began to offer variations on them. For example, they offered programs that were accelerated. They also changed them so that participants could meet with executives in multiple countries (Middleton, 2009).

University personnel designed MBA programs to entice employers as well as students. They were aware that some employers wanted to hire managers who had both technical and managerial expertise. They promised that they would supply candidates who had this profile.

Opponents Respond

The business leaders asked experts in universities to help them identify and train leaders. However, some of them were not satisfied (e.g., Broughton, 2008). They decided to offer their own training. They persuaded professional authors to help them distribute their advice through books.

Some business leaders and authors based their books on the lives of successful entrepreneurs, investors, and managers (e.g., Aronson, 2009; Lipczynski, 2008; Mayo & Nohria, 2005; Schroeder, 2008). Others based them on marketing materials, stock market records, profit reports, and research studies (e.g., Blanchard, Hutson, & Willis, 2008; Gates & Hemingway, 1999; Gladwell, 2008; Khan, 2006; Trump & Zanker, 2007).

Some authors of training books took still another approach: they encouraged aspiring leaders to contemplate academic information. However, they made the information accessible to a broad audience (e.g., Anderson, 2006; Ariely, 2008; Harvard Business School, 2002, 2004; Luecke, 2003; Roberto, 2006).

SCHOOL PRINCIPALS

The early citizens were grateful when religious or community leaders volunteered to organize schools. However, they eventually hired a professional teacher for this task. They asked the teacher to manage a schoolhouse, devise curricula, assemble learning materials, and teach students who ranged from six to eighteen years in age (Giordano, 2009).

As their towns and cities grew, citizens were able to establish scholastic programs for students of different ages. They built grand educational facilities to replace their one-room schoolhouses. They also hired multiple teachers to work in them. They appointed school boards to regulate them.

The school boards were responsible for teachers; they also were responsible for specialists and auxiliary personnel. They provided the directives to hire psychologists, nurses, speech-language pathologists, physical therapists, secretaries, repair persons, truant officers, custodians, groundskeepers, and bus drivers.

As they transformed simple schools into complex bureaucracies, the members of school boards realized that they needed still more professionals; they needed principals to manage their new schools.

Professors Provide Advice

Some early principals were trained within their school systems; they served as apprentices to their current principals. Others went off to study with the professors at normal schools, colleges, and universities.

The professors already were training teachers. They taught them about professional behaviors and the content of curricula. They also taught them about pedagogy and psychology. Some professors encouraged them to become political activists (Fraser, 2007; Hartley & Whitehead, 2006; Herbst, 1989; Ogren, 2005; Whitaker, 2007).

When the professors agreed to train principals, they had to decide on the competencies that they would emphasize. They initially emphasized instruction, curriculum, physical facilities, personnel management, and school organization. However, some of them began to supplement with other competencies.

The education professors encouraged aspiring principals to acquire entrepreneurial attitudes. They directed them to emulate leaders in commerce and industry (Bellamy, 2007; Murphy & Meyers, 2008; Wagner, 2008; Wagner & Kegan, 2006). They also directed them to learn about accounting, law, technology, public relations, strategic planning, fund raising, and political lobbying (e.g., Aquila, 2008; Gorton & Alston, 2009; Lifto & Senden, 2004; Marzano, Waters, & McNulty, 2005; Owings & Kaplan, 2006; Palestini & Palestini, 2005; Thomas, 2008).

Opponents Respond

Some persons did not have confidence in the professor-directed programs. They pointed out that the premiere programs for principals were difficult to discern. Although this situation might have been the result of the modest salaries that principals earned, it also might have resulted from uniformly mediocre programs.

Opponents had additional reasons for questioning professor-directed programs; they claimed that they were too politicized. Liberals suspected that conservatives had influenced the ways in which issues were framed (Anderson, 2007; Giordano, 2009, 2010; Ingersoll, 2003; Kumashiro, 2008; Robbins, 2008). Some of them alleged that they had compromised professors' and students' freedom of speech (Giroux, 2007).

Political conservatives also were upset about professor-directed programs. However, they were worried about the excessive influence of the liberals. They claimed that that the liberals harmed the college students in their own classrooms. They added that they continued to cause harm after these students graduated, became leaders in the schools, and imposed their ideological views on colleagues and children (Bérubé, 2006; Horowitz & Laksin, 2009; Smith, Mayer, & Fritschler, 2008).

Some opponents objected to professor-directed training programs because of their dependence on information from business. They questioned whether business-derived information was genuinely relevant to the schools. They recommended that the professors turn instead to public school personnel for information.

The opponents encouraged aspiring principals to consult with experienced school leaders. They endorsed books in which these leaders shared their personal and professional insights about administration (Dubin, 2006; Goldberg, 2006; Wallace, 2008). They also endorsed books in which principals demonstrated how they had dealt with personnel, facilities, student discipline, and public relations (Gray & Smith, 2007; Hayes, 2000, 2007; Hogg & Merler, 2007).

The opponents counseled prospective principals to avoid the training programs at universities; they advised them to collaborate instead with instructional and auxiliary staffs in schools. They gave them advice about ways to create, expand, and sustain this collaboration (Byrne-Jiménez & Orr, 2007; Dana & Bourisaw, 2006; Spillane & Diamond, 2007).

Some opponents encouraged principals to return to an earlier era and personally train their administrative associates and successors. They also suggested that they designate mentors to provide this training (Allen & Ort, 2008; Knight, 2009; *Mentoring, Coaching, and Collaboration*, 2008; Morse & Schifter, 2009; Reeves, 2009; Sergiovanni, 2009; Walker, 2010).

Opponents of university training programs recommended several routes to leadership. They noted that some of these routes might be especially suitable for women and the members of racial minority groups (Dana & Bourisaw, 2006; Dubin, 2006; Gardiner, Enomoto, & Grogan, 2000; Walker & Byas, 2009).

Opponents of university training programs were aware that professors had an advantage over them because they not only provided training but also academic degrees. They proposed that practitioners be authorized to confer these degrees (Foderaro, 2010).

ANALYZING ADVICE FROM PRACTITIONERS AND PROFESSORS

Persons in sports, the military, and business wished to identify effective leaders. They observed that some leaders had acquired their skills on the job while others had acquired them at universities.

The persons who hired educational leaders were struck by the distinct ways in which leaders were trained. Like colleagues in other fields, they experimented with different types of preparatory programs.

Activity 5.1

You may wish to examine professor-directed leadership programs. You could use Table 5.1.

Table 5.1. Professor-Directed Leadership Programs

Program	*Characteristic*	*Strength*	*Weakness*	*Explanation*
Sports				
Military				
Business				
Education				

Table 5.1 identifies four types of programs: those for sports, the military, business, and education.

Complete the table by noting characteristics of the programs. Additionally, note their strengths and weaknesses. As a final step, explain your answers. You can rely on the information in this chapter, the materials that are cited in it, or other materials.

Activity 5.2

You may wish to examine practitioner-directed leadership programs. You could use Table 5.2.

Table 5.2 identifies four types of programs: those for sports, the military, business, and education. Complete this table by noting characteristics of the programs. Additionally, note their strengths and weaknesses. Finally, explain the bases for your answers.

Activity 5.3

You may wish to examine competencies within training programs. You could use Table 5.3.

Table 5.2. Practitioner-Directed Leadership Programs

Program	*Characteristic*	*Strength*	*Weakness*	*Explanation*
Sports				
Military				
Business				
Education				

Table 5.3 identifies groups that developed training programs for principals. It lists two groups: practitioners and professors. It also lists five competencies: personnel management, facilities management, budgeting, public relations, and political lobbying.

Complete this table by indicating the priority that the groups assigned to the competencies. You can rely on symbols.

Use the symbol − if they assigned low priority. Use the symbol ± for moderate priority and the symbol + for high priority. As a final step, explain your responses.

Activity 5.4

You may wish to examine the ways in which groups responded to school leadership programs. You could use Table 5.4.

Table 5.4 identifies groups that were concerned about the training of principals. It lists six groups: aspiring principals, experienced principals, superintendents, school board members, teachers, and parents.

This table also identifies two types of training programs: professor directed and practitioner directed.

Table 5.3. Competencies in Training Programs for Principals

	*Competency**					
Group	*Personnel*	*Facilities*	*Budget*	*Public Relations*	*Lobbying*	*Rationale*
Practitioners						
Professors						

*– Low Priority
± Moderate Priority
+ High Priority

Table 5.4. Responses to Training Programs for Principals

Group	*Response to**		Explanation
	Professor-Directed Program	*Practitioner-Directed Program*	
Aspiring Principals			
Experienced Principals			
Superintendents			
School Board Members			
Teachers			
Parents			

*− Unsupportive
± Somewhat Supportive
+ Supportive

Complete this table by indicating the ways in which groups responded to programs. You can use symbols.

Use the symbol − if they were unsupportive. Use the symbol ± if they were somewhat supportive and the symbol + if they were supportive. As a final step, explain your responses.

SUMMARY

Persons in numerous fields needed effective leaders. Some of them personally identified and trained candidates; others delegated these tasks to professors. When persons needed effective school leaders, they split into similar groups.

6

Should Educators Wrangle with Philosophers?

> Zeno maintains that, at every moment of its flight, the arrow is at rest. . . . [with] no place or time in which it can move.
>
> —Ernest Sosa & Jaegwon Kim, 1998

A philosopher noted that all arrows had to pass through an infinite series of points. He reasoned that the journeys along these passages prevented them from reaching targets. Scholars applied this mind-bending logic to numerous fields, including education.

MOTIONLESS ARROWS

Zeno was a student of Parmenides, the ancient Greek philosopher. He is best known for his impact on other philosophers. He influenced many of them with a conundrum about archers (Meinwald, 1991; Parmenides & Tarán, 1965; Plato, 1983; Sosa & Kim, 1998).

Zeno noted that archers could identify the halfway points for arrows' trajectories. However, they also could identify the quarter points. They could continue to divide segments hundreds, thousands, tens of thousands, millions, and billions of times.

Zeno asked whether the archers ever would be unable to subdivide arrows' trajectories at least one more time. If they never would reach such points, the opportunities to make partitions would be infinite. However, arrows that had to pass through infinite series of partitions could not reach targets (Mazur, 2007).

After he had posed his paradox, Zeno did not encourage persons to stand between arrows and targets. After all, he was concerned about logic rather than weapons. He hoped that his contemporaries would study his puzzle, form logical insights, and then generalize those insights to other problems.

Scholars were inspired by Zeno's logic. They eventually used it to defend innovative practices in numerous disciplines, including psychology and education. However, their opponents used the identical logic to discount those practices.

SKETCHING WITH THE RIGHT SIDE OF THE BRAIN

Betty Edwards was an education professor with advice for art students. She urged them to disregard stepwise drawing lessons and rely instead on Zen-like activities.

Edwards presented her unconventional activities in a 1970s book. She gave the book a clever title, *Drawing on the Right Side of the Brain*. She advised readers that the activities in it were rooted in research about the localized functions of the neurological hemispheres (Edwards, 1979, 1999).

Professional authors were impressed by Edwards's holistic activities. However, they did not always rely on her justification. Some of them claimed that cognitive psychology provided a better basis for them (Gardner, 1982).

Authors were extremely ambitious when they published books about the neurological basis for creativity (Springer & Deutsch, 1981). Some of them claimed that readers would be able to acquire twin-hemisphere neural power and apply it to their jobs (Wonder & Donovan, 1984). Others promised that they could acquire this power in only thirty days (Harary & Weintraub, 1991).

READING RAPIDLY IN THE WHITE HOUSE

Persons realized that drawing was a complex and difficult process. They anticipated that they would have to practice extensively to become artists. They became excited when they were informed that they could expedite the process by engaging the appropriate neurological hemisphere.

Like drawing, reading was a complex and challenging process. After all, most persons had begun it as youngsters, practiced it in school, and refined it as adults. They became curious when they were advised about a shortcut to faster reading speeds.

Adults who wished to accelerate their reading were excited during the early 1960s. Reporters informed them that the newly elected president, John Kennedy, read six newspapers every morning over breakfast. They explained that he had learned to read at this rate by attending a speed reading course.

Evelyn Wood had offered the commercial course in which Kennedy had enrolled. Although she charged tuition, she guaranteed that she would refund it to participants who did not double their reading speeds. To comply with this guarantee, she measured students' reading speeds during the first and the last sessions of each course.

A *Time* magazine reporter asked Kennedy's instructors about his reading speed at the end of his course. Although they did not have the information, they detected an opportunity to help the reporter, the president, and their business. Aware that the average college student read at three hundred words per minute, they generously speculated that Kennedy read at six hundred to seven hundred words per minute. After Kennedy insisted that this estimate was too low, the reporter doubled it (Reeves, 1993).

Like the eighteenth-century fable about George Washington tossing a coin across the Potomac River, the contemporary story about Kennedy reading six newspapers each morning was repeated frequently. It attracted the attention of believers and skeptics for decades (John F. Kennedy, 2009; Noah, 2000; Reeves, 1993; Suero & Garside, 2001).

IMPROVING ACADEMIC INSTRUCTION

Educators hoped to find new types of academic instruction. They were fascinated by speed reading. Enthusiasts assured them that several hours of instruction could enable persons to double, triple, or quadruple their reading speeds.

Opponents questioned the claims about speed reading. They pointed out that adults had required tens of thousands of hours to reach their current levels of proficiency. They wondered how they could raise those levels in just several hours. They accused the enthusiasts of exaggerating. Nonetheless, they had little influence on consumers, who were more impressed by the testimonials of a charismatic president.

Early Attempts to Accelerate Eye Movements

The 1960s enthusiasts searched for strategies to increase reading rates. However, they were not the first investigators to go on this quest.

Early twentieth-century researchers suspected that inefficient eye movements were a primary reason for reading problems. Even though they informally had observed the ways in which persons moved their eyes during reading, they needed special equipment to continue their explorations.

The researchers designed devices to photograph readers' eyes. One of them was the size of a midsized sedan. It had a lectern at one end and a wooden stirrup at the other. Educators placed a book onto the lectern and a reader's head onto the stirrup. To ensure that the head did not move, they secured it with a leather strap.

After they had positioned books and strapped heads, the researchers aimed narrow beams of light at subjects' eyes. After instructing the subjects to read, they filmed the reflected beams.

Readers focused their eyes on a printed item, made a jump, and then refocused on another item. They exhibited this saccadic pattern across each line of print. They gathered no information while their eyes were in motion; they acquired it only when they were resting.

If a printed line comprised twelve six-letter words, persons who focused on individual letters crossed it in seventy-two muscular movements. Persons who focused on whole words crossed it in just twelve movements; those who focused on phrases crossed it in still fewer movements (Giordano, 2000).

The researchers assumed that the eye movements determined the amount of energy that persons expended. They also reasoned that they limited the reading speeds that they achieved.

The researchers encouraged teachers to photograph and study students' eyes. However, the teachers protested that the diagnostic equipment was expensive and hard to operate. The researchers were able to reduce the cost of diagnostic equipment. They also trained specialists to operate it.

The researchers were pleased when school administrators purchased their equipment and hired specialists. Nonetheless, they still were not completely satisfied. They did not want to simply diagnose readers; they wanted to help them.

The researchers advised educators to complement their diagnostic gear with therapeutic equipment. They developed relatively inexpensive projectors to rhythmically flash phrases at students. Using the projectors like metronomes, the teachers progressively increased the operating speeds and the sizes of the phrases that they displayed.

Early Opponents

Some persons were enthusiastic about strategies and equipment to accelerate eye movements. They believed that they could use them to increase the efficiency of struggling, average, and even superior students. However, business leaders had an additional reason that they were enthusiastic.

The business leaders had been using novel managerial practices to increase the efficiency of factories, farms, transportation networks, retail outlets, and supply centers. They encouraged teachers to use comparable practices in the schools. They judged that speed reading was an ideal practice.

Business leaders viewed technology as another resource that teachers needed to cultivate. They had benefitted professionally by relying on this resource; they assured teachers that they also would benefit. They suggested that they rely more on copying machines, motion picture projectors, radios, typewriters, and adding machines.

Business leaders prodded educators to use the technology that had been developed outside of the schools; they also encouraged them to commission distinctive machines for their classrooms. They approved of the diagnostic equipment for analyzing eye movements and the instructional machines for accelerating them.

Enthusiasts supported greater reliance on technology, a businesslike culture, and the use of speed reading in school. However, their opponents warned that these initiatives would transform schools into instructional factories (Giordano, 2009, 2010).

The opponents preferred to use instructional approaches that were pedagogically and philosophically distinct from speed reading. For example, they used the children's literature approach, which relied on books that reflected students' individual backgrounds, interests, and problems. They also used the children's language approach, which relied on transcripts of students' utterances (Giordano, 2000, 2009).

Recent Attempts to Accelerate Eye Movements

During the early part of the twentieth century, persons were entranced by the prospect of reading more rapidly. They remained fascinated during subsequent eras. Many of them were inspired when a president claimed that a commercial course had enabled him to read at breakneck speeds.

The early educators tried to increase speed by modifying eye movements. The later educators developed additional strategies. For example, they recommended that readers use counterintuitive scanning patterns to change their current habits (Konstant, 2000; Marks Beale & Mullan, 2008; Sutz & Weverka, 2009).

The speed reading instructors wanted students to change the techniques that they had learned in school. They realized that these techniques, which some students had used throughout elementary school, high school, and college, would be difficult to modify. Therefore, they substituted radically different sorts of techniques.

The students in speed reading programs read a line of print from left to right. However, they read the subsequent line from right to left. They continued to use this zigzag pattern as they progressed through passages. They also expanded their focal area and grasped several sentences simultaneously.

Many adolescents and adults were frustrated when they tried to use eccentric reading strategies. They found them especially hard to apply to technical manuals, textbooks, and professional materials (Moidel, 1998; Wechsler & Bell, 2006).

When adolescents and adults were frustrated by speed reading strategies, proponents had a supplementary technique to help them. They urged them to form hypotheses about the content in passages and then try to confirm them. They explained that this procedure had undergirded the commercial speed reading courses that Evelyn Wood had developed (Frank, 1990).

Some enthusiasts recommended that young children use speed reading techniques. One author conveyed his enthusiasm for youthful audiences in his book's title, *Quantum Speed-Reading: Awakening Your Child's Mind* (Tobitani, 2006).

Many enthusiasts used the titles of their books to lure consumers. To convince them that they could easily and rapidly acquire new skills, they made sure that their titles included reassuring phrases. They selected phrases such as *triple your reading speed, speed reading in a week, read faster, recall more, speed reading and maximum recall,* and *increasing reading speed, comprehension, and general knowledge* (Buzan, 2006; Cutler, 1993; Konstant, 2002; Wainwright, 2001).

Novel Equipment and Software

The recent enthusiasts of speed reading have continued to rely on the strategies that were popular during earlier eras. For example, they have continued to rely on the examination and modification of eye movements. However, they did not use the primitive mechanical devices that earlier practitioners employed; they devised more sophisticated and powerful equipment (Hyönä, Radach, & Deubel, 2003; Kaminski & Leigh, 2002; Radach, Kennedy, & Rayner, 2004; Van Gompel, 2007).

The enthusiasts improved the equipment for analyzing eye movements and the projectors for accelerating them. They also developed software to enable teachers to substitute personal computers for projectors.

Enthusiasts regularly identified the top speed reading software programs. They recommended products such as *The Reader's Edge, Ace Reader*

Pro, Rocket Reader, Ultimate Speed Reader, Speed Your Read, IQ Infinite Mind, and *Fluent Reading* (Speed Reading Software Review, 2009; What Is Speed Reading, 2006).

Enthusiasts, entrepreneurs, and marketers advised consumers about popular speed reading programs. They also identified the distinctive features of these programs. They indicated whether they included warm-up exercises, timed tests, comprehension tests, progress reports, and opportunities to regulate the styles, colors, and sizes of fonts. They distinguished those that incorporated flashed or stable presentations, horizontal or vertical formats, partial or full passages, highlighted or nonhighlighted phrases, and automatically or manually adjusted speeds (Speed Reading Software Review, 2009).

Recent Opponents

The early opponents of speed reading objected to its competitive nature; they worried that it would discourage some children. They also objected to its similarities with business practices. Recent opponents have continued to raise these objections. However, they have made additional objections.

Some opponents noted that the diagnosis and altering of eye movement resembled medical practices. They questioned whether the enthusiasts had the training to identify ailments and prescribe treatments (Giordano, 2000).

Some opponents objected to the expense of speed reading programs. They concluded that the benefits were not in proportion to this expense. They suggested that school funds be diverted from speed reading and used for less costly types of instruction, equipment, and curricula (Giordano, 2009, 2010).

The speed reading enthusiasts tried to answer their opponents. They frequently addressed them indirectly: they supplied testimonials from persons who had enrolled in the programs and improved their skills.

Opponents of speed reading were not impressed by testimonials. They compared them to the notoriously unreliable statements about the effectiveness of medical placebos (Giordano, 2010).

VOCATIONAL INSTRUCTION

Some nineteenth-century students were not learning to read, calculate, and write. Because they had not acquired fundamental academic skills, they also had difficulty mastering the advanced skills that they needed to progress in geography, civics, history, literature, and the sciences.

Parents were disturbed when their children struggled. They wanted them to stay in school, graduate, get good jobs, prosper, and lead happy lives. All of these goals could be threatened by academic difficulties.

Employers and leaders in the military also were disturbed by struggling students. They wanted them to succeed so that they would be qualified for critical jobs in business and the armed services.

Politicians joined the groups that were concerned about struggling students. They wanted students to learn so that they eventually could participate in a democratic government. They also hoped that they would prosper and pay local, state, and federal taxes.

Educators shared the concerns about struggling students. However, some of them did not want to provide them with academic help.

Early Proponents

Some educators questioned whether they should offer academic help to challenged students. They judged that they would benefit more from alternative rather than traditional scholastic curricula.

Enthusiasts were excited about vocational curricula. They pointed out that these curricula could address the concerns of parents, business leaders, military leaders, and politicians. Some of them suggested that they be integrated into traditional schools; others suggested that they be offered at independent technical schools (Cremin, 1988; Gordon, 1999; Jeynes, 2007; Kliebard, 1999).

Although several groups supported vocational schools, employers may have been the most ardent advocates. They pressured politicians to fund them.

Early Opponents

Many of the educators were upset about vocational curricula. They were convinced that they were less effective than the traditional curricula. They also were convinced that they would divert money from them.

The supporters of the vocational curricula had a rejoinder: they insisted that vocational curricula were necessary for the many children who failed with the traditional curricula. Some of these children dropped out of school and worked in menial jobs; others became juvenile delinquents, vagrants, alcoholics, drug addicts, or prostitutes (Giordano, 2000).

The opponents of vocational curricula realized that they needed allies. They asked the parents whose children were failing in traditional programs to remain confident in them. They also appealed to other groups. However, they were disheartened by some of their responses.

Employers and military leaders were not impressed by the supplications from the opponents of vocational curricula. They believed that the new curricula would prepare students for civilian and military careers.

African Americans joined the supporters of vocational curricula. They believed that they would help their children earn a living (Fisher, 1967; Spivey, 1978).

Special educators also joined the supporters. They believed that vocational curricula would help students with disabilities become financially and socially independent (Giordano, 2007; Osgood, 2008).

The proponents of vocational curricula attracted additional supporters during World War I. They contended that their curricula were critical for America's economy and its national security. They repeated these contentions during the post–World War I era, World War II, and the cold war. They gloated when their opponents had difficulty retorting (Ben-Porath, 2006; Giordano, 2004).

Recent Proponents

The vocational educators antagonized traditional educators during the early years of the twentieth century. They competed for funds from local communities, states, and the federal government. They continue to compete for these funds today.

Vocational educators currently attract many students to their programs. A 2004 survey revealed that 50 percent of American students were involved in some form of vocational training (United States Department of Education, 2004b).

In spite of the impressive advances that they made, the vocational educators bickered among themselves. They disagreed about the goal of their training. Some of them contended that it was to inform students about a broad range of employment opportunities; others countered that it was to prepare them for specific jobs.

The vocational educators also disagreed about the students for whom their instruction was appropriate. Some of them focused on adolescents and adults; others broadened their focus to encompass younger children (Magisos, 1973; Marland, McClure, & Buan, 1973; Perry & Sherlock, 2008; Wilson & Hayes, 2000).

Some of the vocational educators were entrepreneurs. Although they looked for opportunities to help adults secure specialized jobs, they also looked for opportunities to make profits. They eventually established numerous proprietary schools (Vocational Schools Database, 2010). They even persuaded companies to pay the tuition for employees to attend these schools (Olson, 2010a).

The proponents argued about numerous issues; they even argued about the name with which to designate vocational education. They argued about whether to call it manual, career, adult, trade, industrial, or technical education (Clery, 2008; National Center for Education Statistics, 2002).

Recent Opponents

Opponents have continued to pose questions about vocational programs. They questioned whether their curricula should include academics or concentrate exclusively on job-specific information.

The vocational educators retorted by pointing to instances in which exclusively technical or exclusively scholastic training had helped students. They also identified programs in which both types of education had been integrated cohesively. For example, they noted that many community colleges had blended traditional scholastic programs with vocational training (Greene, 2009).

Opponents made additional accusations against vocational educators. Some of them accused them of excessive regimentation. They claimed that their restrictive structures prevented students from obtaining and retaining jobs in their own communities (Gill, Fluitman, & Dar 2000; Kincheloe, 1999; Middleton, Ziderman, & Van Adams, 1993).

The proponents responded by identifying vocational education programs that were synchronized to community opportunities. Some of them identified programs that prepared students for employment in rural communities; others highlighted those that qualified them for the opportunities in urban locales (Dickar, 2008; Eddy & Murray, 2007; Repetto, 1990; Ritchey, 2008; Stone, 1998).

Proponents of vocational education found additional ways to respond to their opponents. Some of them pointed to programs that had been designed for workers who had been laid off by their local employers (Olson, 2010b). Others highlighted programs that prepared persons for domestic jobs that were changing as a result of international economic pressure (Canning, Godfrey, & Holzer-Zelazewska, 2007; Clarke & Winch, 2007; Green, 2007; Heijke & Muysken, 2000; Hyland & Winch, 2007; Merriam, Courtenay, & Cervero, 2006).

Opponents questioned the ways in which students from minority groups were treated in vocational programs. The vocational educators responded by identifying programs that had been modified for women and racial minority groups (Ginsberg, Shapiro, & Brown, 2004; López, 2003). Some of them highlighted training programs that had been adapted for persons with physical, cognitive, or emotional disabilities (DeFur & Patton, 1999; Loyd & Brolin, 1997; Palomaki, 1981; Pierangelo & Giuliani, 2004).

Opponents were concerned that politicians had an excessive influence on vocational programs. Although proponents publicly decried this influence, they privately cultivated it (Chambers, 2006; Henig & Rich, 2004; Wong, 2007).

ANALYZING ADVICE ABOUT NOVEL INSTRUCTION

The educators who were dissatisfied with typical art activities looked for one that was based on a different sort of pedagogy. Those who were dissatisfied with typical scholastic activities also looked for alternatives. Some of them devised learning activities that they could integrate within their traditional curricula; other devised entirely new types of curricula.

Activity 6.1

You may wish to examine the goals for instructional activities. You could use Table 6.1.

Table 6.1 identifies four types of activities: drawing with the right side of the brain, modifying eye movements, scanning, and completing the job mastery tasks within vocational curricula.

Complete this table by identifying the goals that proponents set for the activities. Additionally, specify the strengths and weaknesses of the

Table 6.1. Strengths and Weaknesses of Instructional Activities

Activity	*Goal*	*Strength*	*Weakness*	*Explanation*
Right-Brain Drawing				
Altered Eye Fixations				
Scanning				
Job Activities				

activities. Finally, explain the bases for your responses. You can rely on information from this chapter, the citations within it, or another source.

Activity 6.2

You may wish to examine the ways in which groups responded to instructional activities. You could use Table 6.2.

Table 6.2 lists seven groups: parents, students, teachers, principals, school board members, employers, and politicians. It also identifies four types of activities: drawing with the right side of the brain, modifying eye movements, scanning, and completing the job mastery tasks within vocational curricula.

Complete this table by indicating the ways in which groups responded to activities. You can rely on symbols.

Use the symbol − if they were not supportive. Use the symbol ± if they were somewhat supportive and the symbol + if they were supportive. As a final step, explain the bases for the symbols that you selected.

Activity 6.3

You can examine the ways in which groups responded to novel instructional activities when these were integrated into traditional academic curricula. You could use Table 6.3.

Table 6.3 lists seven groups: parents, students, teachers, principals, school board members, employers, and politicians.

This table gives you opportunities to identify the ways in which groups responded to an innovative instructional activity: the use of scanning within reading curricula. It also gives you the chance to designate another innovative instructional activity and the traditional curricula into which it was introduced.

Complete the table by indicating the ways in which groups responded to activities. You can use symbols.

Use the symbol − if they were not supportive. Use the symbol ± if they were somewhat supportive and the symbol + if they were supportive. As a final step, explain the bases for the symbols that you selected.

Activity 6.4

You can examine the ways in which groups responded to novel instructional activities when they were incorporated into nontraditional curricula. You could use Table 6.4.

Table 6.4 lists seven groups: parents, students, teachers, principals, school board members, employers, and politicians.

Table 6.2. Responses to Instructional Activities

	*Response to**				
Group	*Right-Brain Drawing*	*Altered Eye Fixations*	*Scanning*	*Job Activities*	*Explanation*
Parents					
Students					
Teachers					
Principals					
School Board Members					
Employers					
Politicians					

*– Unsupportive
± Somewhat Supportive
+ Supportive

Table 6.3. Responses to Academic Activities

	*Response to**		
Group	*Scanning and Reading*	*Other:*	*Explanation*
Parents			
Students			
Teachers			
Principals			
School Board Members			
Employers			
Politicians			

*− Unsupportive
± Somewhat Supportive
+ Supportive

This table gives you chances to indicate the ways in which groups responded to a novel type of instructional activity: the use of job mastery tasks within vocational curricula. It also gives you the chance to designate another novel instructional activity and the nontraditional curricula into which it was introduced.

Table 6.4. Responses to Nonacademic Activities

Group	*Response to**		*Explanation*
	Job Activities and Vocational Curricula	*Other:*	
Parents			
Students			
Teachers			
Principals			
School Board Members			
Employers			
Politicians			

*– Unsupportive
± Somewhat Supportive
+ Supportive

Complete this table by indicating the ways in which groups responded. You can rely on symbols.

Use the symbol − if they were not supportive. Use the symbol ± if they were somewhat supportive and the symbol + if they were supportive. As a final step, explain the bases for the symbols that you selected.

SUMMARY

Educators tried to help students who were struggling in school. Some of them devised novel instructional activities; others devised novel curricula. Both groups generated supporters and opponents.

7

What Motivates Scholars?

The poor invariably accused poverty itself of their destruction.

—Jane Addams, 1912

Critics noted that scholars had personal as well as professional goals. They claimed that their personal goals had an excessive influence on the ways in which they designed, conducted, and shared research. However, the scholars made the same charges against their critics.

A NEW AGE ANTHROPOLOGIST

Carlos Castaneda was an anthropology student at a California university during the 1960s. He attracted international attention with his book *The Teachings of Don Juan: A Yaqui Way of Knowledge*.

Castaneda depicted Don Juan as a spiritual guide who visited alternative worlds. Castaneda claimed that he became a disciple, ingested hallucinatory drugs, and made spiritual journeys with Don Juan.

Although many persons had drug-induced experiences, Castaneda stood out from them. He had been admitted into a reputable doctoral program, had a book published by a scholarly press, and had the support of respected professors.

The editors at the University of California Press published Castaneda's book in 1968. They anticipated that it would be popular. However, they were delighted when it quickly sold over a million copies. Even decades later, it still was selling thousands of copies annually.

Castaneda hastily followed his first book with two more volumes about Don Juan. This trilogy was translated into multiple languages and sold millions of copies (Castaneda, 1968, 1971, 1972).

Castaneda published many more books. He also promoted a commercial program of meditation. However, he could not retain the interest of his audience (Applebome, 1998; Marshall, 2007).

Readers originally were fascinated by Castaneda's scholarly demeanor, engaging narrative style, outrageous stories, and insistence that all of his accounts were true. Nonetheless, they eventually became weary of him. Some of them tired as he recapitulated information from earlier works. Others tired as they lost confidence in his veracity.

Critics suspected that Castaneda fabricated his narratives. After investigating library records from the time that he had been a doctoral student, they noted that he had been in that facility on those dates on which key meetings with Don Juan were supposed to have transpired. They also documented instances in which he lied about his personal life (De Mille, 1976, 1980; Fikes, 1993).

As early as the 1970s, some critics had accused Castaneda of being a charlatan. Even though editors featured him on the cover of *Time* magazine, they highlighted the inconsistencies in his recollections (Don Juan and the Sorcerer's Apprentice, 1973).

After the *Time* magazine incident, Castaneda refused to speak with reporters. Nonetheless, he did conduct seminars for disciples. Some of the disciples admitted that his fabrications were disquieting; others rationalized them as examples of the evasive strategies that he had learned from Don Juan.

Authors wrote books about Castaneda for decades. Some of them extolled his life and teachings; others disputed them (M. R. Castaneda, 1996; Eagle Feather, 2006; Patterson, Allen, & Brinton, 2008; Wallace, 2003).

Loyal disciples of Castaneda chastised followers who left their master and then wrote denigrating books about him. They scolded them for seeking vindication, attention, and money.

AN ENTREPRENEURIAL PSYCHOLOGIST

Edward Thorndike was a prominent New York City psychologist. His professional colleagues acknowledged his prominence when they offered him the presidency of the American Psychological Association. They bestowed this accolade on him before he was even forty years old.

Thorndike conducted research in a new field of study—educational psychology. In fact, he wrote the first textbook on this topic. The original edition was released in 1903; subsequent editions were published for more than six decades (Thorndike, 1903, 1970).

Standardized Tests

Thorndike was a productive author; he also was a prolific creator of tests. His intelligence tests for schoolchildren were extremely popular. Many of his other tests were widely adopted.

Thorndike created tests to measure whether students were learning to read, spell, and calculate. He created additional tests to measure whether they were mastering more elusive academic skills, such as those required to develop handwriting and vocabulary (Thorndike, 1912, 1914, 1921b).

Some educational stakeholders suspected that student learning was declining. They wanted to document the decline and hold educators accountable. They were sure that Thorndike's tests could help them.

Thorndike was flattered that his tests were viewed as useful. However, he also realized that they were profitable. He assured his publishers that he could develop additional profitable products (Giordano, 2005).

Commercial Scholastic Products

Thorndike was aware of the practical problems that teachers and school administrators were facing. He resolved that he would help them.

Thorndike had abilities that qualified him to assist educators. In addition to impressive intelligence, he had rarified organizational skills. He demonstrated his organizational skills when he wrote books for college students and teachers.

Thorndike's books were popular because they contained useful information; they also were popular because of the ways in which they arranged and displayed it. They deftly incorporated introductions, illustrations, summary passages, and charts (Moss & Thorndike, 1949; Thorndike, 1903, 1922, 1940, 1970).

Contemporaries were impressed by the ways in which Thorndike used organizational and formatting techniques to improve his books. However, they had another reason for being impressed. They were struck by his entrepreneurship.

Thorndike displayed business acumen when he created popular materials for reading education. He was aware that teachers used standardized tests to assess the reading levels of students. However, they still had to ascertain the reading levels of books, magazines, and classroom instructional materials. Having already helped them with their students, Thorndike resolved to help them with materials.

Thorndike decided that he would solve this problem scientifically; he would calculate the frequencies with which words occurred in printed materials. Because he was designing a tool for teachers, he chose the materials that they were employing in their classrooms.

Thorndike selected passages from multiple types of materials: classic works of literature, the Bible, children's literature, correspondence, schoolbooks, newspapers, cookbooks, and vocational manuals. Some of his passages, such as those from the Bible, were over three million words in length; others, such as those from vocational manuals, were less than one hundred thousand words (Thorndike, 1921a).

Thorndike displayed the results of his research in a word list. Each word in the list indicated whether it appeared frequently or infrequently. He directed teachers to use the list to classify the words from their own books. He then showed them how to make calculations that would reveal whether those books were suitable for their students.

After he published his word list, Thorndike was pleased with the sales. He continued to publish subsequent editions. In fact, he increased the original list from ten to twenty thousand words; he later increased it to thirty thousand words. These lists were so popular that they were republished for decades (Thorndike, 1921a; Thorndike, 1931; Thorndike & Lorge, 1944, 1968).

Thorndike hoped that teachers would use his word lists to match reading materials to their students' reading levels. However, he detected opportunities to apply them to several business ventures. He used them to transform classic works of literature into graded classroom materials.

Thorndike identified books that were not protected by copyrights. He then used his word lists to rewrite and simplify the vocabulary in them. He identified passages with low-frequency words, eliminated those words, and substituted high-frequency words. As a result, he was able to make those passages easy to read.

Thorndike bowdlerized numerous books. As examples, he rewrote *Andersen's Fairy Tales, The Little Lame Prince, Robinson Crusoe, A Christmas Carol, Black Beauty,* and *The Arabian Nights* (Andersen & Thorndike, 1935; Craik & Thorndike, 1935; Defoe & Thorndike, 1936; Dickens, Thorndike, & Yonge, 1936; Sewell & Thorndike, 1935; Spyri, Thorndike, & Woodward, 1935; Thorndike, 1936).

Thorndike found another opportunity to employ his word lists: he made them the bases for school and home dictionaries. Like his other publications, the dictionaries went through numerous editions (e.g., Thorndike, 1935, 1941, 1942). In fact, they remained profitable long after his death (e.g., Thorndike & Barnhart, 1997, 1999; Thorndike, Palmer, & Ballard, 1973).

A POLITICAL SOCIAL WORKER

Jane Addams had similarities to Thorndike. She was a scholar, lived in one of the largest cities of the era, was internationally acclaimed, and gave advice about the schools.

Addams also exhibited differences from Thorndike. Thorndike searched for principles of learning, conducted validating experiments, and made those experiments the foundation for his educational suggestions. In contrast, Addams was less clear about the bases for her suggestions. She alternatively linked them to psychology, politics, arts, and religion (Addams, 1910, 1912, 1930, 2003).

Addams also stood out from Thorndike because she applied her talents to political rather than entrepreneurial situations. She explained that her suggestions about education had a specific social goal: the elimination of poverty.

Addams believed that persons could end poverty only if they understood its origin. She was convinced that it stemmed from social, legal, and economic injustices. She viewed education as the critical tool for informing persons about those injustices (Addams, 1912).

Politics

Biographers speculated about the factors that influenced Addams. They were curious about those that influenced the problems that she selected and the ways that she solved them.

Some biographers investigated familial and personal events from Addams's childhood (Diliberto, 1999). Others investigated the social, economic, and political events of her adult years (Berson, 2004; Elshtain, 2002; Fischer, Nackenoff, & Chmielewski, 2009; Knight, 2005).

Biographers were struck by Addams's remarkable rhetorical skills. They wondered whether she had been influenced by her contemporaries. Some of them concentrated on her political relationships with reformers; others focused on her sexual relationships with women (Brown, 2004; Deegan, 1988; Hamington, 2004; Jackson, 2009).

Addams displayed a full range of rhetorical techniques. She was conciliatory when religious conservatives depicted her as an atheist and a communist. She responded that she championed the same social changes that they supported. However, she was confrontational when critics pressured her to change her political stances on women's suffrage and international pacifism (Addams, 2003; Addams, Whipps, & Fischer, 2003; Hamington, 2009; Starr, Deegan, & Wahl, 2003).

Hull House

Addams generated a great deal of publicity with Hull House. This was an establishment that combined the facilities of schools with those of social agencies. Although it had classrooms, it also encompassed a gymnasium, playground, library, lunch shop, art museum, music recital hall, infirmary, and bathing area (Addams, 1910, 1930, 2003).

Addams attracted adults as well as children to Hull House. She gave them opportunities to learn English, register to vote, meet with mental health counselors, and join labor unions. She even offered residence to women who had been abandoned or abused.

The politicians, school administrators, and social workers from multiple communities visited Hull House. They hoped to replicate it in their own communities.

REACTIONARY PEDAGOGUES

Phonics-based reading instruction was popular during the late 1800s. It required students to blend the sounds of letters. It gradually replaced alphabet-based instruction, a classroom practice in which students recited the names of letters (Giordano, 2000, 2009).

Although many teachers chose phonics-based or alphabet-based instruction, they had other options. Some of them chose whole-word instruction. These teachers required students to perform repetitive drills until they were able to recognize words spontaneously.

A Literacy Reactionary

Rudolf Flesch studied reading education at Columbia University. After he graduated, he demonstrated a knack for simplifying complex scholastic information, such as Thorndike's system for computing the reading levels of materials (Flesch, 1943).

Teachers who used Thorndike's approach had to extract words from printed materials, look up those words in a long list, and then make time-consuming calculations. Those who employed Flesch's approach selected a short passage, computed the average number of syllables in the words, and the average number of words in the sentences. By plotting these two figures on a graph, they quickly discerned the reading level of that passage (Flesch, 1951).

Flesch eponymously referred to his new procedure as the Flesch formula. Although his opponents conceded that the formula was simple, they protested that it was inaccurate.

Opponents cited encyclopedias, which comprised short words and sentences, as examples of books that the Flesch formula would depict as simple to read. They pointed out that these materials actually were difficult to read because they contained densely compacted information (Giordano, 2000).

Flesch ignored his opponents; he continued to promote his formula. He inspired other scholars, who devised similar procedures (Giordano, 2000).

Flesch also was concerned about instructional techniques. He judged that phonics was the simplest and most effective type of reading instruction. However, he did not give this advice to teachers, school administrators, or professors; he gave it directly to parents.

Flesch wrote a book that tapped into parents' fears. He grabbed their attention with the title: *Why Johnny Can't Read: And What You Can Do about It*. He adjured them to confront the many teachers who were using whole-word instruction. He urged them to demand that they replace whole-word instruction with phonics (Flesch, 1955).

Parents loved Flesch's book. They were attracted to the clear and unpretentious manner in which it simplified a complicated learning problem. They purchased it for decades. They bought so many copies that Flesch did not even update it for thirty years (Flesch, 1986).

Flesch tried to extend his success with other books. He authored writing manuals, compendia of quotations, logic books, rhetorical guides, and study-skill workbooks; he even developed materials for lawyers and business leaders (Flesch, 1957, 1960, 1966, 1972, 1974, 1979).

Competitors tried to duplicate Flesch's achievements. Like him, they proposed simple solutions to complex school problems (Bauerlein, 2008; Sykes, 1995). Like him, they aimed their books at parents. They even selected deferential titles such as *Why Johnny Can't Add* and *Why Johnny Can't Write* (Kline, 1973; Linden & Whimbey, 1990).

Many politicians respected Flesch. Those who were politically conservative agreed with him that reading skills had declined. They also agreed that phonics was a simple and inexpensive way to reverse the decline.

Opponents

Some parents admired the way in which Flesch had identified an inexpensive solution to a chronic instructional problem. However, others characterized his advice as antiquated and ineffective. They preferred different sorts of instructional materials.

Flesch's opponents used varied materials to stimulate students. Some of them ignored standardized reading materials and relied instead on children's books. Others wrote down students' utterances and made these transcriptions into bases for instruction.

His opponents insisted that they had located types of instruction that were more stimulating and effective than phonics. They added that their materials were especially well suited to students who spoke languages other than English (Giordano, 2000, 2009, 2010).

A Historical Reactionary

Flesch claimed that students' reading skills had deteriorated. He specified the cause—the introduction of innovative reading practices. He then specified the solution—a return to earlier instructional practices.

Flesch was a reactionary who protested against the prevailing pedagogy in reading education. However, reactionaries railed against the pedagogy in several other academic disciplines. Some of them were sure that current pedagogy was responsible for students' declining knowledge of history.

Diane Ravitch was a New York City professor and a bureaucrat in the federal Department of Education. She was concerned about history. She contended that students knew little about it.

Ravitch used the results of 1980s standardized history tests to validate her allegations. She was startled that many students could not identify famous historical figures, the events with which they were associated, or even the centuries during which they had lived. She warned that this deficiency would create grave trouble for the students, employers, the government, and the entire nation (Ravitch & Finn, 1987).

Ravitch looked for the reasons that students' knowledge of history had declined. She concluded that pedagogical innovators and politically liberal interest groups had deleted key information from curricula. She added that they then had substituted extraneous information. She claimed that they had confused students, who then had lost sight of their historical heritage (Finn & Ravitch, 2007; Ravitch, 2003, 2007; Ravitch & Finn, 1987).

Politically conservative citizens were upset about students' declining knowledge of history; they also were concerned about their declining interest in it. Many of them blamed feminist groups for removing religious information and replacing it with their political information (Hess, 2008; McGreal, 2009; Sommers, 2000; Survey: U.S. Students, 2008).

Conservative politicians shared the concerns about students' declining interest in history. They also detected a declining commitment to patriotism and traditional American values (Giordano, 2003, 2009, 2010). They became fervent allies of the reactionaries (Bauder, 2007;

Foerstel, 2002; J. C. McKinley, 2010a, 2010b; Robelen, 2010; Shackelford, 2010).

Opponents

Some reactionaries blamed innovative learning materials for students' declining interest in historical facts. However, the innovators were not intimidated by the accusations; they fiercely challenged the reactionaries.

The pedagogical innovators came up with their own explanations for students' declining interest in history. They did not believe that the decline was the result of new learning materials. After noting that contemporary materials had changed little from those in earlier classrooms, they adduced this inertia as a more likely explanation for the students' disinterest.

Although the pedagogical innovators did not observe extensive changes in learning materials, they endorsed those that they did detect. They supported materials that highlighted the relationships between past and current events. They also supported materials that highlighted politics, race, gender, economics, employment, and culture. They gave examples of the types of materials that they recommended.

Pedagogical innovators recommended that teachers use contemporary music to explain recent history. They contended that it could be a tool with which to analyze multiple issues in the community, state, nation, and the world. They identified historical accounts of hip-hop that could stimulate students intellectually and engage them emotionally (George, 1998; Watkins, 2005).

The pedagogical innovators had additional recommendations. They suggested that librarians assemble collections that would appeal to young persons. As examples, they recommended that they collect contemporary music, graphic novels, and video games. They impressed the American Library Association, which published advice about collecting and distributing unconventional materials (Anderson, 2005; Burek Pierce, 2008; McGrath, 2002; Neiburger, 2007).

Some pedagogical innovators urged teachers to change instructional techniques as well as learning materials. For example, they recommended that they create hip-hop melodies and rhymes to help students recollect important historical information (Harrison & Rappaport, 2006).

ANALYZING ADVICE FROM SCHOLARS

Critics pointed out that scholars were motivated by personal as well as professional goals. They worried that their personal goals restricted the problems that they selected, the investigative tools that they employed, and the results that they shared.

Scholars had similar accusations for their critics. They accused them of making one-sided attacks to promote special interests, gain fame, and accumulate wealth.

Activity 7.1

You may wish to examine scholars' goals. You could use Table 7.1.

Table 7.1 identifies scholars associated with anthropology, educational psychology, social work, reading education, and history education. It lists five scholars: Carlos Castaneda, Edward Thorndike, Jane Addams, Rudolf Flesch, and Diane Ravitch.

To complete the table, identify the goals that the scholars set when they designed, conducted, and shared research. Identify their explicit professional goals and their implicit personal goals. As a final step, explain the bases for your answers.

Table 7.1. Explicit and Implicit Goals

	Goal		
Scholar	*Explicit*	*Implicit*	*Explanation*
Carlos Castaneda			
Edward Thorndike			
Jane Addams			
Rudolf Flesch			
Diane Ravitch			

Table 7.2. Influence of Money

Group	Response to*					Rationale
	Castaneda	Thorndike	Addams	Flesch	Ravitch	
Supporters						
Critics						

*− Insignificant Influence
± Moderate Influence
+ Significant Influence

You can complete this table from the information in this chapter, the citations in it, or other sources. You can complete it individually, with another reader, or with a small group of readers.

Activity 7.2

You may wish to investigate whether money had an impact on the ways in which persons responded to scholars. You could rely on Table 7.2.

Table 7.2 identifies two groups: persons who supported scholars and those who criticized them. It also identifies five scholars: Carlos Castaneda, Edward Thorndike, Jane Addams, Rudolf Flesch, and Diane Ravitch.

Complete the table by indicating the degrees to which money influenced persons when they became supporters or critics of the scholars. You can rely on symbols.

Select the symbol − if money had an insignificant influence. Select the symbol ± if it had a moderate influence and the symbol + if it had a significant influence. As a final step, explain the bases for the symbols that you selected.

Activity 7.3

You might wish to specify the ways in which groups responded to critics. You could rely on Table 7.3.

Table 7.3. Responses to Education Scholars

Group	Response to*					Rationale
	Castaneda	Thorndike	Addams	Flesch	Ravitch	
Supporters						
Critics						

*P Parents
T Teachers
S School Administrators
L Liberal Politicians
C Conservative Politicians
B Business Leader

Table 7.3 differentiates persons who supported educational scholars from those who criticized them. It also identifies five education scholars: Carlos Castaneda, Edward Thorndike, Jane Addams, Rudolf Flesch, and Diane Ravitch.

Complete the table by classifying groups as supporters or critics of the scholars. Classify the following groups: parents, teachers, school administrators, politically liberal elected officials, politically conservative elected officials, and business leaders. You can use abbreviations.

Use the letter *P* for parents, *T* for teachers, *S* for school administrators, *L* for politically liberal elected officials, *C* for politically conservative elected officials, and *B* for business leaders. As a final step, explain the bases for your classifications.

SUMMARY

Critics claimed that scholars were distracted by irrelevant issues when they designed, conducted, and shared research. However, the scholars made the identical accusations against their critics.

8

Can Politicians Fix the Schools?

What you make of your education will decide nothing less than the future of this country.

—Barack Obama, 2009

Scholars were concerned about the ways in which persons responded to them. They used rhetorical strategies to win their support. Many of them concentrated on gaining the support of politicians. Although the politicians were impressed by the information from the scholars, they also were impressed by the rhetorical strategies with which they presented it.

APOLITICAL SCHOLARS

Arthur Schopenhauer was a nineteenth-century professor. He attracted listeners when he recommended that males have sex only with each other. However, he soon alienated them when he explained that he endorsed gay behavior only because it might prevent the conception of additional human wretches.

Schopenhauer and his disciples were referred to as philosophical pessimists. They claimed that they were unconcerned about this unflattering epithet. They insisted that they were ready to endure demeaning remarks or ostracism in order to pursue truth (Atwell, 1995; Hannan, 2009; Jacquette, 1996; Tanner, 1999).

POLITICAL SCHOLARS

Some scholars were not bothered by the ways in which professional colleagues and the public responded to their advice; however, most of them did care. They tried to persuade them to agree with them on numerous topics, including the environment, health, and business.

Environment

Environmental scholars offered information about the immediate and long-term impact of the expanding human population. However, they did not elicit the types of responses for which they had hoped. Therefore, they searched for strategies with which to showcase their information (Ball & Johnson, 2010b; Kessel, 2006; Nash, 2006; Ward & Warren, 2007).

Scholars wanted to educate the public about environmental perils. However, they had another motive: they wanted the public to become excited enough to place pressure on politicians. They hoped that the politicians then would provide the legislation, ordinances, and funding to deter perils.

The scholars hoped that politicians would surrender to the public when it demanded environmental reforms. They hoped that they would capitulate in the same way that they had when the public demanded health reforms.

Public Health

Numerous groups worried about health problems. These groups included scholars, doctors, nurses, religious leaders, and parents. Aware that they could not solve problems on their own, they asked politicians for help.

Politicians historically had supported persons who advocated for public health. Some of them were supportive because they genuinely shared their concerns. However, they had additional reasons to join them. They hoped that their rhetorical postures on health issues would win elections; they also hoped that they would advance initiatives that were unrelated to health but important to them (Bennett & DiLorenzo, 2000; Wright, 2005).

Politicians had still more reasons to support public health. They used it to allay anxieties. Aware that some of their constituents were apprehensive about racial groups, they made public health into a pretext for confining minority groups to urban ghettos or shipping them to distant locales (Abel, 2007; Burnstein, 2006; Molina, 2006; Mullan, 1989).

Politicians used public health to promote the financial interests of constituents. They rewarded the doctors, hospital owners, and pharmaceutical manufacturers who assisted them during electoral campaigns (Daschle, Greenberger, & Lambrew, 2008; Dranove, 2008; Halvorson, 2007; Jost, 2007; Terry, 2007).

Politicians insisted that private enterprise was the optimal vehicle for promoting health in a capitalist society. However, critics accused them of selectively advancing the interests of business leaders. They published commentaries, solicited organizational funding, organized demonstrations, and printed diatribes. They even aired accusations in films (Glynn, Weinstein, Weinstein, O'Hara, & Moore, 2007; Weisberg, 2008).

When elected officials took controversial stances on health, they needed allies. They hoped that scholars would support them. They were distressed when their opponents also tried to win endorsements from the scholars (Jackson & Jamieson, 2007; Lee, 2007; United States Senate Special Committee on Aging, 2001).

ENTREPRENEURS

Politicians hoped that persons would be impressed by scholars' confident demeanors. They also hoped that they would be impressed by their advanced academic degrees, research studies, appointments to prestigious universities, and affiliations with scientific institutes.

Like politicians, entrepreneurs realized that scholarly research could be a strategy with which to advance schemes. They viewed business leaders as the targets for some of their schemes. They assured them that they had located scholarly information that would stimulate them personally and benefit them professionally (Ruokonen, 2003).

Although the entrepreneurs were eager to share information with business leaders, they realized that professors were providing this information as well. The entrepreneurs claimed that they had information that was easier to understand and implement than that from professors. Additionally, they provided their information outside of university classrooms; they offered it within seminars, films, software, and books (e.g., Covey, 1989; S. Johnson, 1998; Kaplan Thaler & Koval, 2006; Mortensen, 2008; Rao, 2006).

Simplifying Complex Information

Entrepreneurs had to organize information about business. They tried to present it in formats that every business leader could understand. They also transformed information from business-related fields, such as psychology (Dweck, 2006; McGraw, 1999).

Some of the entrepreneurs even focused on information from philosophy. As with other types of information, they attempted to reduce its complexity. They explained that they could transform it into *new-thought information*. They claimed that this transformed material would help business leaders deal with career and life situations.

The entrepreneurs claimed that the simplified information still was remarkably potent. They assured readers that it would enable them to discern future events, their causes, their consequences, and even ways to control those consequences (Bruce & Wattles, 2007; Byrne, 2006; Kelly, 2007; Mosley, 2006; Twyman, 2008).

Embellishing Everyday Information

Entrepreneurs sometimes relied on personal reminiscences, anecdotes, or stories to convey information. They argued that common-sense notions, traditional assumptions, and populist beliefs were more valuable than scholarly information.

One entrepreneur described an ailing professor who had confided common-sense insights about life's greatest lesson (Albom, 1997). The author of another widely read book used a parable about mice in a maze to illustrate the optimal way to deal with change (S. Johnson, 1998).

Authors claimed that seemingly simple information was profound. They complimented the persons who already were relying on it and encouraged others to follow their examples. They demonstrated how they could apply it to diverse topics (Buffington, 1996; Fulghum, 1988; Johnson & Ruhl, 2007; McKnight-Trontz, 2000).

When the entrepreneurs were challenged by skeptics, they ignored them. Although they lost some of their followers with this response, they retained many others (e.g., Dolby, 2005; Jackson & Jamieson, 2007; Tiede, 2001).

POLITICIANS FIX ROADS

Entrepreneurs hoped to find effective, easily implemented, and inexpensive solutions to problems. Although they genuinely may have wished to solve problems, they had an ulterior motive: they hoped to accumulate wealth.

Government officials were fascinated by the entrepreneurs. Like them, they were searching for effective, easily implemented, and inexpensive solutions to problems. Like them, they had an ulterior motive: they hoped to accumulate political power.

Governmental officials searched for issues that could excite voters, attract financial contributors, and be addressed through legislation, regulations, or government funding.

White-Line Fever

During the 1930s, safety engineers in the California Department of Transportation worried about drivers. They were especially nervous about those who traveled along roads with few distractions on them.

Some roads were uninterrupted by billboards, roadside stands, gas stations, directional signals, fire hydrants, livestock, industrial buildings, shacks, homes, or trees. They even were beyond the range in which motorists could tune in radio broadcasts.

Safety engineers noted that the lines along the centers of isolated roads were the only stimuli on which drivers sometimes could focus. They realized that these pulsating white dashes kept the drivers in their lanes. Nonetheless, they worried that they could have debilitating consequences: they feared that they could lull drivers into hypnotic trances.

Journalists were fascinated when they learned about road hypnosis. They referred to it with a catchy phrase—*white-line fever*. They alerted readers that white-line fever was a bizarre but plausible psychological malady.

Although California road engineers were aware of white-line fever during the 1930s, they did not solve the problem. In fact, they waited twenty years to come up with a solution.

The engineers devised a simple cure: they hammered special nails along driving lanes. These nails, which had large, plastic, convex heads on them, created small bumps. If highway-hypnotized drivers strayed from their lanes, they felt the reverberations from the bumps and awoke (All about Highway, 2008; Kirkley, 2009; Raised Pavement Marker, 2009).

The road nails were technically called raised pavement markers. However, they had another name—highway dots. Because Elbert Botts was the engineer who had invented them, some persons referred to them as Botts Dots.

During the 1960s, California legislators passed laws mandating the use of Botts Dots. Legislators in several other states copied them. The federal government eventually required road engineers to incorporate Botts Dots into all federally funded projects.

Although the Botts Dots had benefits, they also had drawbacks. They could be dislodged by snow-clearing equipment. The loosened markers were dangerous to motorists. Additionally, they left moisture-capturing craters that destroyed roads.

Some politicians judged that road hypnosis would be an effective problem with which to attract voters and financial contributors. They were disappointed when it aroused little interest. They eventually delegated it to engineers.

The engineers initially hoped that the Botts Dots would eliminate road hypnosis. They later devised other products that were safer, more durable, and equally effective (Martin, 2001).

Text Messaging

California engineers waited twenty years to devise a solution for highway hypnosis. Their politicians waited ten years to implement it. Federal bureaucrats waited still longer. Journalists were unperturbed about the sluggish responses. However, they responded differently to another highway problem.

Journalists reported about a 2008 train catastrophe in which the engineer had been sending text messages (Engineer Sent, 2008). They used this incident to alert readers, listeners, and viewers to the problems of text messaging. They demanded that politicians solve the problem immediately.

At the beginning of 2008, only two states banned automobile drivers from using cell phones or other devices to read or send text messages. Less than twenty-four months later, nine states had imposed bans on novice drivers; another eighteen had imposed them on all drivers (Cell Phone and Texting Laws, 2010; Schulte, 2008; Shiffrin & Silberschatz, 2009).

In the summer of 2009, President Obama prohibited federal employees from reading or sending text messages while they were driving. Both liberal and conservative partisans supported him. In fact, legislators from some traditionally conservative states endorsed even more draconian prohibitions (Richtel, 2009).

Politicians recognized that journalists and voters were upset about text messaging. However, they lacked an objective way to estimate the number of text-messaging drivers who were responsible for automobile accidents. Lacking data, they relied on their personal experiences and common sense.

U.S. Transportation Secretary Ray LaHood joined the persons who were concerned about text messaging. He conceded that other politicians had relied on their intuitions when they had taken stances on this problem. However, he emphasized that he personally relied on data from the National Highway Traffic Safety Administration.

LaHood admitted that he did not have information about the drivers who sent text messages. However, he claimed that he did have it about those that were distracted during automobile accidents. He announced that approximately one thousand drivers had died while distracted in 2008. He assumed that a substantial portion of them were sending or receiving text messages (Krewson, 2009; National Highway Traffic Safety Administration, 2009).

In spite of his personal convictions about the scientific way that he had confirmed the dangers of text messaging, LaHood had to deal with skeptics. The skeptics reported about a study from the Insurance Institute for Highway Safety. Personnel at this institute had examined accident claims in states that prohibited drivers from using hand-held communication devices; they also examined them in the states without prohibitions. They found no significant differences between the numbers of claims (White, 2010).

Persons were aware that the data from the Insurance Institute for Highway Safety were counterintuitive; they therefore asked investigators to explain them. The investigators responded that the use of cell phones, even though their use is dangerous, was only one of many distractions.

Some analysts worried about billboards. Others were concerned about garish digital displays along roadsides. Still others worried about the Internet-delivered displays on automobile dashboards. They speculated that drivers had to deal with so many distractions that they were not safer when they avoided only hand-held communication devices (Richtel, 2010a, 2010b; Vance & Richtel, 2010).

POLITICIANS FIX SCHOOL TESTS

Politicians realized that their stances on educational situations could help children, appease voters, and attract financial contributors. The situations on which they took stances involved teachers, methods of instruction, curricula, textbooks, and school policies.

Depending on their goals, politicians defended or attacked situations in the schools. They sometimes had difficulty deciding which type of action would be most advantageous for them. They had particular difficulty deciding whether to defend or attack standardized tests.

Early Advocates

Some pre–World War I politicians wanted to watch the schools more carefully. However, they had difficulty identifying a monitoring technique.

During the war, some believed that they had discovered the perfect procedure—standardized testing.

Politicians wanted to administer standardized tests and publicize the scores that students earned on them. They claimed that they needed the scores to ascertain whether schools were providing a sound foundation for the nation's economy and defense. They added that parents needed them to determine whether schools were meeting their children's needs (Giordano, 2004, 2005).

Politicians had another reason to support tests. They wished to make them part of a plan to reward model schools and teachers. They would reward schools with increased funds; they would reward teachers with job security and bonuses. However, they had to convince critics that this plan made sense.

Later Advocates

Post–World War I politicians had a hard time persuading some constituents to support standardized tests. They had difficulty explaining the bases for some of the items on them. They struggled to defend items that did not resemble the traits that they were supposed to measure.

The discrepancy between test items and the traits they measured was evident on intelligence tests. For example, the puzzle-completion tasks on intelligence tests resembled games more than academic activities.

Although persons were wary of tests because of the peculiar items on them, they were wary because of some other features. They protested that the tests were too expensive, robbed students of instructional time, relied on hermetic statistical procedures, and misrepresented minority students (Giordano, 2005).

Testing advocates were not impressed by their opponents' objections; they continued to endorse tests. They became more powerful after many politicians endorsed them. However, they realized that they would become stronger still with additional allies. They tried to persuade the general public to take their side.

Recent Advocates

Governor George W. Bush was the Republican Party's presidential candidate in 2000. He complained that Democratic strategists had depicted him as unconcerned about schools. He pledged to shatter that stereotype.

Candidate Bush claimed that education was his highest priority. He noted that admiring journalists had referred to him as the education governor and to his state school efforts as the Texas miracle. He pledged that he would expand his gubernatorial achievements and earn a nickname as the education president (Bronner, 1999; Leung, 2004; Lyman, 1999).

After Bush won the election, he proposed to expand tests, distribute their results, and stipulate consequences for schools in which students were failing. He and his associates referred to this set of initiatives as No Child Left Behind (Hess & Petrilli, 2006; Irons & Harris, 2007; United States Department of Education, 2004a).

Bush threatened to withhold federal educational funds from schools that did not embrace his plans (Hess & Finn, 2004, 2007). Many educators protested that he was giving federal authorities too much control over state and local budgets.

The educators had another objection; they insisted that some educational problems could not be solved through standardized tests. They pointed out that inadequately staffed schools, run-down buildings, obsolete equipment, and old textbooks were problems that would not disappear without increased educational funds.

Bush had a rejoinder: he promised to accompany testing with funding. He persuaded an influential Democrat, Senator Edward Kennedy, to cosponsor his plan (Loveless, 2006).

Bush had to find funds for war in Afghanistan, war in Iraq, homeland security, and an economic recession; he had difficulty locating them for No Child Left Behind. Nonetheless, he retained his plan's testing requirements. Educators howled in protest (Abernathy, 2007; Popham, 2004; Rebell & Wolff, 2008; Shaker & Heilman, 2008; Vinovskis, 2009).

POLITICIANS FIX SCHOOL MANAGEMENT

When voters elected George W. Bush, they gave him control of both houses of Congress. He promised to use this advantage to advance education. He explained that he would promote it with two major initiatives: increased testing and expanded funding.

After eight years with a Republican president, voters elected Barack Obama. Like Bush, the new president was given control of both houses. Like his predecessor, he promised to make education a high priority. He described plans that involved budgets and school management.

When Obama pledged to expand school budgets, he elicited loud applause from the members of education unions. However, he did not hear any clapping after he pledged to change the ways that schools were managed (Fitzgerald, 2007).

The union members realized that Obama was committed to a specific school management strategy—the expansion of charter schools. Charter schools were publicly funded but loosely regulated institutions. Union members were uneasy about them because they were exempt from union-negotiated agreements (Fitzgerald, 2007).

Unionized educators were suspicious of charter schools for another reason: they distrusted the many conservative politicians who supported them. They worried that they had used inaccurate information to bolster the reputations of these schools (Gabriel, 2010; Murray, 2010). They feared that they wished to give them a larger share of federal educational funds (Dillon, February 24, 2010; Push-Back on Charter Schools, 2010).

Unlike the educators, parents generally were supportive of charter schools. Those who were dissatisfied with public education already could send their children to home schools or private schools. They viewed charter schools as another valuable option.

Educators were upset with elected officials for politicizing charter schools. However, they employed the same strategy. Both sides revealed the degree to which they would politicize charter schools when they wrote books. They peppered the titles with emotional phrases about *educational renewal, hope, hype, opportunities, miracles, spin cycles,* and *hoaxes* (Buckley & Schneider, 2007; Cookson & Berger, 2002; Corwin & Schneider, 2005; Finn, Manno, & Vanourek, 2000; Henig, 2008; Nathan, 1996).

The educators who were upset about charter schools were delighted when a high-profile proponent changed her mind. Diane Ravitch, who had served as an administrator in the federal Department of Education, explained that she changed her mind about charter schools after she concluded that they did not genuinely affect educational success (Ravitch, 2010a, 2010b).

POLITICIANS FIX SCHOOL FUNDING

As a presidential candidate for the Democratic Party, Barack Obama depended on the teacher unions; he needed their endorsements, financial support, and votes. However, he realized that he could not win the election if he only had their help. He also needed endorsements, financial support, and votes from political independents; he even might need the support of some Republicans.

Like his predecessor, Obama did not want to be stereotyped. However, he was concerned that he would be depicted as a puppet of the teachers' unions. He was aware of the damage that this depiction had caused Jimmy Carter during the 1970s (Giordano, 2010).

Wishing to appear decisive and independent, candidate Obama pledged that he would support charter schools. After he won the election, he honored this pledge. However, he made other controversial suggestions.

Although Obama wished to change some of the features of No Child Left Behind, he recommended that it be maintained. He also suggested that teachers be awarded merit pay and that student performance on standardized tests serve as one of the criteria for assigning it (Dillon, March 13, 2010; King & Martinez, 2010; Paulson, 2010).

Struck by some of Obama's nonstereotypical educational policies, journalists sarcastically referred to him as Bush III. They taunted that he might alienate the teachers' unions (Anderson, 2009; Shih, 2010; Whitmire & Rotherham, 2009).

Obama promised to expand standardized testing, change school management, and increase educational funding. However, he did not focus the same amount of effort on all of these initiatives.

Early in his administration, he tried to stimulate the economy with nearly eight billion dollars. He earmarked more than 10 percent of this money for education (American Recovery and Reinvestment Act, 2009; Giordano, 2010; GovTrack.us. H.R. 1—111th Congress, 2009).

Critics lambasted the president for incorporating education into an economic stimulus bill. They complained that educational spending would have minimal impact on economic recovery. They also complained that the money would be disbursed with scant accountability (Giordano, 2010).

A year after he signed the stimulus bill, Obama turned his attention to the staffs at schools with chronic dropout problems. He advised community leaders to either retrain or fire these staffs. He added that he would channel nearly a billion dollars to schools that followed his advice (Zeleny, 2010).

ANALYZING ADVICE FROM POLITICIANS

Critics sometimes belittled scholars. They predicted that the nineteenth-century pessimists, who disavowed procreation, would leave distasteful treatises as their only progeny. The pessimists retorted that they were unconcerned about the opinions of critics.

Although the pessimists spurned critics, other scholars cared deeply about them. In fact, they took measures to cultivate their support. They especially were concerned about politicians, who crafted legislation and supplied resources.

The politicians were impressed by the scholars' information and persuasive strategies. They decided to use them to achieve their own goals.

Activity 8.1

You may wish to examine scholars' persuasive strategies. You could use Table 8.1.

Table 8.1 lists three types of problems: those related to the environment, health, and business. Complete this table by identifying samples of scholars' advice. Also identify their persuasive strategies.

You can use abbreviations to represent persuasive strategies. Use *S* for simplifying complex information, *E* for embellishing everyday information, and *O* for other strategies. As a final step, explain the bases for your responses.

You could complete the table by yourself, with another reader, or with a small group of readers. You could rely on information from this chapter, the citations in it, or other resources.

Activity 8.2

You might wish to analyze politicians' persuasive strategies. You could use Table 8.2.

Table 8.1. Scholars Use Persuasive Strategies

Problem	*Advice*	*Strategy**	*Explanation*
Environment			
Health			
Business			

**S* Simplify
E Embellish
O Other

Table 8.2. Politicians Use Persuasive Strategies for Road Problems

Problem	*Advice*	*Strategy **	*Explanation*
White-Line Fever			
Text Messaging			

**S* Simplify
E Embellish
O Other

Table 8.2 lists two types of road problems: white-line fever and text messaging. Complete the table by identifying samples of politicians' advice. Also identify their persuasive strategies.

You can use abbreviations to represent persuasive strategies. Use *S* for simplifying complex information, *E* for embellishing everyday information, and *O* for other strategies. As a final step, explain the bases for your responses.

Activity 8.3

You might wish to analyze the persuasive strategies that politicians used when they were dealing with school problems. You could use Table 8.3.

Table 8.3 identifies three types of school problems: those related to testing, management, and funding. Complete the table by identifying samples of politicians' advice. Also identify their persuasive strategies.

Table 8.3. Politicians Use Persuasive Strategies for Education Problems

Problem	*Advice*	*Strategy**	*Explanation*
Testing			
Management			
Funding			

**S* Simplify
E Embellish
O Other

You can use abbreviations to represent persuasive strategies. Use *S* for simplifying complex information, *E* for embellishing everyday information, and *O* for other strategies. As a final step, explain the bases for your responses.

Activity 8.4

You might wish to analyze the ways in which presidents set educational priorities. You could use Table 8.4.

Table 8.4 lists two presidents: George W. Bush and Barack Obama. It also identifies three educational issues: standardized testing, school management, and federal funding. Complete this table by identifying the priorities that the presidents assigned to the issues.

You can rely on symbols. Use the symbol − for low priority. Use the symbol ± for moderate priority and the symbol + for high priority. Finally, explain the bases for your responses.

Activity 8.5

You might wish to examine the ways in which presidents used educational policies to influence constituents. You could use Table 8.5.

Table 8.4. Presidents Set Education Priorities

President	Priority of*			Explanation
	Testing	Management	Funding	
George W. Bush				
Barack Obama				

*– Low
± Moderate
+ High

Table 8.5 lists two presidents: George W. Bush and Barack Obama. It also identifies three types of educational policies: those related to standardized testing, school management, and federal funding. Complete this table by identifying groups to which the presidents were attentive when they crafted their policies.

You can use symbols. Use the symbol *U*+ for groups that promoted the interests of unionized teachers and the symbol *U*– for those that did not. Use the symbol *M*+ for groups that promoted the interests of racial/ethnic minorities and *M*– for those that did not. Use the symbol *C*+ for groups that promoted conservative fiscal practices and *C*– for those that did not.

As a final step, explain the bases for your answers.

SUMMARY

The scholars who disapproved of the schools tried to increase their influence; they hoped that allies would help them. They recruited voters, special interest groups, and politicians.

Table 8.5. Presidents Use Education to Influence Constituents

President	*Policy**			*Explanation*
	Testing	*Management*	*Funding*	
George W. Bush				
Barack Obama				

**U+* Promote Unions
U− Do Not Promote Unions
M+ Promote Minorities
M− Do Not Promote Minorities
C+ Promote Conservative Fiscal Practices
C− Do Not Promote Conservative Fiscal Practices

9

Do Critics Offer Helping Hands?

It is naughty to knock the schools.

—William McAndrew, 1878

Critics looked for school problems. They detected them in facilities, equipment, textbooks, tests, teachers, principals, curricula, instructional strategies, policies, and funding. They also recommended ways to eliminate them.

A HELPING HAND

The Haizhu Bridge is situated in the Chinese city of Guangzhou. It is famous for its design and practicality; it is infamous for the number of persons who scale it.

During a three-week period in 2009, ten persons climbed and threatened to jump from this bridge. In each instance, police cordoned off the site, halted traffic, and urged the climbers to come down safely.

When the eleventh person ascended the Haizhu Bridge, commuters were concerned. Some of them worried about the climber; they approved of the police officers, firefighters, medical personnel, emergency workers, and equipment on the scene. Others worried about the traffic jam; they fretted about the inconvenience it created for them.

One motorist was upset because the climber was still on the bridge after more than four hours. He decided to take charge. He left his car, slipped through the emergency barrier, removed his shoes, embraced a vertical beam, shimmied along it, and emerged next to the climber. Once he was in position, he extended a hand.

The man on the bridge assumed that the motorist was a police officer. He carefully balanced himself and reached out. However, he realized that he had made a mistake when the motorist hurled him downwards.

When he was asked why he had flung the man from the bridge, the motorist replied that the climber had been acting selfishly. He explained that he had no sympathy when a man's "action violates a lot of public interests" (Would-Be Jumper, 2009).

EARLY SCHOOL CRITICS

The persons who criticized the schools initially focused on physical facilities and resources. They were upset about buildings, instructional equipment, textbooks, playgrounds, sports arenas, gyms, vocational shops, libraries, and school vehicles.

Some early critics focused on personnel. They were upset about teachers, school administrators, nurses, psychologists, truant officers, reading specialists, speech-language pathologists, clerical workers, custodians, groundskeepers, and bus drivers.

The critics also focused on funding. Some of them insisted that school administrators did not have the money to repair facilities, purchase equipment, and hire personnel. However, others retorted that school administrators were short on money because they were wasting their current budgets.

Educators sometimes trusted critics. They trusted those who recommended funds to build new facilities and hire new employees. They trusted those who wanted to increase their salaries and expand their benefits.

Educators were wary when critics blamed them for problems. They questioned those who wanted to make changes in management, instruction, curricula, assessment, policies, and spending. They worried that they were looking after their own interests rather than those of educators and students.

The school critics assured the educators that they truly were offering them a helping hand. They encouraged them to grasp it.

Novelists

Some of the early school critics were novelists. In *The Evolution of "Dodd": A Pedagogical Story*, William Smith described an incompetent teacher. He metaphorically referred to her as Miss Stone.

Miss Stone was "dull intellectually" and known for "detesting severe study." She decided to devote her "spare and somewhat stale energies to fitting herself for primary [school] work" (Smith, 1884, p. 17). She aspired to school employment because she lacked the "personality, individuality, and character" to resist a bureaucracy in which she would have the opportunity to follow a "pattern made and prepared by a pattern maker" (p. 245).

William Stead (1894) also was concerned about the schools. He entitled his book, *If Christ Came to Chicago*. He indicated in this title that he would examine education from a highly distinctive perspective.

Stead described a hypothetical visit by Christ to the nineteenth-century city. He probably surprised few readers when he depicted Christ as upset with the many residents who had been raised as Christians but who had abandoned their religion's principles.

Stead may have jolted readers when he wrote that Christ would be fascinated with politics. He explained that Christ would want to review the tax system with which the politicians funded the Chicago schools. He assured them that he would be disappointed.

Upton Sinclair was still another novelist who was perturbed about Chicago's schools. When he published *The Jungle* in 1906, he blamed industrialists and bankers for creating school problems. He also criticized university administrators for participating in a decadent system that involved all levels of education (Sinclair, 1922, 1971).

Sinclair was disappointed that he could not change the schools with fiction; he eventually organized a utopian community. The residents within it shared economic and social responsibilities, including those affecting education (Arthur, 2006; Bausum, 2007; Mattson, 2006).

Educational Scholars

John Dewey was a philosopher who wrote about the schools. He even established an experimental school at which he conducted scholastic experiments.

Dewey was annoyed with most of the public school teachers. He particularly disliked the emphasis that they placed on reading. He scolded them for requiring young children to read before their "sense organs and connected nerve and motor apparatus" were sufficiently developed (Dewey, 1898).

Although Dewey tolerated reading for older children, he still referred to it as a nineteenth-century fetish. He warned that tradition-minded teachers and parents assumed that reading "marked the distinction between the educated and the uneducated man." Although he was convinced that many progressive minds no longer held this assumption, he warned that in rural regions "the old state of things still persists" (Dewey, 1898, p. 316).

Dewey also questioned books. Using a financial metaphor, he explained that "the capital handed down from past generations, and upon whose transmission the integrity of civilization depends, is no longer amassed in those banks termed books." He added that intellectual capital was "in active and general circulation, at an extremely low rate of interest" (1898, p. 317).

Like Dewey, Charles Henderson (1902) wished to make dramatic changes in the schools. He based many of his recommendations on a philosophical conviction that civic life, religion, morality, ethics, and education were interconnected. However, he provided more than a philosophical rationale; he claimed that the schools needed to change because employers, civic leaders, religious leaders, and parents were disappointed in them and demanded changes.

Henderson added that even students were disappointed in the schools. He explained that they demonstrated their disappointment in a straightforward fashion: they simply dropped out.

Gillette (1910) was another scholar who demanded school changes. He identified the vocational training movement as the best way to make them. He reported that the federal government, the National Education Association, professors of education, and journalists had concluded that vocational training provided an alternative to the "useless material contained in our school curricula" (p. 1).

Scholars from Diverse Fields

J. M. Rice was a nineteenth-century physician who examined the Chicago schools. Although he conceded that these schools were respected as some of the finest in the Midwest, he claimed that they did not deserve that reputation. In fact, he alleged that the instruction in them was "by far the most absurd I have ever witnessed" (1893, p. 202).

Chicago's business leaders listened carefully to Rice. They were aware that their peers in Boston, New York, and Philadelphia already had made impressive cultural, architectural, social, economic, civic, and educational achievements. They realized that they would have to improve their local schools if they hoped to replicate those achievements (Flanagan, 2002; Merriner, 2004; Miller, 1996; Sawislak, 1995; Spinney, 2000; Waldheim & Rüedi Ray, 2005; Zukowsky & Thorne, 2004).

Although business leaders may have had civic reasons to improve the schools, they also had selfish reasons. They relied on the schools to supply them with executives, managers, technicians, and secretaries. They urged school administrators to equip graduates with vocational skills.

The early twentieth-century business leaders endorsed vocational schools. In fact, those in Chicago commissioned special textbooks for them. They also paid a former superintendent to tour Europe, observe vocational schools, and advise them about ways to replicate those programs (Cooley, 1911).

G. Stanley Hall (1911) was an influential psychologist. His professional stature was evident when his peers selected him to serve as the first president of the American Psychological Association. However, Hall was also an influential school critic.

Hall wrote extensively about personnel problems. Some of these problems, such as those created by teachers without professional training, were widely acknowledged. Others, such as those resulting from the excessive "feminization" of the workforce, revealed his own idiosyncrasies.

Hall was concerned that the "prevalent methods of teaching are open to very grave criticism" (1911, p. 609). He warned educators to take this criticism seriously because opponents were using it to erode school funding.

Hall was concerned about curricula. Even though he acknowledged that the students in the public schools were learning "a vast body of things," he insisted they forgot it "when school life ends" (1911, p. 617). He claimed that this problem resulted from the many scholastic "heirlooms" that they encountered in their curricula.

RESPONDING TO EARLY CRITICS

Some school critics were persuasive. Those who wrote fiction were able to remind parents of their experiences in the school. They encouraged them to protect their children from similarly unpleasant episodes.

Although persons who disagreed with school critics did not write best-selling novels, they sometimes made editorialized retorts in their memoirs.

A California superintendent wrote enthusiastically about the teachers whose classrooms he had visited during the late 1800s and early 1900s. He reported that they were equipping their students with invaluable knowledge and skills. Although he conceded that they were stressed by larger classes, he boasted that they still were keeping "even pace." He reassured readers that "all of the [scholastic] omens are auspicious" (Swett, 1969, 1911, p. 258).

One retired teacher described his positive experiences in a rural New England community. He wrote rhapsodically that "there is no better place to bring up a boy than on a farm, especially if that farm is located in the midst of an intelligent community with a good rural school" (Mowry, 1908, p. 9).

Although the New England teacher was pleased with educators, curricula, and instruction, he was upset about the increasing number of immigrant children. He explained that they came from families with "extreme differences" in "language, social life, morals, and religion." He added that they also demonstrated "totally un-American" political attitudes (Mowry, 1908).

Educators

Colleagues in higher education defended the teachers and school administrators who were being attacked. Painter (1886) was a professor of education who wrote a history of the American schools. He claimed that the critics had excited few sympathizers but numerous opponents. He added that their opponents were exhibiting an "impulsion" of positive feelings about the schools.

Shoup (1891) was another professor who had written a history of education. He insisted that the schools of the United States could not be criticized because they were internationally recognized for their "beneficent influence."

In spite of reassurances from professors, some educators worried about the critics. They especially worried about those that were attracting sizeable audiences. A group of educators in Massachusetts complained that the critics were luring large groups by arousing "a growing feeling of inadequacy of the existing public school system." They added that they were accusing the schools of failing to prepare students for "modern industrial and social conditions" (Wright, Mather, & Swaysland, 1906, p. 5).

The Massachusetts educators wished to ascertain the feelings of constituents for themselves. They were pleased after they located numerous citizens who were proud of their state's schools and who were glad to pay the relatively high cost for maintaining them.

Educators who minimized the influence of critics may have been mistaken, Pollyannaish, or disingenuous. Elsa Denison (1912), who was a political activist and director of an alternative school, did not underestimate the power that critics brandished. She admitted that she was startled by the "abuse" that they were aiming at schools.

Denison judged that the school critics were credible because they did not appear to have ulterior motives. She noted that one school administrator attracted publicity by contending that "a revolution is necessary in present methods of education." She added that a physician created a stir by characterizing the schools as "physical menaces" (Denison, 1912, p. 8).

Denison asked citizens to rally around the schools. She asked them to support them because they were the "bulwarks of democracy." She asked them to support teachers because they continually were making improvements in the schools.

Journalists

Joseph King was president of the national News Enterprise Association. This nineteenth-century society was a precursor to the media organizations that distributed stories, photos, and cartoons to newspapers and magazines.

King was annoyed at the journalists who were assaulting the schools. He was particularly upset at those who were describing teachers as incompetent. He remonstrated that it was unfair for them to "represent [teachers] as unattractive to children." He claimed that they were using this rhetoric only because they knew it would attract readers.

King might have revealed a bit of doubt about his proschool campaign when he noted that even if the school criticism was valid, "it would be poor public policy to admit it" (Joseph King, as quoted by McAndrew, 1878, pp. 551–52). However, he immediately covered his rhetorical faux pas by insisting that the criticism was categorically false.

RECENT SCHOOL CRITICS

Critics have continued to examine the schools; they have continued to discern problems. In fact, the problems that they recently detected are similar to the early problems.

Personnel

Numerous critics have shared their opinions about teachers. Some attempted to be evenhanded; others did not conceal their political interests. However, they agreed that any attempt to judge teachers was contentious (Horn, 2002).

Many school critics used the titles of their books to editorialize the central messages in them. One author chose the title, *Smart Kids, Bad Schools: 38 Ways to Save America's Future.* To ensure that readers understood his feelings about the degree to which teachers were responsible for bad schools, he gave the chapter on school personnel a confrontational title: "The Way Teachers Need to Be Treated, Trained, and Rewarded" (Crosby, 2008).

Some recent critics have repeated the nineteenth-century allegations about dysfunctional teachers. They added that today's teachers differ because they can rely on unions to protect them. They blamed the unions for discouraging professional achievement, scholastic excellence, student-centered learning, fiscal efficiency, and educational reform (Brimelow, 2003; Lieberman, 1997; Paige, 2006).

The critics even identified the ideal way to differentiate competent from incompetent teachers. Because they did not trust school administrators, they proposed to use the scores that students earned on standardized tests. They were sure that these scores would reveal whether teachers were meeting their expectations (Evers & Walberg, 2004).

Curricula

The recent critics have worried about incompetent teachers. They also worried about teachers who abused curricula; they worried about those who introduced inappropriate content or omitted critical content from them.

The critics wished to specify the information in curricula; they also wanted to ascertain whether it then was actually shared with students. They argued fiercely about the place of religious information in the curricula.

Early in the twentieth century, critics detected an erosion of information about Christianity from the schools. They had difficulty halting the wear, which was aggravated by changing social mores, scientific attitudes, and court interventions (Giordano, 2009).

Like the early critics, their successors tried to halt the removal of religious information from schools. In fact, some of them wished to restore some of the information that already had been deleted. They argued that restoration was appropriate because teachers had a responsibility to instruct students about the historical and social aspects of religion (Greenawalt, 2005; Head, 2005; Thomas, 2007).

The disputes about religion in the schools had an impact on numerous types of curricula, including those in the sciences. At the beginning of the twentieth century, some state legislators used religion as the rationale for excising information about evolution from science curricula. They were distressed when the courts struck down their restrictions. They were even more distressed when they barred the inclusion of biblical information within curricula.

To get around the courts, advocates of religion in schools argued that Bible-based accounts of creation were plausible scientific theories. They reasoned that they were as appropriate in science curricula as evolutionary theories (Giordano, 2009, 2010).

Many of the critics who detected a decline in religion also detected a decline in patriotism. They feared that this decline would weaken the traditional values on which the nation had been founded.

Critics demanded that curricula foster loyalty to the United States, its international interests, its system of government, and its economic structure. To ensure that this type of information was available, they wanted it embedded in textbooks (Bauder, 2007; Foerstel, 2002; Gaddy, Hall, & Marzano, 1996; J. C. McKinley, 2010a, 2010b; Shackelford, 2010; Westheimer, 2007).

Politically conservative school critics identified history textbooks that complemented the curricula that they had in mind (e.g., Scweikart & Allen, 2007). They also singled out those with which they disagreed (e.g., Stefoff & Zinn, 2007a, 2007b; Zinn, 2005).

School Policies

Critics were concerned about fundamental educational issues such as academic failure, school dropout, gang membership, and drug use. They also were concerned about ancillary issues. In fact, they believed that the ways in which children responded to ancillary issues had a far-reaching impact. They used school uniforms as an illustration.

Enthusiasts alleged that the students who wore uniforms demonstrated low rates of academic failure, school dropout, gang membership, and drug use. Sure that the uniforms were responsible, they advised public school administrators to make them mandatory (Giordano, 2010).

Critics had additional school policies that they wished to change; they wanted to alter those that dealt with bullies. Some of them wanted policies that would suspend or expel the bullies. Others wanted policies that would require on-campus police, locker searches, video monitoring, metal detectors, transparent backpacks, and drug-sniffing dogs (Beane, 1999, 2009; Lee, 2004).

Critics wished to change the policies affecting homework. They were convinced that homework developed habits that helped the students while they were in school and then after they graduated.

The critics added that homework could be made less onerous. They wrote prohomework books for teachers, parents, and children (Canter & Hausner, 1988; De Groat, 2000; Gutman, 2006; Hong & Milgram, 2000; Klein & McKinley, 2004; Painter, 2003; Stein, 2007; Yorinks & Egielski, 2009).

Funding

Critics recently have detected problems in personnel, curricula, and policies. They also have recommended solutions. They almost always tied their solutions to funding. Although some of them alleged that school problems stemmed from the shortage of funds, many alleged that they resulted from the abuse of them (Hess, 2004; Murray, 2008).

Critics asked politicians for assistance. One group advised them to increase funds; others counseled them to impose greater accountability on them. Politicians had to pick the side to which they would listen (Anderson, 2007; Giordano, 2010; United States Department of Education, 2007; Vinovskis, 2009).

The critics who demanded accountability had a plan: they directed the politicians to couple school funds to students' test scores. They predicted that this coupling would promote academic achievement and equity (Grubb, 2009; Hanushek, 2006; Hanushek & Lindseth, 2009).

The critics who endorsed accountability were pleased when politicians listened to their suggestions. They had additional advice: they urged them to create competition among public school educators. They explained that they could stimulate competition by establishing charter schools, subsidizing commercial schools, and reimbursing parents for the tuition they paid to private schools (Finn, Manno, & Vanourek, 2000; Hill, 2006; Walberg & Bast, 2003; Weil, 2000, 2002).

RESPONDING TO RECENT CRITICS

School critics upset educators when they accused them of incompetence. They infuriated them when they accused them of using labor organizations to shield ineptitude. They anticipated that the educators would retort.

Personnel

The educators disputed the antiunion allegations. They pointed to instances in which unions had helped workers who had been treated unfairly. They pointed to instances in which they had promoted workplace diversity, equitable salaries, employee health care, and retirement benefits (Hannaway & Rotherham, 2006; Loveless, 2000; Peterson & West, 2003).

Educators also highlighted ways in which their unions helped students. They documented their early and recent advocacy of students with disabilities as well as students from racial, ethnic, gender, religious, and economic minorities (Giordano, 2009).

Curricula

Educators disagreed when critics characterized them as opponents of patriotic curricula. Although they conceded that they opposed some curricula, they insisted that they focused only on those that were inaccurate or chauvinistic. They argued that students would not develop balanced views of national and international affairs unless they were exposed to curricula that revealed complex social, economic, and international issues (Robbins, 2008; Westheimer, 2007).

Educators also disagreed with the critics who claimed that they had suppressed religion. They argued that they had not challenged religion itself but rather efforts to promote sectarian interests (Apple, 2006; Debray, 2006; Howell, 2005; Kumashiro, 2008).

School Policies

Educators admitted that they had opposed certain policies, including those mandating school uniforms. They explained that they did not object to the uniforms themselves but rather to the assumption that they were an adequate response to complicated social, economic, and emotional problems (Giordano, 2010).

Some educators admitted that they had objected to homework policies. However, they explained that their reasoning was similar to that which had guided their response to uniforms. They dismissed some homework policies as simple attempts to solve complex problems (Bennett & Kalish, 2006; Buell, 2004; Kohn, 2006; Kralovec & Buell, 2000).

Educators frequently were at odds about safety policies. They insisted that policies be connected to behavioral, emotional, social, and economic issues. They objected to those that depended excessively on transparent backpacks, metal detectors, drug-sniffing dogs, or electronic surveillance (Almond, 2008; Barton, 2009; Hopkins, 2004; Jimerson & Furlong, 2006; Shafii & Shafii, 2001).

Funding

School critics disconcerted educators because they recommended controversial solutions to problems. They also disconcerted them because of the audience that they attracted. Their audience included scholars, government bureaucrats, religious leaders, parents, journalists, military leaders, community leaders, business leaders, and politicians.

Educators were concerned that some of their constituents might become hostile to them. Nonetheless, they fretted particularly about business leaders and politicians. They worried about business leaders because they could generate publicity; they worried about politicians because they could limit their funding.

Blaming Business Leaders

Educators were pleased when business leaders showed interest in the schools and then lobbied for improved facilities, upgraded equipment, new textbooks, and larger budgets (McNeal & Oxholm, 2009; Shipps, 2006; Wagner, 2008).

Educators were upset when business leaders accused them of failing to spend their funds wisely. They were extremely upset when they urged them to alter their management styles and copy those of executives in industry, logistics, and commerce (Boyles, 2005; Brower, 2006; Franklin, Bloch, & Popkewitz, 2004; Kohn & Shannon, 2002).

Some educators accused business leaders of meddling in affairs about which they had insufficient knowledge. They communicated their annoyance in books. They gave them titles such as *The Blackboard and the Bottom Line: Why Schools Can't Be Businesses, None of Our Business: Why Business Models Don't Work in Schools,* and *Why Is Corporate America Bashing Our Public Schools?* (Cuban, 2004; Emery & Ohanian, 2004; England, 2003).

Blaming Politicians

Some educators distrusted business leaders because of the culture that they represented, the problems that they highlighted, and the solutions that they proposed. They distrusted politicians for similar reasons. However, they also worried about the politicians' motives (Irons & Harris, 2007; McGuinn, 2006; Rebell & Wolff, 2008).

Educators acknowledged that politicians needed to be involved in the schools. Nonetheless, they accused them of using that involvement to benefit their own political interests (Eisler, 2000; Gold, 2007; Hawley, 2007; Johnson & Salz, 2008; McGrath, 2005; R. Moore, 2006; Noddings, 2007; Rothstein, 2004; Sarason, 1990; Schmoker, 2006; Shapiro, 2006).

Educators pointed to assessment as an instance in which politicians had behaved selfishly. They claimed that they selected stances on it to advance their own goals (Comer, 2004; English & Steffy, 2001; Gallagher, 2007; Noddings, 2007; Sloan, 2008).

Educators identified additional instances in which politicians had behaved inappropriately. They claimed that selfish motives explained their stances on charter schools (Berends, Springer, & Walberg, 2008; Fuller, 2000; Push-Back on Charter Schools, 2010; Weil, 2000). They claimed that these motives also explained their stances on the diversion of government funds to private schools (Belfield & Levin, 2005; Boyles, 2005; Bracey, 2002; Giordano, 2009, 2010; Good & Braden, 2000; Levin, 2001; Saltman, 2000; Wilson, 2006).

ANALYZING ADVICE FROM SCHOOL CRITICS

Early and recent critics were distressed about situations in the schools. Novelists communicated their alarm through fiction, journalists through anecdotes, and scholars through systematically gathered observations.

The critics pinpointed problems with physical facilities, equipment, textbooks, personnel, curricula, policies, and funding. After they had identified problems, they suggested remedies.

Educators were not sure about the critics' motives. They listened to them when they thought that they were genuinely concerned about them and their students; they ignored them when they thought they had ulterior motives.

The critics were upset when educators ignored them; they asked parents, business leaders, and politicians to help discipline them. However, they were frustrated because educators asked these same groups for assistance.

Activity 9.1

You may wish to examine the issues that early school critics investigated. You could use Table 9.1.

Table 9.1 lists four critical groups: novelists, journalists, scholars from education, and scholars from fields other than education.

Complete this table by identifying issues about which the groups were concerned. You can use abbreviations.

Use the letters *MA* for materials (e.g., facilities/equipment/textbooks), *PE* for personnel, *CU* for curriculum, *SP* for school policies, and *FN* for funding.

As a final step, provide explanations for your answers. You can complete the table with the information in this chapter, the resources that are cited in it, or other resources.

Activity 9.2

You may wish to examine the influence of the early school critics. You could use Table 9.2.

Table 9.2 identifies groups that critics attempted to influence. It lists four groups: parents with children in the schools, educators, business leaders, and politicians. It also identifies critics. It lists four types: novelists, journalists, education scholars, and scholars from fields other than education.

Complete the table by indicating the ways in which groups viewed critics. You can use symbols.

Table 9.1. Early School Critics

Group	*Issue**	*Explanation*
Novelists		
Journalists		
Scholars—Education		
Scholars—Other		

**MA* Materials
PE Personnel
CU Curriculum
SP School Policies
FN Funding

Use the symbol − if they viewed them as not influential. Use the symbol ± if they viewed them as moderately influential and the symbol + if they viewed them as highly influential. As a final step, explain the bases for your answers.

Activity 9.3

You may wish to compare the issues on which early and recent critics concentrated. You could use Table 9.3.

Table 9.3 identifies five types of issues: those related to materials (e.g., facilities/equipment/textbooks), personnel, curricula, school policies, and funding.

Complete the table by indicating the importance that the critics assigned to the issues. You can rely on symbols.

Table 9.2. Responses to Critics

Group	*Responses to**				*Explanation*
	Novelists	*Journalists*	*Scholars—Education*	*Scholars—Noneducation*	
Parents					
Educators					
Business Leaders					
Politicians					

* − Not Influential
± Moderately Influential
+ Highly Influential

Table 9.3. Early and Recent School Critics

Critics	*Response to**					*Rationale*
	Materials	*Personnel*	*Curricula*	*Policies*	*Funding*	
Early						
Recent						

* – Unimportant
± Moderately Important
± Very Important

Table 9.4. Educators Respond to Recent Critics

Issue	*Allegation*	*Response to**	*Explanation*
Materials			
Personnel			
Curricula			
Policies			
Funding			

*– Disagreed
± Mixed Response
± Agreed

Use the symbol − if they depicted them as unimportant. Use the symbol ± if they depicted them as moderately important and the symbol + if they depicted them as very important. As a final step, explain the bases for your answers.

Activity 9.4

You might wish to examine the ways in which educators responded to allegations from recent critics. You could use Table 9.4.

Table 9.4 identifies five types of allegations: those related to materials (e.g., facilities/equipment/textbooks), personnel, curricula, school policies, and funding.

Complete the table by identifying critical allegations. Also indicate the ways in which educators responded. You can use symbols.

Use the symbol + if the educators disagreed with the allegations. Use the symbol ± if they demonstrated a mixed response and the symbol + if they agreed. As a final step, explain your answers.

Activity 9.5

You may wish to examine the ways in which groups responded to the issues that recent school critics raised. You could use Table 9.5.

Table 9.5 identifies three groups: parents with children in the schools, business leaders, and politicians. It also identifies issues on which critics concentrated. It lists five types: issues related to materials (e.g., facilities/equipment/textbooks), personnel, curricula, school policies, and funding.

Complete the table by indicating the importance that groups assigned to the issues. You can rely on symbols.

Use the symbol − if they viewed them as unimportant. Use the symbol ± if they viewed them as somewhat important and the symbol + if they viewed them as important. As a final step, explain the bases for your answers.

SUMMARY

Critics made recommendations about school reform. They strengthened their recommendations by gathering supportive parents, business leaders, and politicians.

Table 9.5. Responses to Recent Critics

Critics	*Response to**					*Rationale*
	Materials	*Personnel*	*Curricula*	*Policies*	*Funding*	
Parents						
Business Leaders						
Politicians						

* − Unimportant
± Somewhat Important
+ Important

10

Is Education Like Dieting?

Results not typical.

—Phrase accompanying testimonials
by Jenny Craig dieters, JennyCraig.com, 2009

Business leaders supported commercial diets that were profitable. However, they were chastised for conflicts of interest. When elected officials supported diets that were politically profitable, they also were chastised.

DIETS

Americans worried about their weights. They revealed that concern by spending over sixty billion dollars annually on dieting products and services (Adams, 2005; Fletcher, 2006; Media Influence, 2009).

Americans also revealed a concern about weight when they focused on certain celebrities. They focused on Kirstie Alley with unusual intensity.

Kirstie Alley

Kirstie Alley played Lieutenant Saavik in a popular 1980s film *Star Trek II: The Wrath of Khan* (Shatner et al., 2002, 1982). She appeared in other films for decades. She eventually starred in a television series that mirrored aspects of her personal life.

The show, which was entitled *Fat Actress*, highlighted the professional challenges of overweight actors (Alley, Callen, Harris, Hampton, & Truesdell, 2005). Alley later used the reputation that she had gained from the show to secure a different type of employment; she began to work in the weight-loss business.

Alley took a position promoting the Jenny Craig diet. This diet gave clients chances to consult with counselors. It provided them with convenient, premeasured, and tasty rations of food. It guaranteed them that they would remain healthy, avoid hunger pangs, and lose weight (JennyCraig.com, 2009).

Alley claimed that she had lost fifty pounds with her new diet. She discussed her success in television interviews and on commercials. She even wrote a book about the ways in which she had handled her weight problems (Alley, 2005; Warner, 2005).

Although Alley did lose weight, she then regained it. In fact, she eventually grew very large. Like her losses, her gains were publicized extensively.

Journalists wrote demeaning articles about Alley; they supplemented them with unflattering photos. They could not conceal their glee when she was terminated by the Jenny Craig Company (Kirstie Checks, 2009).

Some journalists wrote about Alley because they thought that her misfortunes would titillate mean-spirited audiences. However, others thought that her weight problems would evoke empathy.

Like the journalists, entrepreneurs realized that Alley could be an invaluable asset. They signed her to another weight-themed television show and made her the spokesperson for her own brand of diet products (Dawn, 2010; Kirstie Alley, 2010; Stanley, 2010; Tan, 2010).

Entrepreneurs

The importance that Americans assigned to weight control is indicated by the money that they spent on it. They purchased numerous products, including books. Although the amount that they allocated for books is difficult to specify, it is reflected in the statistics about best-selling volumes.

A 2008 report identified the books that had sold the most copies during a fifteen-year period. The top seller was a Harry Potter novel. However, the volume with the second highest sales was a dieting book—*Dr. Atkins' New Diet Revolution* (Atkins, 1970; *USA Today*'s Best-Selling, 2008).

The Atkins diet manual was not the sole dieting book on the best-seller list. The top fifty volumes included five other dieting books; the next fifty volumes included another five (Agatston, 2004a, 2004b; Atkins, 1972; Carey, 2008; Daley, 1994; Eades & Eades, 2000; McGraw, 2003; Roizen & Oz, 2006; Sears & Lawren, 1995; Steward, Andrews, Bethea, & Balart, 1998).

Books about diets were profitable. However, they became more profitable when they were linked to additional products. Entrepreneurs connected them to drinks, energy bars, snacks, meals, seasonings, dietary supplements, drugs, cooking utensils, newsletters, magazines, seminars, computer programs, CDs, and DVDs (Bijlefeld & Zoumbaris, 2003).

The entrepreneurs made impressive profits from dieting books, products, and services. Those at the Jenny Craig Company reported that their profits exceeded two hundred million dollars during 2003, which was the last year that their stock was publically traded (Warner, 2005).

Investors in dieting companies conceded that these businesses were profitable. However, they rejoined that they also were effective. In fact, they argued that they were profitable precisely because they were effective. They still had a hard time convincing their critics.

Critics

Critics challenged commercial dieting books, products, and services. They asked how so many diverse plans could all be based on sound nutritional advice. They found nutrition experts who agreed with them (Jibrin, 1998; Lankford, 2007; Levitt, 2009).

Critics came up with additional reasons for opposing the dieting industry. They noted that the business leaders who managed it were committed to corporate and consumer interests. They gave examples of business leaders who had been unable to deal with these conflicting interests (Bijlefeld & Zoumbaris, 2003; Snyderman, 2009).

The critics denigrated faddish diets, such as those that required persons to dine at fast food restaurants or eat specially formulated cookies (Ellin, 2010). They predicted that consumers would regain any weight they had lost after they resumed their normal eating regimens (Beck, 2009). They buttressed this prediction with statements from disgruntled clients (Kolata, 2007; Taubes, 2007; Warner, 2005).

The authors of dieting books were bothered by accusations about temporary weight loss. They made sure that their titles included reassuring phrases: *thin forever, permanent weight loss, lose weight and keep it off, fat loss that lasts forever*, or *last diet you'll ever need* (Atkins, 2003; Bauer & Svec, 2009; Beck, 2007; Eisenson & Binks, 2007; Fletcher, 2006; Reno, 2007; Smith, 2006; Somers, 2005; Zuckerbrot, 2006).

DISCREDITING CRITICS

The professionals in many fields worried that they would be discredited for succumbing to conflicts of interest. They tried to separate their personal and professional interests.

Physicians wished to help their patients and succeed in their businesses. Worried about the damages that would sustain from conflicting interests, they attempted to avoid even the appearance that their professional and personal goals conflicted (Emanuel, 2003; Kassirer, 2005; Snodgrass, 2006).

Many professionals shared the concerns of the medical community. Lawyers and elected government officials displayed anxiety when they were accused of conflicting interests. Some defended themselves convincingly; others were less effective (e.g., Cohen, 2007; Davis & Stark, 2001; Monroe, Miller, & Tobis, 2008; Moore, 2005; Pruchno & Smyer, 2007; Sharp, 2006).

Journalists

Journalists were another group that worried about conflicts of interest. They were vulnerable when they made subjective judgments about films, books, art, restaurants, vacation destinations, automobiles, computers, and television programs. They anticipated that they would be accused of displaying biased and unprofessional attitudes (Bilton, 2010; David Pogue Responds, 2009; Dwyer, 2009; Green, 2008; Rubinstein, 2006).

Persons berated journalists when they reported about art, services, and products; they also criticized them when they reported about the government. Some of them complained that political reporters were influenced too heavily by conservatives; others insisted that they were influenced excessively by liberals (Alterman, 2003; B. C. Anderson, 2005; Baumgartner & Francia, 2008; Beinhart, 2005; Henry, 2007; Jamieson & Waldman, 2003; Kallen, 2004; Kuypers, 2006; Ruschmann, 2006; Sheppard, 2008).

Some persons reproached journalists for the ways in which they reported about minority groups. They alleged that they showed biases when they presented information about women, individuals with disabilities, members of some races, and participants in select religions (Davenport, 2009; Falk, 2008; Giordano, 2007; Hammersley, 2006; Sloan & Mackay, 2007).

Entrepreneurs

Professional authors accused dieting entrepreneurs of using questionable practices. They contended that they were blinded by opportunities to gain profits (Bijlefeld & Zoumbaris, 2003; Jibrin, 1998; Lankford, 2007; Snyderman, 2009).

The dieting entrepreneurs counterattacked. They noted that the persons who wrote exposés had their own conflicts of interest; they claimed that they were compromised by opportunities to sell books and advance their careers.

Although some dieting entrepreneurs confronted their critics, others sidestepped them. A spokesperson for the Atkins Diet demonstrated a way to execute this maneuver. She acknowledged that she did not know enough about nutrition to address the concerns of the experts. However, she responded that attacks on her diet merely demonstrated that it, like all other diets, was controversial (Common Atkins Diet Criticism, 2009).

POLITICIANS ADDRESS DIETS

Health professionals made recommendations about commercial diets. However, they confused members of the public because their recommendations were frequently irreconcilable. They even confused them about the groups at which their recommendations were targeted.

The health professionals were sure that consumers needed their advice. They revealed that conviction in surveys. In one survey, more than 80 percent of these professionals ranked excessive weight as the most serious health problem in America (McAllister, 2007).

Members of the public responded to weight issues differently than the health professionals. They underscored their differences when they did not select excessive weight as one of their top health problems; they underscored them more emphatically when those who were obese insisted that they were normal sized (Miller et al., 2008).

Persons' views about their weights were linked to numerous factors. Although they were connected to physical traits, they also were connected to social, economic, geographic, cultural, ethnic, and psychological traits (Costin, 2007; Dalrymple, 2010; Gura, 2007; Keel, 2006; Peña & Bacallao, 2000; Phillips, 1996; Savage, 2008).

Many adults were unable to determine whether they were carrying excessive weight. They were not alone; their children also could not make this calculation. Some children became confused while playing or viewing sports (Dosil, 2008; Lask & Bryant-Waugh, 2007). Others became confused while studying or viewing models (Cottle, 2007; Inness, 2003; Lask & Bryant-Waugh, 2007; Tiemeyer, 2007).

Authors noted that children and teenagers were confused about their weight. They wrote books about the problems that their misperceptions created. They aimed them at parents, teachers, health professionals, young adults, adolescents, and children (Bjorklund, 2005; Orr, 2007; Strada, 2001; Vander Hook, 2001; Vollstadt, 1999; Wagner, 2007).

Health professionals worried about excessive weight; they resolved to publicize their worries. They persuaded journalists and professional authors to assist them. However, they also persuaded politicians.

Reducing Fats

When politicians decided to address weight-related problems, they could have focused on genes. After all, they had been advised that genes played an important and sometimes determinant role in body weight (Blaming Genes, 2008; Henderson, 2008). However, they worried that some constituents might be unable to comprehend these factors.

New York City politicians wanted to concentrate on food ingredients that were harmful and that voters could comprehend. They selected fats. They had been advised about the nutritional consequences of six types: trans fats, monounsaturated fats, polyunsaturated fats, saturated fats, omega-3 fatty acids, and dietary cholesterol (Mayo Clinic, 2009).

The politicians were interested in the popular trans fats. These fats were popular for two reasons: they were inexpensive and they had great flavor. However, they created the cholesterol that contributed to heart disease.

Politicians discouraged New York City restaurateurs from frying food in trans fats. After they were ignored, they imposed a citywide ban. They generated local and national attention (Lueck & Severson, 2006; Severson, 2007).

Politicians in Chicago decided to copy the New York City ban. However, they faced stiffer opposition. They realized that their proposal would fail because of resistance from the business leaders who owned small and midsized eateries. Even though they redrafted the proposal so that it affected only restaurants that grossed more than twenty million dollars annually, they could not appease their opponents (Vagnoni, 2006).

Politicians sometimes devised ingenious bans. In one community, they banned restaurateurs from using toys to market high-fat foods (J. McKinley, 2010). In other communities, they banned trans fats from both restaurants and school cafeterias. By 2009, they had enacted these dual ordinances in numerous cities and two populous states (Black, 2008; Trans Fat, 2009).

Reducing Calories

Elected officials wished to promote their constituents' health; they also wished to promote their own political goals. Although they had some success with trans fats campaigns, they were disappointed because of the many persons who resisted them. They assumed that they had not fully understood the campaigns.

Politicians wished to endorse a diet that would have broad support. They searched for one with a simple-to-comprehend rationale. Some of them believed that a calorie diet would be ideal.

Low-calorie diets were readily comprehensible. The most popular early- and mid-twentieth-century diets had focused exclusively on calories. They had equated calorie intake with sugar consumption. They employed a simple algorithm: eat sugar and put on weight—avoid it and lose weight (Critser, 2003; Libal, 2006; Lillien, 2009; Rolls, 2007; Taubes, 2007).

The New York politicians realized that a sugar-consumption campaign would oversimplify complex health problems. Nonetheless, they hoped that it would appeal to voters because of its simple rationale. They had another reason to be optimistic.

The politicians realized that some voters had resisted the trans fat campaign because of the government's role in it. They hoped that they would support an anticalorie campaign if the government was less involved. They proposed that restaurant owners simply display calorie counts (Calorie Posting, 2009).

Some critics still objected. They reminded the politicians of the government-mandated warnings on cigarette packages. Characterizing the tobacco warnings as ineffective, they predicted that the menu warnings would be equally ineffective. They even conducted studies to validate their predictions (Calorie Counters, 2010; Downs, Loewenstein, & Wisdom, 2009).

Some critics of the calorie ordinance had studied excessive eating. They seemed to agree with the politicians when they conceded that posting calories would make obese restaurant patrons feel guilty. However, they predicted that they would gorge themselves later. They warned that the new ordinance inadvertently might promote weight gain (Saul, 2008).

After New York City's calorie ordinance became effective, proponents and opponents tried to assess its influence. Although they disagreed about whether it was effective, they conceded that it generated a great deal of publicity. This attention may have benefitted New York City's consumers; it definitely benefitted its politicians (Hartocollis, 2009).

Federal politicians were impressed by New York City's calorie ordinance; they incorporated similar measures into health overhaul legislation in 2010. They required restaurant chains that had more than twenty sites to post calorie counts on their menus. Although they did not require them to display information about fats, they insisted that they have it available for patrons (Bernstein, 2010; Jalonick, 2010; Spencer & Wang, 2010).

Reducing Salt

The New York City politicians designed additional dieting campaigns. They were aggressive on some occasions. They were aggressive when they tried to discourage residents from drinking sugar-based soft drinks; they imposed a penny-per-ounce tax (Healthy Solution, 2010).

The politicians were less aggressive when they tried to reduce use of salt. Aware that they had been castigated for mixing health with politics, they decided to refrain from directly regulating this seasoning (Moss, 2010; Tierney, 2009, 2010).

The politicians resolved to make residents aware of the dangers of excessive salt consumption (NYC Mayor Declares War, 2009; New York City Department of Health and Mental Hygiene, 2009; New York City Starts Push, 2009; New York Preps for Battle, 2009). They also resolved to pressure food packagers and restaurateurs to reduce salt (Adamy, 2010; Neuman, 2010).

EXPERT AND AMATEUR CRITICS

Iron Chef was a popular 1990s Japanese television program. It was aired in numerous countries; it became the prototype for several other programs (Hoketsu, 2001; Television Food Network, 2004, 2009; Yukich et al., 2002).

The show was divided into three parts. The first part recounted the saga of Chairman Kaga. This individual resembled the wealthy, powerful, and eccentric antagonist in a famous karate movie, *Enter the Dragon* (Weintraub et al., 1973).

Enter the Dragon featured Bruce Lee, the incomparable martial arts star. A mysterious figure invited Lee to a stadium where he competed in death matches against the world's fiercest fighters.

Iron Chef featured accomplished chefs. Chairman Kaga had invited the chefs to compete in culinary clashes. The competitions took place within a special "kitchen stadium."

The initial portion of each episode introduced Kaga and the chefs who were competing on that episode. The second portion featured the chefs at work. Commentators discussed the ways in which they selected and combined ingredients. They emphasized the flavors, aromas, textures, freshness, and costs of their rare ingredients.

The third segment featured critics. They evaluated the contestants' dishes on the bases of presentation, taste, and originality.

When the show premiered in 1993, the evaluation panels comprised three members. When the last episode aired in 1999, they had expanded to five members. Nonetheless, the early and later panels comprised similar types of members.

Each *Iron Chef* panel contained one expert food critic. This person, who might have been a professional restaurant reviewer, was opinionated and pretentious.

Each panel also contained amateur critics. The amateurs included movie stars, baseball players, authors, sumo wrestlers, hosts of television shows, artists, and business leaders. They spoke plainly and spontaneously about the dishes.

In view of the show's hyperbolic premise, some fans may have been uninterested in the panels' verdicts. Like professional wrestling fans, they may have enjoyed the histrionics too much to be concerned about their validity (Beekman, 2006; Hackett, 2006; Kluck, 2009; Sammond, 2005).

Although some fans suspended critical judgment while listening to verdicts, others truly were concerned. They may have cared because they had confidence in the panels. They approved of a mixture that gave an advantage to the engaging and open-minded amateur critics. They may have decided to tune in regularly precisely because the amateurs prevailed.

ANALYZING ADVICE FROM NONEDUCATIONAL CRITICS

Dietary critics provided diverse and frequently contradictory advice. They tried to increase their influence through supporters. They tried to attract support from journalists, entrepreneurs, and politicians.

School critics were in similar situations. They made multiple and frequently incompatible recommendations. They tried to increase their influence through allies. They asked journalists, entrepreneurs, and politicians to join them.

Activity 10.1

You may wish to look for conflicts of interest among persons who gave advice. You could rely on Table 10.1.

Table 10.1 identifies groups that were concerned about diets. It lists two groups: entrepreneurs and politicians.

Complete the table by estimating their conflicting interests. You can rely on symbols. Select the symbol − to indicate low conflicts of interest. Select the symbol ± for moderate conflicts and the symbol − for high conflicts. As a final step, explain the bases for your responses.

Activity 10.2

You may wish to look for conflicts of interest when groups gave advice about varied topics. You could rely on Table 10.2.

Table 10.2 identifies two groups: enthusiasts and their critics. It also identifies issues about which they were concerned. It identifies two non-

Table 10.1. Conflicts of Interest among Diet Enthusiasts

Group	*Conflicts**	*Explanation*
Entrepreneurs		
Politicians		

*– Low
± Moderate
+ High

Table 10.2. Conflicts of Interest among Enthusiasts and Critics

	*Conflicts**		
Issue	*Enthusiasts*	*Critics*	*Explanation*
Commercial Diets			
Trans Fats Bans			
Education			

*– Low
± Moderate
+ High

educational issues: commercial diets and political bans on trans fats. It gives you the chance to choose another issue. Choose an issue related to education.

Complete the table by estimating conflicting interests. You can rely on symbols.

Use the symbol − to indicate low conflicts of interest. Use the symbol ± for moderate conflicts and the symbol + for high conflicts. As a final step, explain the bases for your responses.

Activity 10.3

You might wish to examine the ways in which groups responded to critics. You could use Table 10.3.

Table 10.3 identifies groups that were targeted by critics. It lists four groups: television viewers, consumers, voters, and parents.

This table also identifies four types of incidents: television programs, commercial diets, politician-backed dieting campaigns, and educational initiatives. The table already specifies the television incident—*Iron Chef*. You can specify the other incidents.

Complete the table by identifying the ways in which groups responded to expert and populist critics during each incident. You can rely on symbols.

Use the symbol − if they viewed them as insignificant. Use the symbol ± if they viewed them as moderately significant and the symbol + if they viewed them as significant. Finally, explain the bases for the symbols that you selected.

SUMMARY

When business leaders invested in dieting enterprises, they were accused of succumbing to conflicting interests. The politicians who mounted dieting campaigns faced similar accusations.

Table 10.3. Responses to Critics

Group	*Incident*	*Response to**		*Explanation*
		Expert	*Populist*	
Viewing Audience	Television Program: *Iron Chef*			
Consumers	Commercial Diet:			
Voters	Political Dieting Campaign:			
Parents	Schools:			

*– Insignificant
± Moderately Significant
+ Significant

References

Abel, E. K. (2007). *Tuberculosis and the politics of exclusion: A history of public health and migration to Los Angeles*. New Brunswick, NJ: Rutgers University Press.

Abernathy, S. F. (2007). *No Child Left Behind and the public schools*. Ann Arbor, MI: University of Michigan Press.

Adams, C. (2003). *Women's suffrage: A primary source history of the women's rights movement in America*. New York: Rosen Central Primary Source.

Adams, M. (2005, March 30). U.S. weight loss market worth $46.3 billion in 2004—Forecast to reach $61 billion by 2008. Naturalnews.com. Retrieved October 21, 2009, from: http://www.naturalnews.com/006133.html.

Adamy, J. (2010, April 21). Will low-salt pretzels taste just as good? *Wall Street Journal* [national edition], D1–D2. Retrieved April 22, 2010, from: http://online.wsj.com/article/SB10001424052748703763904575196283015020398.html.

Addams, J. (1910). *Twenty years at Hull-house: With autobiographical notes*. New York: Macmillan.

Addams, J. (1912). *Twenty years at Hull-house: With autobiographical notes*. New York: Macmillan. Retrieved October 29, 2009, from: http://digital.library.upenn.edu/women/addams/hullhouse/hullhouse.html.

Addams, J. (1930). *The second twenty years at Hull-house, September 1909 to September 1929, with a record of a growing world consciousness*. New York: Macmillan.

Addams, J. (2003). *The selected papers of Jane Addams* (M. Bryan, B. Bair, & M. de Angury, Eds.). Urbana, IL: University of Illinois Press.

Addams, J., Whipps, J. D., & Fischer, M. (2003). *Jane Addams's writings on peace*. Bristol, UK: Thoemmes Press.

Agatston, A. S. (2004a). *The South Beach diet cookbook*. Emmaus, PA: Rodale.

Agatston, A. S. (2004b). *The South Beach diet: Good fats good carbs guide*. Emmaus, PA: Rodale.

Aitken, I. (2006). *Encyclopedia of the documentary film*. New York: Routledge.

Albom, M. (1997). *Tuesdays with Morrie: An old man, a young man, and life's greatest lesson*. New York: Doubleday.

Aleccia, J. (2009, November 11). Va. teen suffers rare illness after swine flu shot. MSNBC.com. Retrieved November 11, 2009, from: http://www.msnbc.msn.com/id/33845867/ns/health-cold_and_flu.

All about highway hypnosis, road hypnosis, white line fever. (2008, November 2). Blogspot.com. Retrieved October 6, 2009, from: http://freearticlehelp.blogspot.com/2008/11/all-about-highway-hypnosis-road.html.

Allen, D., & Ort, S. W. (2008). *Coaching whole school change: Lessons in practice from a small high school*. New York: Teachers College Press.

Allen, W., Farrow, M., Sontag, S., Bellow, S., Horgan, P., Willis, G., Morse, S. E., & Hyman, D. (2001). *Zelig* [Film]. Los Angeles, CA: MGM. (Original film released in 1983.)

Alley, K. (2005). *How to lose your ass and regain your life: Reluctant confessions of a big-butted star*. Emmaus, PA: Rodale.

Alley, K., Callen, B., Harris, R., Hampton, B., & Truesdell, K. (2005). *Fat actress: The complete first season*. Los Angeles, CA: Showtime Entertainment.

Almond, L. (Ed.). (2008). *School violence*. Detroit, MI: Greenhaven Press.

Alterman, E. (2003). *What liberal media?: The truth about bias and the news*. New York: Basic Books.

Altshuler, L. (2006). *The bird-flu primer: The guide to being prepared and surviving an avian flu pandemic*. New York: Sterling & Ross.

American Academy of Child and Adolescent Psychiatry. (1994, February). Policy statement of facilitated communication. American Academy of Child and Adolescent Psychiatry Newsletter. Retrieved July 27, 2009, from: http://www.aacap.org/cs/root/policy_statements/facilitated_communication.

American Academy of Pediatrics. (1998). American Academy of Pediatrics auditory integration training and facilitated communication for autism. *Pediatrics*, 102, 431–33.

American Association on Mental Retardation. (1994). AAMR board approves policy on facilitated communication. *AAMR News & Notes*, 7 (1), 1.

American Psychological Association. (1994, August 14). Council policy manual. Retrieved July 27, 2009, from: http://www.apa.org/about/governance/council/policy/chapter-11.aspx#facilitated-communication.

American Recovery and Reinvestment Act of 2009. (2009). U.S. Government Printing Office. Retrieved on March 28, 2009, from: http://www.gpo.gov/fdsys/pkg/PLAW-111publ5/content-detail.html.

American Speech-Language-Hearing Association. (1995). Facilitated communication [position statement]. Retrieved July 27, 2009, from: http://www.asha.org/docs/html/PS1995-00089.html.

Andersen, H. C., & Thorndike, E. L. (1935). *Andersen's fairy tales*. New York: Appleton-Century.

Anderson, B. C. (2005). *South Park conservatives: The revolt against liberal media bias*. Washington, DC: Regnery.

Anderson, C. (2006). *The long tail: Why the future of business is selling less of more*. New York: Hyperion.

Anderson, L. (2007). *Congress and the classroom: From the Cold War to "No Child Left Behind."* University Park, PA: Pennsylvania State University Press.

Anderson, N. (2009, September 25). Unions criticize Obama's school proposals as "Bush III." *Washington Post*. Retrieved August 13, 2010, from: http://www.washingtonpost.com/wp-dyn/content/article/2009/09/24/AR2009092403197.html.

Anderson, S. B. (2005). *Extreme teens: Library services to nontraditional young adults*. Westport, CT: Libraries Unlimited.

Andreff, W., & Szymanski, S. (Eds.). (2006). *Handbook on the economics of sport*. Elgar original reference. Cheltenham, UK: Edward Elgar.

Apple, M. W. (2006). *Educating the "right" way: Markets, standards, God, and inequality*. New York: Routledge.

Applebome, P. (1998, August 19). Mystery man's death can't end the mystery; Fighting over Carlos Castaneda's legacy. *New York Times* [New York edition], E1. Retrieved October 30, 2009, from: http://www.nytimes.com/1998/08/19/arts/mystery-man-s-death-can-t-end-mystery-fighting-over-carlos-castaneda-s-legacy.html?sec=&spon=&pagewanted=1.

Aquila, F. D. (2008). *School law for K–12 educators: Concepts and cases*. Thousand Oaks, CA: Sage.

Ariely, D. (2008). *Predictably irrational: The hidden forces that shape our decisions*. New York: Harper.

Armfield, J. M. (2007, December 9). When public action undermines public health: A critical examination of antifluoridationist literature. *Australia and New Zealand Health Policy*. Retrieved August 4, 2009, from: http://anzhealthpolicy.com/content/4/1/25.

Armstrong, T. (1998). *Awakening genius in the classroom*. Alexandria, VA: Association for Supervision and Curriculum Development.

Aronson, M. (2009). *Bill Gates: A twentieth-century life*. New York: Viking.

Arthur, A. (2006). *Radical innocent: Upton Sinclair*. New York: Random House.

Astin, A. W. (1977). *Four critical years*. San Francisco: Jossey-Bass.

Astin, A. W. (1993). *What matters in college? Four critical years revisited*. San Francisco: Jossey-Bass.

Atkins, R. C. (1970). *Dr. Atkins' new diet revolution: The high calorie way to stay thin forever*. New York: McKay.

Atkins, R. C. (2003). *Atkins for life: The complete controlled carb program for permanent weight loss and good health*. New York: St. Martin's Press.

Atwell, J. E. (1995). *Schopenhauer on the character of the world: The metaphysics of will*. Berkeley, CA: University of California Press.

Augmentative and alternative communication. (2009, December 4). Assistivetech.net. Retrieved April 7, 2010, from: http://atwiki.assistivetech.net/index.php/Augmentative_and_alternative_communication.

Auster, P. (2005). *Collected prose: Autobiographical writings, true stories, critical essays, prefaces, and collaborations with artists*. New York: Picador.

Austin, T. (2007). *Watching the world: Screen documentary and audiences*. Manchester, UK: Manchester University Press.

Ayres, I. (2001). *Pervasive prejudice?: Unconventional evidence of race and gender discrimination*. Chicago: University of Chicago Press.

Baez, J., Howd, J., & Pepper, R. (2007). *The gay and lesbian guide to college life: A comprehensive resource for lesbian, gay, bisexual, and transgender students and their allies*. New York: Random House.

Bagshaw, S., & Oates, D. (2008). *Brighton graffiti*. Munich: Prestel.

Balkin, J. M., & Ackerman, B. A. (Eds.). (2001). *What* Brown v. Board of Education *should have said: The nation's top legal experts rewrite America's landmark civil rights decision*. New York: New York University Press.

Ball, J., & Johnson, K. (2010a, February 10). Climate group admits mistakes. *Wall Street Journal*. Retrieved August 13, 2010, from: http://online.wsj.com/article/SB10001424052748704182004575055703697897576.html?KEYWORDS=Climate±group+admits+to+making+mistakes.

Ball, J., & Johnson, K. (2010b, February 26). Push to oversimplify at climate panel. *Wall Street Journal* [national edition], A1, A12. Retrieved February 26, 2010, from: http://online.wsj.com/article/SB100014240527487041881045750836813 19834978.html.

Bamberger, A. (2010). Art, money, Shepard Fairey, Banksy and the quest for clarity. Artbusiness.com. Retrieved April 16, 2010, from: http://www.artbusiness.com/osoqfairbank.html.

Bank, B. J., & Hall, P. M. (Eds.). (1997). *Gender, equity, and schooling: Policy and practice*. New York: Garland.

Barbera, R. J. (2009). *The cost of capitalism: Understanding market mayhem and stabilizing our economic future*. New York: McGraw-Hill.

Bartholomew. (2009, October 25). Our indivisible environment. *Wall Street Journal* [national edition], A17. Retrieved October 26, 2009, from: http://online.wsj.com/article/SB10001424052748704500604574485341504345488.html.

Barton, E. A. (2009). *Leadership strategies for safe schools*. Thousand Oaks, CA: Corwin Press.

Bauder, J. (2007). *Censorship*. Detroit, MI: Greenhaven Press.

Bauer, J., & Svec, C. (2009). *Joy's life diet: Four steps to thin forever*. New York: Harper-Collins.

Bauerlein, M. (2008). *The dumbest generation: How the digital age stupefies young Americans and jeopardizes our future (Or, don't trust anyone under 30)*. New York: Tarcher/Penguin.

Baumgartner, J. C., & Francia, P. L. (2008). *Conventional wisdom and American elections: Exploding myths, exploring misconceptions*. Lanham, MD: Rowman & Littlefield.

Bausum, A. (2007). *Muckrakers: How Ida Tarbell, Upton Sinclair, and Lincoln Steffens helped expose scandal, inspire reform, and invent investigative journalism*. Washington, DC: National Geographic.

Beane, A. L. (1999). *The bully free classroom: Over 100 tips and strategies for teachers K–8*. Minneapolis, MN: Free Spirit.

Beane, A. L. (2009). *Bullying prevention for schools: A step-by-step guide to implementing a successful anti-bullying program*. San Francisco: Jossey-Bass.

Beck, M. (2009, December 7). How the cookie diet crumbles. *Wall Street Journal*, D1, D2. Retrieved December 7, 2009, from: http://online.wsj.com/article/SB10001424052748704825504574581812455177846.html.

Beck, M. N. (2007). *The four-day win: End your diet war and achieve thinner peace.* Emmaus, PA: Rodale.

Becker, L. M. (2004). *How to manage your postgraduate course.* New York: Palgrave-Macmillan.

Beckwith, D. W. (2009). *A new day in the Delta: Inventing school desegregation as you go.* Tuscaloosa: University of Alabama Press.

Beekman, S. (2006). *Ringside: A history of professional wrestling in America.* Westport, CT: Praeger.

Beinhart, L. (2005). *Fog facts: Searching for truth in the land of spin.* New York: Nation.

Belfield, C. R., & Levin, H. M. (2005). *Privatizing educational choice: Consequences for parents, schools, and public policy.* Boulder, CO: Paradigm.

Bellamy, G. T. (2007). *Principal accomplishments: How school leaders succeed.* New York: Teachers College Press.

Bellingham, L., & Bybee, J. A. (2008). *Food styling for photographers: A guide to creating your own appetizing art.* Amsterdam: Elsevier/Focal Press.

Bennett, J. T., & DiLorenzo, T. J. (2000). *From pathology to politics: Public health in America.* New Brunswick, NJ: Transaction.

Bennett, S., & Kalish, N. (2006). *The case against homework: How homework is hurting our children and what we can do about it.* New York: Crown.

Ben-Porath, S. R. (2006). *Citizenship under fire: Democratic education in times of conflict.* Princeton, NJ: Princeton University Press.

Benson, T. W., & Snee, B. J. (2008). *The rhetoric of the new political documentary.* Carbondale, IL: Southern Illinois University Press.

Benz, C. (2006). *College reading.* Boston: Houghton Mifflin.

Berends, M., Springer, M. G., & Walberg, H. J. (Eds.). (2008). *Charter school outcomes.* New York: Erlbaum.

Bernanke warns about creating new bubbles. (2010, January 3). MSNBC.com. Retrieved January 3, 2010, from: http://www.msnbc.msn.com/id/34673368/ns/business-stocks_and_economy.

Bernstein, S. (2010, March 23). Health care overhaul will put calorie counts on more menus. *Chicago Tribune.* Retrieved March 24, 2010, from: http://www.chicagotribune.com/news/sc-biz-0324-calories--20100323,0,7791625.story.

Berra, Y., & Kaplan, D. (2008). *You can observe a lot by watching: What I've learned about teamwork from the Yankees and life.* Hoboken, NJ: Wiley.

Berraho, M., Nejjari, C., Elrhazi, K., El Fakir, S., Tessier, J., & Ouédraogo, N. (2006). Measuring levels of professionally-related stress in taxi drivers in Fes, Morocco (Original tile in French). *Sante Publique,* 3, 375–87. Retrieved July 6, 2009, from: http://www.labmeeting.com/paper/27012909/berraho-2006-measuring-levels-of-professionally-related-stress-in-taxi-drivers-in-fes-morocco.

Bersoff, D. N. (2008). *Ethical conflicts in psychology.* Washington, DC: American Psychological Association. (Original work published in 1999.)

Berson, R. K. (2004). *Jane Addams: A biography.* Westport, CT: Greenwood Press.

Bérubé, M. (2006). *What's liberal about the liberal arts? Classroom politics and "bias" in higher education.* New York: Norton.

Bethell, T. (2005). *The politically incorrect guide to science.* Washington, DC: Regnery.

Beukelman, D. R., Yorkston, K. M., & Reichle, J. (Eds.). (2000). *Augmentative and alternative communication for adults with acquired neurologic disorders*. Baltimore, MD: Paul Brookes.

Bijlefeld, M., & Zoumbaris, S. K. (2003). *Encyclopedia of diet fads*. Westport, CT: Greenwood Press.

Biklen, D. (1993). *Communication unbound: How facilitated communication is challenging traditional views of autism and ability/disability*. New York: Teachers College Press.

Biklen, D., & Cardinal, D. N. (1997). *Contested words, contested science: Unraveling the facilitated communication controversy*. New York: Teachers College Press.

Bilton, N. (2010, February 24). *Yelp is sued after dispute over a review*. Bits. Retrieved March 1, 2010, from: http://bits.blogs.nytimes.com/2010/02/24/yelp-is-sued-after-dispute-over-a-review/?scp=2&sq=ebooks&st=cse.

Bily, C. A. (2006). *Global warming*. San Diego, CA: Greenhaven Press.

Bjorklund, R. (2005). *Eating disorders*. New York: Marshall-Cavendish-Benchmark.

Black, J. (2008, July 26). Calif. becomes 1st state to enact trans fat ban. *Washington Post*. Retrieved October 22, 2009, from: http://www.washingtonpost.com/wp-dyn/content/article/2008/07/25/AR2008072502308.html.

Blaming genes for obesity. (2008, July 28). Newscientist.com. Retrieved October 22, 2009, from: http://www.newscientist.com/blog/shortsharpscience/2008/07/blaming-genes-for-obesity.html.

Blanchard, K. H., Hutson, D., & Willis, E. (2008). *The one minute entrepreneur: The secret to creating and sustaining a successful business*. New York: Currency/Doubleday.

Bogle, K. A. (2008). *Hooking up: Sex, dating, and relationships on campus*. New York: New York University Press.

Boon, T., & Rotha, P. (2008). *Films of fact: A history of science in documentary films and television*. London: Wallflower Press.

Borden, M. E., Burlinson, M. A., & Kearns, E. R. (1995). *In addition to tuition: The parents' survival guide to freshman year of college*. New York: Facts on File.

Borenstein, S. (2009, October 26). Global cooling? Statisticians reject claims that climate trend is shifting. Taragana.com. Retrieved October 27, 2009, from: http://blog.taragana.com/n/ap-impact-global-cooling-statisticians-reject-claims-that-climate-trend-is-shifting-207434/.

Boushey, A. (2004). *Parent to parent: Information and inspiration for parents dealing with autism and Asperger's syndrome*. London: Jessica Kingsley.

Boushey, A. (2007). *Talking teenagers: Information and inspiration for parents of teenagers with autism or Asperger's syndrome*. London: Jessica Kingsley.

Bowen, W. G., & Levin, S. A. (2003). *Reclaiming the game: College sports and educational values*. Princeton, NJ: Princeton University Press.

Boyles, D. (2005). *Schools or markets? Commercialism, privatization, and school-business partnerships*. Mahwah, NJ: Erlbaum.

Bracey, G. W. (2002). *The war against America's public schools: Privatizing schools, commercializing education*. Boston: Allyn & Bacon.

Bray, C. (2010, January 12). Cuomo seeks data on bonuses. *Wall Street Journal* [national edition], A4. Retrieved January 12, 2010, from: http://online.wsj.com/article/SB10001424052748703652104574652433778946994.html.

Brimelow, P. (2003). *The worm in the apple: How the teacher unions are destroying American education*. New York: HarperCollins.

Brody, C. M. (Ed.). (2000). *Gender consciousness and privilege*. London: Falmer Press.

Bronner, E. (1999, May 28). Texas school turnaround: How much Bush credit? *New York Times*. Retrieved October 12, 2009, from: http://partners.nytimes.com/library/politics/camp/052899wh-gop-bush.html.

Broughton, P. D. (2008). *Ahead of the curve: Two years at Harvard Business School*. New York: Penguin.

Brower, R. (2006). *Whose business is school reform? Letting the experts drive school improvement*. Lanham, MD: Rowman & Littlefield.

Brown v. Board of Education of Topeka. (1954). 347 U.S. 483.

Brown, V. (2004). *The education of Jane Addams*. Philadelphia: University of Pennsylvania Press.

Brownell, S. (2008). *Beijing's games: What the Olympics mean to China*. Lanham, MD: Rowman & Littlefield.

Bruce, A., & Wattles, W. D. (2007). *Beyond the secret: The definitive unauthorized guide to the secret*. New York: Disinformation.

Bryant, P. W., & Underwood, J. (2007). *Bear: The hard life and good times of Alabama's coach Bryant*. Chicago, IL: Triumph.

Bryce, R. (2009, September 7). Windmills are killing our birds: One standard for oil companies, another for green energy sources. *Wall Street Journal*. Retrieved October 26, 2009, from: http://online.wsj.com/article/SB10001424052970203706604574376543308399048.html.

Bryce, R. (2010, March 2). The brewing tempest over wind power. *Wall Street Journal* [national edition], A23. Retrieved March 3, 2010, from: http://online.wsj.com/article/SB10001424052748704240004575085631551312608.html.

Buckley, J., & Schneider, M. (2007). *Charter schools: Hope or hype?* Princeton, NJ: Princeton University Press.

Buell, J. (2004). *Closing the book on homework: Enhancing public education and freeing family time*. Philadelphia: Temple University Press.

Buffington, P. W. (1996). *Cheap psychological tricks: What to do when hard work, honesty, and perseverance fail*. Atlanta, GA: Peachtree.

Burek Pierce, J. (2008). *Sex, brains, and video games: A librarian's guide to teens in the twenty-first century*. Chicago: American Library Association.

Burkhart, A. M., & Stein, R. A. (2008). *Law school success in a nutshell: A guide to studying law and taking law school exams*. St. Paul, MN: Thomson/West.

Burns, K. (2005). *New York street art*. Berlin: Gestalten Verlag.

Burns, T., & Sinfield, S. (2008). *Essential study skills: The complete guide to success at university*. Los Angeles: Sage.

Burnstein, D. E. (2006). *Next to godliness: Confronting dirt and despair in Progressive Era New York City*. Urbana, IL: University of Illinois Press.

Buzan, T. (2006). *The speed reading book: The revolutionary approach to increasing reading speed, comprehension and general knowledge*. London, UK: BBC.

Byrd, C. (2006). *Potentially harmful: The art of American censorship*. Atlanta: Georgia State University.

Byrne, R. (2006). *The secret*. New York: Atria.

Byrne-Jiménez, M., & Orr, M. T. (2007). *Developing effective principals through collaborative inquiry*. New York: Teachers College Press.

Calorie counters. (2010, February 10). *New York Times* [New York edition], A26. Retrieved May 2, 2010, from: http://www.nytimes.com/2010/02/03/opinion/03wed4.html.

Calorie posting regulations. (2009, October 22). New York City Department of Health and Mental Hygiene. Retrieved October 22, 2009, from: http://www.nyc.gov/html/doh/html/inspect/insp-calorie-posting.shtml.

Camerota, R. (2008). *Graffiti Japan*. West New York, NJ: Mark Batty.

Campbell, L., & Campbell, B. (2009). *Mindful learning: 101 proven strategies for student and teacher success*. Thousand Oaks, CA: Corwin.

Canning, M., Godfrey, M., & Holzer-Zelazewska, D. (2007). *Vocational education in the new EU member states: Enhancing labor market outcomes and fiscal efficiency*. Washington, DC: World Bank.

Cannon, J. M. (1994). *Time and chance: Gerald Ford's appointment with history*. New York: HarperCollins.

Canter, L., & Hausner, L. (1988). *Homework without tears*. New York: Harper Perennial.

Carafoli, J. F., & Smith, R. (1992). *Food photography and styling*. New York: Amphoto.

Carey, A. (2008). *Champions body for life: 12 weeks to mental and physical strength*. New York: Collins.

Carr, M. P. (2009). *The prepared parent's operational manual: Sending your child to college*. Washington, DC: Dicmar.

Carter, C., Bishop, J., & Kravits, S. L. (2006). *Keys to success: Building successful intelligence for college, career, and life*. Upper Saddle River, NJ: Pearson/Prentice Hall.

Cassidy, T., Jones, R. L., & Potrac, P. (2004). *Understanding sports coaching: The social, cultural and pedagogical foundations of coaching practice*. New York: Routledge.

Castaneda, C. (1968). *The teachings of Don Juan: A Yaqui way of knowledge*. Berkeley, CA: University of California Press.

Castaneda, C. (1971). *A separate reality: Further conversations with Don Juan*. New York: Simon & Schuster.

Castaneda, C. (1972). *Journey to Ixtlan: The lessons of Don Juan*. New York: Simon & Schuster.

Castaneda, M. R. (1996). *A magical journey with Carlos Castaneda*. Victoria, British Columbia, Canada: Millenia.

CDC: U.S. swine flu deaths surpass 350 with 44,000 confirmed illnesses. (2009, July 31). Foxnews.com. Retrieved August 13, 2010, from: http://www.foxnews.com/story/0,2933,535926,00.html.

Cell phone and texting laws. (2010, August). Governors Highway Safety Association. Retrieved August 13, 2010, from: http://www.ghsa.org/html/stateinfo/laws/cellphone_laws.html.

Chambers, S. (2006). *Mayors and schools: Minority voices and democratic tensions in urban education*. Philadelphia, PA: Temple University Press.

Chanan, M. (2007). *The politics of documentary*. London: British Film Institute.

Chang, J. (2005). *Can't stop, won't stop: A history of the hip-hop generation*. New York: St. Martin's Press.

Chemtob, C. M., Hamada, R. S., Bauer, G., Torigoe, R. Y., & Kinney, B. (1988). Patient suicide: Frequency and impact on psychologists. *Professional Psychology: Research and Practice*, 19, 416–20.

Chen, J., Chang, W., Chang, W., & Christiani, D. (2005). Occupational factors associated with low back pain in urban taxi drivers. *Occupational Medicine*, 55, 535–40.

Child vaccine safety concerns persist. (2010, March 1). *Baltimore Sun*. Retrieved March 1, 2010, from: http://weblogs.batimoresun.com/health/2010/03/parents_and_child_vaccine_safe.html.

Chinn, S. (2008). Hail taxi drivers! *New Scientist*, 198 (2660), 20–21.

Clarke, L., & Winch, C. (Eds.). (2007). *Vocational education: International approaches, developments and systems*. London, UK: Routledge.

Clery, S. B. (2008). *Postsecondary career/technical education: Changes in the number of offering institutions and awarded credentials from 1997 to 2006*. Washington, DC: United States Department of Education.

Clotfelter, C. T. (2004). *After* Brown: *The rise and retreat of school desegregation*. Princeton, NJ: Princeton University Press.

Cluck, B. (2001). *Play better baseball for girls: Winning techniques for players and coaches*. Lincolnwood, IL: Contemporary Books.

Cohen, C. B. (2007). *Renewing the stuff of life: Stem cells, ethics, and public policy*. Oxford, UK: Oxford University Press.

Cohen, I., Dennison, P. E., Dennison, G., & Goldsmith, M. (2002). *Hands on: How to use Brain Gym in the classroom*. Ventura, CA: Edu-Kinesthetics.

Cohen, R. M., & Scheer, S. (1997). *The work of teachers in America: A social history through stories*. Mahwah, NJ: Lawrence Erlbaum Associates.

Comer, J. P. (2004). *Leave no child behind: Preparing today's youth for tomorrow's world*. New Haven, CT: Yale University Press.

Common Atkins diet criticism. (2009). Atkins-diet-advisor.com. Retrieved October 20, 2009, from: http://www.atkins-diet-advisor.com/atkins-diet-criticism.html.

Cookson, P. W., & Berger, K. (2002). *Expect miracles: Charter schools and the politics of hope and despair*. Cambridge, MA: Westview Press.

Cooley, E. (1911). Foreword. In G. Kerschensteiner & A. J. Pressland, *Education for citizenship: Prize essay*. Chicago: Rand McNally.

Cooper, J. M. (2001). *Breaking the heart of the world: Woodrow Wilson and the fight for the League of Nations*. Cambridge, UK: Cambridge University Press.

Cooper, M., & Chalfant, H. (2009). *Subway art: 25th anniversary edition*. San Francisco: Chronicle.

Cooper, S. (2006). *Selfless cinema?: Ethics and French documentary*. London: Legenda.

Correlations of divorce rates with other factors. (2009). Divorce Reform Page. Retrieved July 7, 2009, from: http://www.divorcereform.org/cor.html#anchor614195.

Corwin, R. G., & Schneider, J. (2005). *The school choice hoax: Fixing America's schools*. Westport, CT: Praeger.

Costin, C. (2007). *The eating disorder sourcebook: A comprehensive guide to the causes, treatments, and prevention of eating disorders*. New York: McGraw-Hill.

Cottle, M. (2007). The fashion industry should not be held responsible for eating disorders. In V. Wagner (Ed.), *Eating disorders*. Detroit, MI: Greenhaven Press.

Covey, S. R. (1989). *The 7 habits of highly effective people: Restoring the character ethic*. New York: Free Press.

Craik, D. M. M., & Thorndike, E. L. (1935). *The little lame prince*. New York: Appleton-Century.

Cremin, L. A. (1988). *American education: The metropolitan experience, 1876–1980*. New York: Harper & Row.

Critser, G. (2003). *Fat land: How Americans became the fattest people in the world*. Boston, MA: Houghton-Mifflin.

Crosby, B. (2008). *Smart kids, bad schools: 38 ways to save America's future*. New York: Thomas Dunne Books.

Crossley, R. (1994). *Facilitated communication training*. New York: Teachers College Press.

Cuban, L. (2004). *The blackboard and the bottom line: Why schools can't be businesses*. Cambridge, MA: Harvard University Press.

Cunningham, K. (2009). *Diseases in history: Flu*. Greensboro, NC: Morgan Reynolds.

Cunningham, M. (2005). *The art of the documentary: Ten conversations with leading directors, cinematographers, editors, and producers*. Berkeley, CA: New Riders.

Curran, M., Newhan, R., & Lopez, A. (2007). *Coaching baseball successfully*. Champaign, IL: Human Kinetics.

Cutler, W. E. (1993). *Triple your reading speed*. New York: Prentice Hall.

Daley, R. (1994). *In the kitchen with Rosie: Oprah's favorite recipes*. New York: Knopf.

Dalrymple, T. (2010, May 1). Our big problem. *Wall Street Journal*. Retrieved May 1, 2010, from: http://online.wsj.com/article/SB1000142405274870442350457512281013855148.html.

Dalziel, J. R., & Job, R. F. (1997). Motor vehicle accidents, fatigue and optimism bias in taxi drivers. *Accident Analysis and Prevention*, 29, 489–94.

Dana, J. A., & Bourisaw, D. (2006). *Women in the superintendency: Discarded leadership*. Lanham, MD: Rowman & Littlefield Education.

Daschle, T., Greenberger, S. S., & Lambrew, J. M. (2008). *Critical: What we can do about the health-care crisis*. New York: Thomas Dunne.

Davenport, C. (2009). *Media bias, perspective, and state repression: The Black Panther Party*. Cambridge, UK: Cambridge University Press.

David Pogue responds to critics over "conflict of interest" accusations. (2009, September 23). Edibleapple.com. Retrieved October 20, 2009, from: http://www.edibleapple.com/david-pogue-responds-to-critics-over-conflict-of-interest-accusations/.

Davis, D. (2004). An insider's look at food photography: "If you can shoot food, you can shoot anything!" Shutterbug.com. Retrieved July 12, 2009, from: http://www.shutterbug.com/features/1204insider/.

Davis, J. (2008). *The Olympic Games effect: How sports marketing builds strong brands*. Singapore: Wiley.

Davis, M. (2005). *The monster at our door: The global threat of avian flu*. New York: New Press.

Davis, M., & Stark, A. (2001). *Conflict of interest in the professions*. Practical and professional ethics series. Oxford, UK: Oxford University Press.

Dawn, R. (2010, March 15). Big laughs in Kirstie Alley's new reality show. Reuters .com. Retrieved March 16, 2010, from: http://www.reuters.com/article/idUSTRE 62F08920100316.

De Groat, D. (2000). *Jingle bells, homework smells*. New York: HarperCollins.

De Mille, R. (1976). *Castaneda's journey: The power and the allegory*. Santa Barbara, CA: Capra Press.

De Mille, R. (1980). *The Don Juan papers: Further Castaneda controversies*. Santa Barbara, CA: Ross-Erikson.

De Seife, E. (2007). *This is Spinal Tap*. London: Wallflower Press.

Deas, D., & Clark, A. (2009). Youth binge drinking: Progress made and remaining challenges. *Journal of the American Academy of Child & Adolescent Psychiatry*, (48), 679–80.

Debray, E. H. (2006). *Politics, ideology, & education: Federal policy during the Clinton and Bush administrations*. New York: Teachers College Press.

Deegan, M. J. (1988). *Jane Addams and the men of the Chicago school, 1892–1918*. New Brunswick, NJ: Transaction Books.

Defoe, D., & Thorndike, E. L. (1936). *Robinson Crusoe*. New York: Appleton-Century.

DeFrank, T. M., & Ford, G. R. (2007). *Write it when I'm gone: Remarkable off-the-record conversations with Gerald R. Ford*. New York: Putnam's Sons.

DeFur, S., & Patton, J. R. (Eds.). (1999). *Transition and school-based services: Interdisciplinary perspectives for enhancing the transition process*. Austin, TX: PRO-ED.

DeMause, N., & Cagan, J. (2008). *Field of schemes: How the great stadium swindle turns public money into private profit* (rev. ed.). Lincoln: University of Nebraska Press. (Original work published in 1998.)

Denison, E. (1912). *Helping school children: Suggestions for efficient cooperation with the public schools*. New York: Harper.

Dennison, P. E. (2006). *Brain gym and me: Reclaiming the pleasure of learning*. Ventura, CA: Edu-Kinesthetics.

Dennison, P. E., & Dennison, G. (1986). *Brain gym: Simple activities for whole brain learning*. Glendale, CA: Edu-Kinesthetics.

Dennison, P. E., & Dennison, G. (1994). *Brain gym*. Ventura, CA: Edu-Kinesthetics.

Dent, H. S. (2009). *The great depression ahead: How to prosper in the crash following the greatest boom in history*. New York: Free Press.

DeSantis, A. D. (2007). *Inside Greek U: Fraternities, sororities, and the pursuit of pleasure, power, and prestige*. Lexington: University Press of Kentucky.

Dewey, J. (1898). The primary education fetich [sic]. *Forum*, 25, 315–28.

Dick, A. (2009, September 16). Help wanted. *Wall Street Journal*, A15.

Dickar, M. (2008). *Corridor cultures: Mapping student resistance at an urban high school*. New York: New York University Press.

Dickens, C., Thorndike, E. L., & Yonge, C. M. (1936). *A Christmas carol*. New York: Appleton-Century.

Diliberto, G. (1999). *A useful woman: The early life of Jane Addams*. New York: Scribner.

Dilley, P. (2002). *Queer man on campus: A history of non-heterosexual college men, 1945 to 2000*. New York: RoutledgeFalmer.

Dillon, S. (2010, February 24). As U.S. aid grows, oversight is urged for charter schools. *New York Times* [New York edition], A16. Retrieved March 25, 2010, from: http://www.nytimes.com/2010/02/25/education/25educ.html.

Dillon, S. (2010, March 13). Obama calls for major change in education law. *New York Times* [New York edition], A1. Retrieved March 15, 2010, from: http://www.nytimes.com/2010/03/14/education/14child.html.

DiMaggio, A. R. (2008). *Mass media, mass propaganda: Examining American news in the "War on Terror."* Lanham, MD: Lexington.

Dixon, S. (2007). *Digital performance: A history of new media in theater, dance, performance art, and installation*. Cambridge, MA: MIT Press.

Dolby, S. K. (2005). *Self-help books: Why Americans keep reading them*. Urbana: University of Illinois Press.

Don Juan and the sorcerer's apprentice. (1973, March 5). *Time*. Retrieved October 30, 2009, from: http://www.time.com/time/magazine/article/0,9171,903890,00.html.

Dosil, J. (Ed.). (2006). *The sport psychologist's handbook: A guide for sport-specific performance enhancement*. Chichester, UK: Wiley.

Dosil, J. (2008). *Eating disorders in athletes*. Chichester, UK: Wiley.

Douglas, D. M. (2005). *Jim Crow moves north: The battle over northern school segregation, 1865–1954*. New York: Cambridge University Press.

Downs, J. S., Loewenstein, G., & Wisdom, J. (2009, November 13). Eating by the numbers. *New York Times* [New York edition], A31. Retrieved November 13, 2009, from: http://www.nytimes.com/2009/11/13/opinion/13lowenstein.html.

Doyle, L. (2010, April 8). Robert Rubin, raise your right hand. Benzinga.com. Retrieved April 12, 2010, from: http://www.benzinga.com/213432/robert-rubin-raise-your-right-hand.

Dranove, D. (2008). *Code red: An economist explains how to revive the healthcare system without destroying it*. Princeton, NJ: Princeton University Press.

Du Pré, L., Miles, T. R., & Gilroy, D. E. (2008). *Dyslexia at college*. London: Routledge.

Dubin, A. E. (2006). *Conversations with principals: Issues, values, and politics*. Thousand Oaks, CA: Sage.

Dweck, C. S. (2006). *Mindset: The new psychology of success*. New York: Random House.

Dwyer, S. (2009, October 9). Open forum Friday: Should film critics be allowed to accept free stuff? Filmjunk.com. Retrieved March 3, 2010, from: http://www.filmjunk.com/2009/10/09/open-forum-friday-should-film-critics-be-allowed-to-accept-free-stuff/.

Eades, M. R., & Eades, M. D. (2000). *The protein power lifeplan*. New York: Warner.

Eagle Feather, K. (2006). *On the Toltec path: A practical guide to the teachings of Don Juan Matus, Carlos Castaneda, and other Toltec seers*. Rochester, VT: Bear.

Eastman Kodak Company. (1967). *Studio techniques for portrait photography*. Rochester, NY: Author.

Eddy, P. L., & Murray, J. P. (Eds.). (2007). *Rural community colleges: Teaching, learning, and leading in the heartland*. San Francisco: Jossey-Bass.

Educational flash cards. (2009, December 11). Amazon.com. Retrieved December 11, 2009, from: http://www.amazon.com/s/qid=1260542507/ref=sr_nr_seeall_16?ie=UTF8&rs=&keywords=educational%20flash%20cards&rh=i%3Aaps%2Ck%3Aeducational%20flash%20cards%2Ci%3Atoys-and-games.

Edu-K of South Africa. (2009). Brain Gym International. Retrieved July 25, 2009, from: http://images.google.com/imgres?imgurl=http://www.eduk.org.za/images/eduk_influence.GIF&imgrefurl=http://www.eduk.org.za/&usg=__FTpTwjnmmYj7Fxoz4W6b_h-ZXjw=&h=509&w=520&sz=46&hl=en&start=8&um=1&tbnid=kkSN6LU8d4TcFM:&tbnh=128&tbnw=131&prev=/images%3Fq%3Dbrain%2Bgym%26hl%3Den%26rls%3Dcom.microsoft:en-us%26sa%3DX%26um%3D1.

Edwards, B. (1979). *Drawing on the right side of the brain: A course in enhancing creativity and artistic confidence*. Los Angeles: Tarcher.

Edwards, B. (1999). *The new drawing on the right side of the brain*. New York: Tarcher/Putnam.

Eisenson, H., & Binks, M. (2007). *The Duke diet: The world-renowned program for healthy and lasting weight loss*. New York: Ballantine.

Eisler, R. T. (2000). *Tomorrow's children: A blueprint for partnership education in the 21st century*. Boulder, CO: Westview Press.

Ellin, A. (2010, January 27). Forget Jenny Craig: Hit the drive-thru. *New York Times* [New York edition], E1. Retrieved May 2, 2010, from: http://www.nytimes.com/2010/01/28/fashion/28SKIN.html?adxnnl=1&adxnnlx=1272916842-GriX1tZocfI9LcDhE3x/fg.

Ellis, J. C., & McLane, B. A. (2005). *A new history of documentary film*. New York: Continuum.

Elshtain, J. B. (2002). *Jane Addams and the dream of American democracy: A life*. New York: Basic Books.

Emanuel, E. J. (Ed.). (2003). *Ethical and regulatory aspects of clinical research: Readings and commentary*. Baltimore: Johns Hopkins University Press.

Emery, K., & Ohanian, S. (2004). *Why is corporate America bashing our public schools?* Portsmouth, NH: Heinemann.

Engineer sent text 22 seconds before fatal train crash. (2008, October 1). CNN.com. Retrieved October 8, 2009, from: http://www.cnn.com/2008/US/10/01/train.crash.probe/.

England, C. M. (2003). *None of our business: Why business models don't work in schools*. Portsmouth, NH: Heinemann.

English, F. W., & Steffy, B. E. (2001). *Deep curriculum alignment: Creating a level playing field for all children on high-stakes tests of educational accountability*. Lanham, MD: Scarecrow.

Epstein, A. (2003). *Sports law*. Clifton Park, NY: Thomson/Delmar.

Erlauer, L. (2003). *The brain-compatible classroom: Using what we know about learning to improve teaching*. Alexandria, VA: Association for Supervision and Curriculum Development.

Essenberg, B. (2003). Violence and stress at work in the transport sector. Geneva, Switzerland: International Labour Office. Retrieved July 6, 2009, from: http://www.ilo.org/public/english/dialogue/sector/papers/transport/wp205.pdf.

Essex, C., & McKitrick, R. (2007). *Taken by storm: The troubled science, policy, and politics of global warming*. Toronto: Key-Porter.

Evers, W. M., & Walberg, H. J. (2004). *Testing student learning, evaluating teaching effectiveness*. Stanford, CA: Hoover Institution Press.

Ex-Fannie Mae execs try to defend track record. (2010, April 9). Naplesnews.com. Retrieved April 12, 2010, from: http://www.naplesnews.com/news/2010/apr/09/ex-fannie-mae-execs-try-defend-track-record/.

Facilitated Communication Institute. (2009). Inclusion institutes. Retrieved July 27, 2009, from: http://www.inclusioninstitutes.org/.

Falk, E. (2008). *Women for president: Media bias in eight campaigns*. Urbana: University of Illinois Press.

Farmer, V. L. (2003). *The black student's guide to graduate and professional school success*. Westport, CT: Greenwood Press.

Farndon, J. (2005). *Bird flu*. New York: Disinformation.

Fed considers sweeping limits on bank pay. (2009, September 18). *New York Times*. Retrieved September 21, 2009, from: http://dealbook.blogs.nytimes.com/2009/09/18/fed-considers-limits-on-bank-pay/.

Fernald, G. M. (1943). *Remedial techniques in basic school subjects*. New York: McGraw-Hill.

Fernald, G. M., & Keller, H. B. (1936). *On certain language disabilities: Their nature and treatment*. Baltimore, MD: Williams & Wilkins.

Fertman, C. I. (2009). *Student-athlete success: Meeting the challenges of college life*. Sudbury, MA: Jones-Bartlett.

Fewer Americans see solid evidence of global warming. (2009, October 22). Pew Research Center. Retrieved October 27, 2009, from: http://people-press.org/report/556/global-warming.

Figley, C. R. (2002). *Treating compassion fatigue*. New York: Brunner-Routledge.

Fikes, J. C. (1993). *Carlos Castaneda, academic opportunism and the psychedelic sixties*. Victoria, British Columbia, Canada: Millenia.

Financial Crisis Inquiry Commission. (2010, April 9). Financial Crisis Inquiry Commission: United States of America. Retrieved April 12, 2010, from: http://fcic.gov/.

Finn, C. E., Manno, B. V., & Vanourek, G. (2000). *Charter schools in action: Renewing public education*. Princeton, NJ: Princeton University Press.

Finn, C. E., & Ravitch, D. (Eds.). (2007). *Beyond the basics: Achieving a liberal education for all children*. Washington, DC: Fordam Institute.

Fischer, M., Nackenoff, C., & Chmielewski, W. E. (Eds.). (2009). *Jane Addams and the practice of democracy*. Urbana: University of Illinois Press.

Fisher, B. M. (1967). *Industrial education: American ideals and institutions*. Madison: University of Wisconsin Press.

Fisher, M. C. (2006). *Immunizations & infectious diseases: An informed parent's guide*. Washington, DC: American Academy of Pediatrics.

Fitzgerald, T. (2007, July 5). Obama tells teachers he supports merit pay. Philly.com. Retrieved October 15, 2009, from: http://www.philly.com/philly/news/8335627.html.

Fizel, J. (2006). *Handbook of sports economics research*. Armonk, NY: Sharpe.

Flanagan, M. A. (2002). *Seeing with their hearts: Chicago women and the vision of the good city, 1871–1933*. Princeton, NJ: Princeton University Press.

Flashcard exchange. (2009, December 11). Tuolumne Technology Group. Retrieved December 11, 2009, from: http://www.flashcardexchange.com/.

Flawed 1976 national "swine flu" influenza immunization program. (2005, February 22). Suburban Management Emergency Project. Retrieved August 3, 2009, from: http://www.semp.us/publications/biot_reader.php?BiotID=177.

Flesch, R. (1943). *Marks of readable style: A study in adult education*. New York: Teachers College, Columbia University.

Flesch, R. (1951). *How to test readability*. New York: Harper.

Flesch, R. (1955). *Why Johnny can't read: And what you can do about it*. New York: Harper & Row.

Flesch, R. (1957). *How you can be a better student*. New York: Sterling.

Flesch, R. (1960). *How to write, speak, and think more effectively*. New York: Harper.

Flesch, R. (1966). *The new book of unusual quotations*. New York: Harper & Row.

Flesch, R. (1972). *Say what you mean*. New York: Harper & Row.

Flesch, R. (1974). *Rudolf Flesch on business communications: How to say what you mean in plain English*. New York: Barnes & Noble.

Flesch, R. (1979). *How to write plain English: A book for lawyers and consumers*. New York: Harper & Row.

Flesch, R. (1981). *Why Johnny still can't read: A new look at the scandal of our schools*. New York: Harper & Row.

Flesch, R. (1986). *Why Johnny can't read: And what you can do about it* (rev. ed). New York: Harper & Row.

Fletcher, A. (2006, February 14). Obesity rocketing despite record diet food spending. Foodnavigator.com. Retrieved October 20, 2009, from: http://www.foodnavigator.com/Science-Nutrition/Obesity-rocketing-despite-record-diet-food-spending.

Fletcher, A. M. (2006). *Weight loss confidential: How teens lose weight and keep it off—And what they wish parents knew*. Boston: Houghton Mifflin.

Flippo, R. F., & Caverly, D. C. (2000). *Handbook of college reading and study strategy research*. Mahwah, NJ: Lawrence Erlbaum.

Fluoridated water: Questions and answers. (2005, June 29). National Cancer Institute. Retrieved August 4, 2009, from: http://www.cancer.gov/cancertopics/factsheet/Risk/fluoridated-water.

Foderaro, L. W. (2010, April 18). Alternate path for teachers gains ground. *New York Times* [New York edition], A1, A22. Retrieved April 21, 2010, from: http://www.nytimes.com/2010/04/19/education/19regents.html.

Foerstel, H. N. (2002). *Banned in the U.S.A.: A reference guide to book censorship in schools and public libraries*. Westport, CT: Greenwood Press.

Foster, G., Greyser, S. A., & Walsh, B. (2006). *The business of sports: Text and cases on strategy and management*. Mason, OH: Thomson/South-Western.

Franek, R. (2008). *The best 368 colleges*. New York: Princeton Review.

Frank, S. D. (1990). *Remember everything you read: The Evelyn Wood 7-day speed reading and learning program*. New York: Times.

Frank, S. J. (1997). *Learning the law: Success in law school and beyond*. Secaucus, NJ: Carol.

Franklin, B. M., Bloch, M. N., & Popkewitz, T. S. (2004). *Educational partnerships and the state: The paradoxes of governing schools, children, and families*. New York: Palgrave-Macmillan.

Franklin, J. H. (2005). *Mirror to America: The autobiography of John Hope Franklin*. New York: Farrar, Straus & Giroux.

Fraser, J. W. (2007). *Preparing America's teachers: A history*. New York: Teachers College Press.

Freeman, R. (2006). *Study skills for psychology: Succeeding in your degree*. London: Sage.

Freitas, D. (2008). *Sex and the soul: Juggling sexuality, spirituality, romance, and religion on America's college campuses*. Oxford, UK: Oxford University Press.

Friedman, T. L. (2008). *Hot, flat, and crowded: Why we need a green revolution—And how it can renew America*. New York: Farrar, Straus & Giroux.

Fry, K. (2003). *Constructing the heartland: Television news and natural disaster*. Cresskill, NJ: Hampton Press.

Fulghum, R. (1988). *All I really need to know I learned in kindergarten: Uncommon thoughts on common things*. New York: Villard.

Fuller, B. (2000). *Inside charter schools: The paradox of radical decentralization*. Cambridge, MA: Harvard University Press.

Fullerton, S. (2007). *Sports marketing*. Boston: McGraw-Hill/Irwin.

Gaber, P. (1998). "Just trying to be human in this place": The legal education of twenty women. *Yale Journal of Law and Feminism*, 10, 165–258.

Gabriel, T. (2010, May 1). Despite push, success at charter schools is mixed. *New York Times* [New York edition], A1. Retrieved May 2, 2010, from: http://www.nytimes.com/2010/05/02/education/02charters.html.

Gaddy, B. B., Hall, T. W., & Marzano, R. J. (1996). *School wars: Resolving our conflicts over religion and values*. San Francisco: Jossey-Bass.

Gallagher, C. W. (2007). *Reclaiming assessment: A better alternative to the accountability agenda*. Portsmouth, NH: Heinemann.

Gambetta, D., & Hamill, H. (2005). *Streetwise: How taxi drivers establish their customers' trustworthiness*. New York: Russell Sage.

Ganz, N., & Manco, T. (2004). *Graffiti world: Street art from five continents*. New York: Abrams.

Ganzi Licata, P. (2003, February 23). Big, brutish and gas-guzzling: A low-key protest of S.U.V.'s. *New York Times* [New York edition, Section 14LI], 3. Retrieved July 31, 2009, from: http://www.nytimes.com/2003/02/23/nyregion/big-brutish-and-gas-guzzling-a-low-key-protest-of-suv-s.html.

Gardiner, M. E., Enomoto, E., & Grogan, M. (2000). *Coloring outside the lines: Mentoring women into school leadership*. Albany: State University of New York Press.

Gardner, F. L., & Moore, Z. E. (2006). *Clinical sport psychology*. Champaign, IL: Human Kinetics.

Gardner, H. (1982). *Art, mind, and brain: A cognitive approach to creativity*. New York: Basic Books.

Garone, E. (2009, September 16). In search of cachet. *Wall Street Journal*, A16.

Gastman, R., Rowland, D., & Sattler, I. (2006). *Freight train graffiti*. New York: Abrams.

Gastman, R., & Teri, S. (2007). *Los Angeles graffiti*. New York: Mark Batty.

Gates, B., & Hemingway, C. (1999). *Business @ the speed of thought: Using a digital nervous system*. New York: Warner.

George, N. (1998). *Hip hop America*. New York: Viking.

Gerhard, J. F. (2001). *Desiring revolution: Second-wave feminism and the rewriting of American sexual thought, 1920 to 1982*. New York: Columbia University Press.

Gill, I. S., Fluitman, F., & Dar, A. (2000). *Vocational education and training reform: Matching skills to markets and budgets*. Washington, DC: World Bank/Oxford University Press.

Gillette, J. M. (1910). *Vocational education*. New York: American Book Company.

Gillingham, A., & Stillman, B. W. (1997). *The Gillingham manual: Remedial training for students with specific disability in reading, spelling, and penmanship*. Cambridge, MA: Educators Publishing Service.

Gilmore, S. (2008). *Feminist coalitions: Historical perspectives on second-wave feminism in the United States*. Urbana: University of Illinois Press.

Ginsberg, A. E., Shapiro, J. P., & Brown, S. P. (2004). *Gender in urban education: Strategies for student achievement*. Portsmouth, NH: Heinemann.

Giordano, G. (2000). *Twentieth-century reading education: Understanding practices of today in terms of patterns of the past*. London, UK: Elsevier/JAI Press.

Giordano, G. (2003). *Twentieth-century textbook wars: A history of advocacy and opposition*. New York: Peter Lang.

Giordano, G. (2004). *Wartime schools: How World War II changed American education*. New York: Peter Lang.

Giordano, G. (2005). *How testing came to dominate American schools: The history of educational assessment*. New York: Peter Lang.

Giordano, G. (2007). *American special education: A history of early political advocacy*. New York: Peter Lang.

Giordano, G. (2009). *Solving education problems effectively: A guide to using the case method*. Lanham, MD: Rowman & Littlefield.

Giordano, G. (2010). *Cockeyed education: A case method primer*. Lanham, MD: Rowman & Littlefield.

Giroux, H. A. (2007). *The university in chains: Confronting the military-industrial -academic complex*. Boulder, CO: Paradigm.

Gladwell, M. (2008). *Outliers: The story of success*. New York: Little, Brown.

Glazer, N. (1987). On subway graffiti in New York. In N. Glazer & M. Lilla (Eds.), *The public face of architecture: Civic culture and public spaces* (pp. 371–80). New York: Free Press.

Glazer, N., & Lilla, M. (Eds.). (1982). *The public face of architecture: Civic culture and public spaces*. New York: Free Press.

Global consumers vote Al Gore, Oprah Winfrey and Kofi Annan most influential to champion global warming cause: Nielsen survey. (2007, July 7). Nielsen.com. Retrieved January 9, 2010, from: http://hk.nielsen.com/news/20070707.shtml.

Global swine flu deaths top 1,100. (2009, August 5). CNN.com. Retrieved August 5, 2009, from: http://edition.cnn.com/2009/HEALTH/08/05/swine.flu.deaths/.

Global warming with the lid off. (2009, November 24). *Wall Street Journal*. Retrieved November 25, 2009, from: http://online.wsj.com/article/SB10001424052748704888404574547730924988354.html.

Glynn, K. R., Weinstein, H., Weinstein, B., O'Hara, M., & Moore, M. (2007). *Sicko* [Film]. New York: Weinstein.

Goewey, D. (2005). "Careful, you may run out of planet": SUV's and the exploitation of the American myth. In S. Maasik & J. F. Solomon (Eds.), *Signs of life in the USA: Readings on popular culture for writers* (pp. 119–29). Boston: Bedford/St. Martin's Press.

Gogol, S. (2002). *Hard fought victories: Women coaches making a difference*. Terre Haute, IN: Wish.

Gold, B. A. (2007). *Still separate and unequal: Segregation and the future of urban school reform*. New York: Teachers College Press.

Goldberg, M. F. (2006). *Insider's guide to school leadership: Getting things done without losing your mind*. San Francisco: Jossey-Bass.

Good, T. L., & Braden, J. S. (2000). *The great school debate: Choice, vouchers, and charters*. Mahwah, NJ: Erlbaum.

Gordon, H. R. D. (1999). *The history and growth of vocational education in America*. Boston: Allyn & Bacon.

Gore, A. (2006). *An inconvenient truth: The planetary emergency of global warming and what we can do about it*. New York: Rodale.

Gorton, R. A., & Alston, J. A. (2009). *School leadership and administration: Important concepts, case studies & simulations*. Boston: McGraw-Hill.

Gosling, P., & Noordam, B. (2006). *Mastering your PhD: Survival and success in the doctoral years and beyond*. New York: Springer.

Gottlieb, L. (2008). *Graffiti art styles: A classification system and theoretical analysis*. Jefferson, NC: McFarland.

Gourevitch, P., & Morris, E. (2008). *Standard operating procedure*. New York: Penguin.

GovTrack.us. H.R. 1—111th Congress. (2009). American Recovery and Reinvestment Act of 2009. GovTrack.us (Database of Federal Legislation). Retrieved March 28, 2009, from: http://www.govtrack.us/congress/bill.xpd?bill=h111-1.

GRAFFITAGE: Development of a new anti-graffiti system based on traditional concepts, preventing damage of architectural heritage materials. European Commission. (2008, August 1). Retrieved February 8, 2010, from: http://ec.europa.eu/research/fp6/ssp/graffitage_en.htm.

Gray, D. L., & Smith, A. E. (2007). *Case studies in 21st century school administration: Addressing challenges for educational leadership*. Thousand Oaks, CA: Sage.

Green, F. (2007). *Recent developments in the economics of training*. Cheltenham, UK: Edward Elgar.

Green, T. (2008, January 18). Viveros-Faune and the *Village Voice*'s ethics problem. Modern Art Notes. Retrieved October 20, 2009, from: http://www.artsjournal.com/man/2008/01/the_vvviverosfaune_ethical_tra.html.

Greenawalt, K. (2005). *Does God belong in public schools?* Princeton, NJ: Princeton University Press.

Greene, D. (2001). *Audition success: An Olympic sports psychologist teaches performing artists how to win*. New York: Routledge. (Original work published in 1998.)

Greene, J., & Moline, K. (2006). *The bird flu pandemic: Can it happen? Will it happen? How to protect yourself and your family if it does*. New York: Thomas Dunne.
Greene, K. (2009, April 17). Savvy schools. *Wall Street Journal*. Retrieved April 1, 2010, from: http://online.wsj.com/article/SB123972559135117421.html.
Greenfield, R. (2006). *Timothy Leary: A biography*. Orlando: Harcourt.
Gregory, G., & Parry, T. (2006). *Designing brain-compatible learning*. Thousand Oaks, CA: Corwin Press.
Grévy, F. (2008). *Graffiti Paris*. New York: Abrams.
Grigsby, M. (2009). *College life through the eyes of students*. Albany, NY: SUNY Press.
Grocer, S. (2010, January 14). Banks set for record pay. *Wall Street Journal* [national edition], A1, A4. Retrieved January 14, 2010, from: http://online.wsj.com/article/SB10001424052748704281204575003351773983136.html.
Grody, S. (2006). *Graffiti LA: Street styles and art*. New York: Abrams.
Grubb, W. N. (2009). *The money myth: School resources, outcomes, and equity*. New York: Russell Sage Foundation.
Guest, C., McKean, M., Shearer, H., & Reiner, R. (1984). *This is Spinal Tap* [Film]. Los Angeles, CA: Embassy.
Gunn, A. M. (2008). *Encyclopedia of disasters: Environmental catastrophes and human tragedies*. Westport, CT: Greenwood Press.
Gura, T. (2007). *Lying in weight: The hidden epidemic of eating disorders in adult women*. New York: HarperCollins.
Guth, R. A. (2010, April 23). Gates rethinks his war on polio. *Wall Street Journal* [national edition], A1, A16. Retrieved April 24, 2010, from: http://online.wsj.com/article/SB10001424052702303348504575184093239615022.html.
Gutman, D. (2006). *The homework machine*. New York: Simon & Schuster.
Hackett, T. (2006). *Slaphappy: Pride, prejudice, & professional wrestling*. New York: Ecco.
Halberstam, D. (2005). *The education of a coach*. New York: Hyperion.
Hall, G. S. (1911). *Educational problems*. New York: Appleton.
Halvorson, G. C. (2007). *Health care reform now!: A prescription for change*. San Francisco: Jossey-Bass.
Hamachek, A. L. (2007). *Coping with college: A guide for academic success*. Upper Saddle River, NJ: Pearson/Prentice Hall.
Hamington, M. (2004). *Embodied care: Jane Addams, Maurice Merleau-Ponty, and feminist ethics*. Urbana: University of Illinois Press.
Hamington, M. (2009). *The social philosophy of Jane Addams*. Urbana: University of Illinois Press.
Hamm, T. (2008). *The new blue media: How Michael Moore, MoveOn.org, Jon Stewart and company are transforming progressive politics*. New York: New Press.
Hammersley, M. (2006). *Media bias in reporting social research?: The case of reviewing ethnic inequalities in education*. London: Routledge.
Hampe, B. (2007). *Making documentary films and videos: A practical guide to planning, filming, and editing documentaries*. New York: Holt.
Hand, R. J. (2006). *Terror on the air!: Horror radio in America, 1931–1952*. Jefferson, NC: McFarland.
Hannaford, C. (1995). *Smart moves: Why learning is not all in your head*. Arlington, VA: Great Ocean.

Hannan, B. (2009). *The riddle of the world: A reconsideration of Schopenhauer's philosophy*. Oxford, UK: Oxford University Press.

Hannaway, J., & Rotherham, A. J. (Eds.). (2006). *Collective bargaining in education: Negotiating change in today's schools*. Cambridge, MA: Harvard Education Press.

Hansen, R. S., & Hansen, K. (2008). *The complete idiot's guide to study skills*. New York: Alpha.

Hanushek, E. A. (2006). *Courting failure: How school finance lawsuits exploit judges' good intentions and harm our children*. Stanford, CA: Education Next Books.

Hanushek, E. A., & Lindseth, A. A. (2009). *Schoolhouses, courthouses, and statehouses: Solving the funding-achievement puzzle in America's public schools*. Princeton: Princeton University Press.

Harary, K., & Weintraub, P. (1991). *Right-brain learning in 30 days: The whole mind program*. New York: St. Martin's Press.

Hardiman, M. M. (2003). *Connecting brain research with effective teaching: The brain-targeted teaching model*. Lanham, MD: Scarecrow Press.

Hardy, D. T., & Clarke, J. (2004). *Michael Moore is a big fat stupid white man*. New York: HarperCollins.

Hargreaves, S. (2008). *Study skills for dyslexic students*. Los Angeles: Sage.

Harpur, J., Lawlor, M., & Fitzgerald, M. (2004). *Succeeding in college with Asperger syndrome*. London: Jessica Kingsley.

Harris, M. B. (Ed.). (1997). *School experiences of gay and lesbian youth: The invisible minority*. New York: Harrington Park Press.

Harrison, B., & Rappaport, A. (2006). *Hip-hop U.S. history*. Kennebunkport, ME: Cider Mill.

Hartley, D., & Whitehead, M. (2006). *Teacher education*. London, UK: Routledge.

Hartocollis, A. (2009, October 6). Calorie postings don't change habits, study finds. *New York Times* [New York edition], A26. Retrieved October 22, 2009, from: http://www.nytimes.com/2009/10/06/nyregion/06calories.html.

Hartwig, W. C. (2009). *Med school Rx: Getting in, getting through, getting on with doctoring*. New York: Kaplan.

Harvard Business School. (2002). *Hiring and keeping the best people*. Boston: Harvard Business School Press.

Harvard Business School. (2004). *Harvard business essentials: Managing projects large and small: The fundamental skills for delivering on budget and on time*. Boston: Harvard Business School Press.

Harvard study: Strong link between fluoridated water and bone cancer in boys. (2006, October 13). Alex Jones' Infowars.net. Retrieved August 4, 2009, from: http://www.infowars.net/articles/October2006/131006Fluoridated.htm.

Hawkes, N., & Seggar, J. F. A. (2000). *Celebrating women coaches: A biographical dictionary*. Westport, CT: Greenwood Press.

Hawley, W. D. (Ed.). (2007). *The keys to effective schools: Educational reform as continuous improvement*. Thousand Oaks, CA: Corwin Press.

Hayes, W. (2000). *Real-life case studies for school administrators*. Lanham, MD: Scarecrow Press.

Hayes, W. (2007). *All new real-life case studies for school administrators*. Lanham, MD: Rowman & Littlefield.

Hays, J. N. (2005). *Epidemics and pandemics: Their impacts on human history*. Santa Barbara, CA: ABC-CLIO.

Head, T. (Ed.). (2005). *Religion and education*. San Diego, CA: Greenhaven Press.

Healey, J. R. (2008, February 25). Plug-in cars could actually increase air pollution. *USA Today*. Retrieved October 26, 2009, from: http://www.usatoday.com/tech/products/environment/2008-02-25-plug-in-hybrids-pollution_N.htm.

Healthy solution: Taxing sodas. (2010, March 9). *New York Times* [New York edition], A22. Retrieved March 10, 2010, from: http://www.nytimes.com/2010/03/09/opinion/09tue3.html.

Heijke, J. A. M., & Muysken, J. (2000). *Education and training in a knowledge based economy*. New York: St. Martin's Press.

Heise, M. R. (2007). *The story of San Antonio Independent School Dist. v. Rodriguez: School finance, local control, and constitutional limits*. Ithaca, NY: Cornell Law School. Retrieved November 27, 2009, from: http://scholarship.law.cornell.edu/lsrp_papers/76/.

Henderson, C. H. (1902). *Education and the larger life*. Boston: Houghton-Mifflin.

Henderson, M. (2008, February 7). Genes not poor diet blamed for most cases of childhood obesity. *Times*. Retrieved October 22, 2009, from: http://www.timesonline.co.uk/tol/news/science/article3321748.ece.

Henig, J. R. (2008). *Spin cycle: How research is used in policy debates: The case of charter schools*. New York: Russell Sage Foundation.

Henig, J. R., & Rich, W. C. (Eds.). (2004). *Mayors in the middle: Politics, race, and mayoral control of urban schools*. Princeton, NJ: Princeton University Press.

Henry, N. (2007). *American carnival: Journalism under siege in an age of new media*. Berkeley, CA: University of California Press.

Herbst, D., & Howe, B. (2007). *Soccer: How to play the game: The official playing and coaching manual of the United States Soccer Federation*. New York: Universe Publishing.

Herbst, J. (1989). *And sadly teach: Teacher education and professionalization in American culture*. Madison: University of Wisconsin Press.

Hertsgaard, M., & Frazer, P. (1999, February 17). Fear of fluoride: Questions about the safety of this cavity-fighting chemical aren't just for right-wing conspiracists anymore. Salon.com. Retrieved August 4, 2009, from: www.salon.com/news/1999/02/17news.html.

Hess, F. M. (2004). *Common sense school reform*. New York: Palgrave-Macmillan.

Hess, F. M. (2008). Still at risk: What students don't know, even now. Washington, DC: Common Core.org. Retrieved November 4, 2009, from: http://www.commoncore.org/_docs/CCreport_stillatrisk.pdf.

Hess, F. M., & Finn, C. E. (Eds.). (2004). *Leaving no child behind?: Options for kids in failing schools*. New York: Palgrave-Macmillan.

Hess, F. M., & Finn, C. E. (Eds.). (2007). *No remedy left behind: Lessons from a half-decade of NCLB*. Washington, DC: AEI Press.

Hess, F. M., & Petrilli, M. J. (2006). *No Child Left Behind primer*. New York: Peter Lang.

Heumann, J., & Murray, R. L. (2006, Winter). *Dark Days*: A narrative of environmental adaptation. *Jump Cut: A Review of Contemporary Media*, 48. Retrieved

July 13, 2009, from: http://www.ejumpcut.org/archive/jc48.2006/DarkDays/index.html.

Hill, P. T. (Ed.). (2006). *Charter schools against the odds*. Stanford, CA: Education Next Books.

Hogan, J. M. (2006). *Woodrow Wilson's western tour: Rhetoric, public opinion, and the League of Nations*. College Station: Texas A&M University Press.

Hogg, M., & Merler, M. (2007). *Tales from the principal's office: Case studies in school administration*. Vancouver, British Columbia, Canada: Pacific Educational Press.

Hogshead-Makar, N., & Zimbalist, A. S. (2007). *Equal play: Title IX and social change*. Philadelphia, PA: Temple University Press.

Hoketsu, K. (2001). *Iron chef: The official book*. New York: Berkley.

Holtz, L. (2006). *Wins, losses, and lessons: An autobiography*. New York: William Morrow.

Hong, E., & Milgram, R. M. (2000). *Homework, motivation, and learning preference*. Westport, CT: Bergin & Garvey.

Hopkins, B. (2004). *Just schools: A whole school approach to restorative justice*. London, UK: J. Kingsley.

Horn, R. A. (2002). *Understanding educational reform: A reference handbook*. Santa Barbara, CA: ABC-CLIO.

Horowitz, D. (2007). *Indoctrination U: The left's war against academic freedom*. New York: Encounter.

Horowitz, D., & Laksin, J. (2009). *One-party classroom: How radical professors at America's top colleges indoctrinate students and undermine our democracy*. New York: Crown-Forum.

Houchin, K. E. (2009). *Fuel the spark: 5 guiding values for success in law school & beyond*. Garden City, NY: Madeeasy.

Housman, J. (2001). *The MBA jungle B-school survival guide*. Cambridge, MA: Perseus.

Howell, W. G. (2005). *Besieged: School boards and the future of education politics*. Washington, DC: Brookings Institution Press.

Hu, S., Scheuch, K. L., Schwartz, R. A., Gayles, J. G., & Li, S. (2008). *Reinventing undergraduate education: Engaging college students in research and creative activities*. San Francisco: Wiley/Jossey-Bass.

Huer, M. B., & Lloyd, L. (1990). AAC users' perspectives on augmentative and alternative communication. *Augmentative & Alternative Communication*, 6, 242–49.

Hundal, P., & Lukey, P. (2003). *"Now you know me think more": A journey with autism using facilitated communication techniques*. London, UK: Kingsley.

Hurtig, R., & Downey, D. (2008). *Augmentative and alternative communication in acute and critical care settings*. San Diego, CA: Plural.

Hyland, T., & Winch, C. (2007). *A guide to vocational education and training*. New York: Continuum.

Hyönä, J., Radach, R., & Deubel, H. (Eds.). (2003). *The mind's eye: Cognitive and applied aspects of eye movement research*. Amsterdam: North-Holland.

In the matter of the motion to admit Miss Lavinia Goodell to the Bar of this Court. (1875). 39 Wis. 232, 1875 WL 3615 (Wis.), 20 Am. Rep. 42.

Ingersoll, R. M. (2003). *Who controls teachers' work?: Power and accountability in America's schools*. Cambridge, MA: Harvard University Press.

Inness, S. A. (Ed.). (2003). *Disco divas: Women and popular culture in the 1970s*. Philadelphia: University of Pennsylvania Press.

Irons, E. J., & Harris, S. (2007). *The challenges of No Child Left Behind: Understanding the issues of excellence, accountability, and choice*. Lanham, MD: Rowman & Littlefield.

Irons, P. H. (2002). *Jim Crow's children: The broken promise of the* Brown *decision*. New York: Viking.

Jackson, B., & Jamieson, K. H. (2007). *UnSpun: Finding facts in a world of disinformation*. New York: Random House.

Jackson, S. (2009). Toward a queer social welfare studies: Unsettling Jane Addams. In M. Fischer, C. Nackenoff, & W. E. Chmielewski (Eds.), *Jane Addams and the practice of democracy* (pp. 143–64). Urbana: University of Illinois Press.

Jacobson, J. W., Foxx, R. M., & Mulick, J. A. (2005a). Facilitated communication: The ultimate fad treatment. In J. W. Jacobson, R. M. Foxx, & J. A. Mulick (Eds.), *Controversial therapies for developmental disabilities: Fad, fashion, and science in professional practice* (pp. 363–84). Mahwah, NJ: Erlbaum.

Jacobson, J. W., Foxx, R. M., & Mulick, J. A. (Eds.). (2005b). *Controversial therapies for developmental disabilities: Fad, fashion, and science in professional practice*. Mahwah, NJ: Erlbaum.

Jacquette, D. (1996). *Schopenhauer, philosophy, and the arts*. Cambridge, UK: Cambridge University Press.

Jalonick, M. C. (2010, March 23). US law to make calorie counts hard to ignore. Physorg.com. Retrieved March 24, 2010, from: http://www.physorg.com/news 188576523.html.

James, A. N. (2007). *Teaching the male brain: How boys think, feel, and learn in school*. Thousand Oaks, CA: Corwin.

James, A. N. (2009). *Teaching the female brain: How girls learn math and science*. Thousand Oaks, CA: Corwin.

Jamieson, K. H., & Waldman, P. (2003). *The press effect: Politicians, journalists, and the stories that shape the political world*. Oxford, UK: Oxford University Press.

Jarvis, M. (1999). *Sport psychology*. London, UK: Routledge.

JennyCraig.com. (2009). Weight loss testimonials. Retrieved October 15, 2009, from: http://www.jennycraig.com/.

Jensen, E. (2006). *Enriching the brain: How to maximize every learner's potential*. San Francisco: Jossey-Bass.

Jensen, E. (2007). *Introduction to brain-compatible learning*. Thousand Oaks, CA: Corwin Press.

Jerrard, R., & Jerrard, M. (1998). *The grad school handbook: An insider's guide to getting in and succeeding*. New York: Berkley.

Jeynes, W. (2007). *American educational history: School, society, and the common good*. Thousand Oaks, CA: Sage.

Jibrin, J. (1998). *The unofficial guide to dieting safely*. New York: Macmillan.

Jimerson, S. R., & Furlong, M. J. (Eds.). (2006). *The handbook of school violence and school safety: From research to practice*. Mahwah, NJ: Erlbaum.

Johansen, B. E. (2006). *Global warming in the 21st century*. Westport, CT: Praeger.

John F. Kennedy: The 35th president of the United States. (2009, September 2). John F. Kennedy Library and Museum. Retrieved September 2, 2009, from: http://

www.jfklibrary.org/Historical+Resources/Biographies+and+Profiles/Biographies/John+F.+Kennedy+The+35th+President+of+the+United+States+Page+4.htm.

Johnson, C. K. (2010, March 1). 1 in 4 parents buys unproven vaccine-autism link. HuffingtonPost.com. Retrieved March 1, 2010, from: http://www.huffingtonpost.com/2010/03/05/1-in-4-parents-buys-unpro_n_487912.html.

Johnson, D. M. (2009, November 27). Secondary PTSD warrants discussion after Fort Hood Massacre. *Southern Maryland Online*. Retrieved August 13, 2010, from: http://somd.com/news/headlines/2009/10875.shtml.

Johnson, H. L., & Salz, A. (2008). *What is authentic educational reform? Pushing against the compassionate conservative agenda*. New York: Erlbaum.

Johnson, K. (2006, June 30). When aerosol outlaws became insiders: Graffiti art at the Brooklyn Museum. *New York Times*. Retrieved July 30, 2009, from: http://www.nytimes.com/2006/06/30/arts/design/30graf.html.

Johnson, K. (2009, November 25). Climate action urged amid controversy. *Wall Street Journal* [national edition], A4. Retrieved November 25, 2009, from: http://online.wsj.com/article/SB125911350443163363.html.

Johnson, R. A., & Ruhl, J. M. (2007). *Living your unlived life: Coping with unrealized dreams and fulfilling your purpose in the second half of life*. New York: Jeremy Tarcher/Penguin.

Johnson, S. (1998). *Who moved my cheese?: An a-mazing way to deal with change in your work and in your life*. New York: Putnam's Sons.

Johnson, W. B., & Huwe, J. M. (2003). *Getting mentored in graduate school*. Washington, DC: American Psychological Association.

Jost, T. S. (2007). *Health care at risk: A critique of the consumer-driven movement*. Durham, NC: Duke University Press.

Kadison, R., & DiGeronimo, T. F. (2004). *College of the overwhelmed: The campus mental health crisis and what to do about it*. San Francisco: Jossey-Bass.

Kallen, S. A. (2004). *Media bias*. San Diego, CA: Greenhaven Press.

Kaminski, H. J., & Leigh, R. J. (Eds.). (2002). *Neurobiology of eye movements: From molecules to behavior*. New York: New York Academy of Sciences.

Kaplan Thaler, L., & Koval, R. (2006). *The power of nice: How to conquer the business world with kindness*. New York: Currency/Doubleday.

Kassirer, J. P. (2005). *On the take: How America's complicity with big business can endanger your health*. New York: Oxford University Press.

Keel, P. K. (2006). *Eating disorders*. New York: Chelsea House.

Kelly, K. (2007). *The secret of the secret: Unlocking the mysteries of the runaway bestseller*. New York: Thomas Dunne/St. Martin's Press.

Kerchner, C. T., Koppich, J., & Weeres, J. G. (1998). *Taking charge of quality: How teachers and unions can revitalize schools: An introduction and companion to* United mind workers. San Francisco: Jossey-Bass.

Kershaw, S. (2009, December 23). Using menu psychology to entice diners. *New York Times* [New York edition], D1. Retrieved December 23, 2009, from: http://www.nytimes.com/2009/12/23/dining/23menus.html.

Kessel, A. S. (2006). *Air, the environment and public health*. Cambridge, UK: Cambridge University Press.

Kessler, A. (2009, September 23). Bank pay controls aren't the answer. *Wall Street Journal* [national edition], A25.

KET. (2007). *Graffiti planet: The best graffiti from around the world*. London, UK: Michael O'Mara.

Khan, S. (2006). *P.U.S.H. for success*. London, UK: Vermilion.

Kincheloe, J. L. (1999). *How do we tell the workers? The socioeconomic foundations of work and vocational education*. Boulder, CO: Westview Press.

King, N., & Martinez, B. (2010, March 15). Obama outlines sweeping education revamp. *Wall Street Journal*. Retrieved March 15, 2010, from: http://online.wsj.com/article/SB10001424052748703780204575119214011184980.html.

Kirk, N. (2002). *Beauty therapy: Study skills*. London: Hodder & Stoughton.

Kirkley, W. (2009, October 6). Can anyone get hypnotized? Esortment.com. Retrieved October 6, 2009, from: http://www.essortment.com/articles/hypnotize-anyone_4545.htm.

Kirstie Alley: The official site. (2010). Kirstiealley.com. Retrieved March 16, 2010, from: http://www.kirstiealley.com/.

Kirstie checks into fat farm. (2009, October 5). *National Enquirer*. Retrieved October 19, 2009, from: http://www.nationalenquirer.com/kirstie_alley_huge_checks_into_fat_farm_death_fear/celebrity/67436.

Klein, A., & McKinley, J. (2004). *Homework hassles*. New York: Scholastic.

Kliebard, H. M. (1999). *Schooled to work: Vocationalism and the American curriculum, 1876–1946*. New York: Teachers College Press.

Kline, M. (1973). *Why Johnny can't add: The failure of the new math*. New York: St. Martin's Press.

Kluck, T. (2009). *Headlocks and dropkicks: A butt-kicking ride through the world of professional wrestling*. Santa Barbara, CA: Praeger.

Kluger, J. (2004). *Splendid solution: Jonas Salk and the conquest of polio*. New York: Putnam's Sons.

Knight, J. (2009). *Coaching: Approaches and perspectives*. Thousand Oaks, CA: Corwin Press.

Knight, L. W. (2005). *Citizen: Jane Addams and the struggle for democracy*. Chicago: University of Chicago Press.

Koch, H. (1970). *The panic broadcast: Portrait of an event*. Boston: Little, Brown.

Kohn, A. (2006). *The homework myth: Why our kids get too much of a bad thing*. Cambridge, MA: Da Capo.

Kohn, A., & Shannon, P. (2002). *Education, inc.: Turning learning into a business*. Portsmouth, NH: Heinemann.

Koichi, D., Masaharu, K., Tomoko, T., Shoji, W., & Keizo, S. (2000). Research findings on stress and fatigue among taxi drivers. *Research and Practice in Forensic Medicine*, 43, 377–81.

Kolata, G. B. (1999). *Flu: The story of the great influenza pandemic of 1918 and the search for the virus that caused it*. New York: Farrar, Straus & Giroux.

Kolata, G. B. (2007). *Rethinking thin: The new science of weight loss—And the myths and realities of dieting*. New York: Farrar, Straus, & Giroux.

Konstant, T. (2000). *Speed reading*. Lincolnwood, IL: NTC/Contemporary Publishing.

Konstant, T. (2002). *Speed reading in a week*. London, UK: Hodder & Stoughton.

Kontos, L., & Brotherton, D. (2008). *Encyclopedia of gangs*. Westport, CT: Greenwood Press.

Koocher, G. P., & Keith-Spiegel, P. (2008). *Ethics in psychology and the mental health professions: Standards and cases*. Oxford, UK: Oxford University Press.

Kposowa, A. J., & D'Auria, S. (2009, June 18). Association of temporal factors and suicides in the United States, 2000–2004. *Social Psychiatry and Psychiatric Epidemiology*. Retrieved July 8, 2009, from: http://www.springerlink.com/content/d236q44ut3582v91/.

Kralovec, E., & Buell, J. (2000). *The end of homework: How homework disrupts families, overburdens children, and limits learning*. Boston: Beacon Press.

Krewson, J. (2009, September 30). NHTSA: Distracted driving caused 6,000 deaths in 2008. Jalopnik.com. Retrieved October 8, 2009, from: http://jalopnik.com/5371255/nhtsa-distracted-driving-caused-6000-deaths-in-2008.

Krüger, A., & Murray, W. J. (2003). *The Nazi Olympics: Sport, politics, and appeasement in the 1930s*. Urbana: University of Illinois Press.

Krugman, P. R. (2009). *The return of depression economics and the crisis of 2008*. New York: Norton.

Krzyzewski, M., & Spatola, J. K. (2009). *The gold standard: Building a world-class team*. New York: Business Plus.

Kumar, S. (2006). *Sticker nation: The big book of subversive stickers, Vol. 1*. New York: Disinformation.

Kumashiro, K. K. (2008). *The seduction of common sense: How the right has framed the debate on America's schools*. New York: Teachers College Press.

Kuypers, J. A. (2006). *Bush's war: Media bias and justifications for war in a terrorist age*. Lanham, MD: Rowman & Littlefield.

Lancet's vaccine retraction. (2010, February 3). *Wall Street Journal* [national edition], A16. Retrieved February 3, 2010, from: http://online.wsj.com/article/SB10001424052748704022804575041544115791952.html.

Landry, T., & Lewis, G. (1990). *Tom Landry: An autobiography*. Grand Rapids, MI: Zondervan.

Lankford, R. D. (2007). *Can diets be harmful?* Detroit: Greenhaven Press.

Lapchick, R. E. (1996). *Sport in society: Equal opportunity or business as usual?* Thousand Oaks, CA: Sage.

Larner, J. (2006). *Forgive us our spins: Michael Moore and the future of the left*. Hoboken, NJ: Wiley.

Lask, B., & Bryant-Waugh, R. (Ed.). (2007). *Eating disorders in childhood and adolescence*. London: Routledge.

Latto, J., & Latto, R. (2009). *Study skills for psychology students*. Maidenhead, UK: Open University Press.

Leary, T. (1990). *Flashbacks: A personal and cultural history of an era—An autobiography*. Los Angeles: Tarcher.

Lee, C. (2004). *Preventing bullying in schools: A guide for teachers and other professionals*. London, UK: Paul Chapman.

Lee, R. A. (2007). *From snake oil to medicine: Pioneering public health*. Westport, CT: Praeger.

Lenhart, S. A. (2004). *Clinical aspects of sexual harassment and gender discrimination: Psychological consequences and treatment interventions*. New York: Brunner-Routledge.

Lenskyj, H. (2003). *Out on the field: Gender, sport, and sexualities*. Toronto, Ontario, Canada: Women's Press.

Leung, R. (2004, August 25). The "Texas Miracle." CBSnews.com. Retrieved October 12, 2009, from: http://www.cbsnews.com/stories/2004/01/06/60II/main591676.shtml.

Levin, H. M. (Ed.). (2001). *Privatizing education: Can the marketplace deliver choice, efficiency, equity, and social cohesion?* Boulder, CO: Westview Press.

Levine, A., & Cureton, J. S. (1998). *When hope and fear collide: A portrait of today's college student*. San Francisco: Jossey-Bass.

Levitt, H., Coles, R., Harris, A., & Hoshino, M. (1987). *In the street: Chalk drawings and messages, New York City, 1938–1948*. Durham, NC: Duke University Press.

Levitt, S. (2009, October 9). Bend these weight-loss rules. MSN.com. Retrieved October 19, 2009, from: http://health.msn.com/weight-loss/articlepage.aspx?cp-documentid=100246375>1=31036.

Levitt, S. D., & Dubner, S. J. (2009). *SuperFreakonomics: Global cooling, patriotic prostitutes, and why suicide bombers should buy life insurance*. New York: William Morrow.

Lewis, M. (2009). *Panic: The story of modern financial insanity*. New York: Norton.

Libal, A. (2006). *Fats, sugars, and empty calories: The fast food habit*. Philadelphia: Mason Crest.

Lieberman, M. (1997). *The teacher unions: How the NEA and AFT sabotage reform and hold students, parents, teachers, and taxpayers hostage to bureaucracy*. New York: Free Press.

Lifto, D. E., & Senden, J. B. (2004). *School finance elections: A comprehensive planning model for success*. Lanham, MD: Scarecrow Education.

Lillien, L. (2009). *Hungry girl: 200 under 200: 200 recipes under 200 calories*. New York: St. Martin's Griffin.

Linden, M. J., & Whimbey, A. (1990). *Why Johnny can't write: How to improve writing skills*. Hillsdale, NJ: Erlbaum.

Lipczynski, J. (2008). *Business*. Chicago: Chicago Review Press.

Liptak, A. (2009, August 29). Supreme Court to revisit "Hillary" documentary. *New York Times*. Retrieved August 30, 2009, from: http://www.nytimes.com/2009/08/30/us/30scotus.html.

Liptak, A. (2010, January 21). Justices, 5–4, reject corporate spending limit. *New York Times* [New York edition], A1. Retrieved January 22, 2010, from: http://www.nytimes.com/2010/01/22/us/politics/22scotus.html.

Lomborg, B. (2007). *Cool it: The skeptical environmentalist's guide to global warming*. New York: Knopf.

López, N. (2003). *Hopeful girls, troubled boys: Race and gender disparity in urban education*. New York: Routledge.

Loveless, T. (Ed.). (2000). *Conflicting missions?: Teachers unions and educational reform*. Washington, DC: Brookings Institution Press.

Loveless, T. (2006). The peculiar politics of No Child Left Behind. *Brown Center on Education Policy: Brookings Institution*. Retrieved August 13, 2010, from: http://www.brookings.edu/views/papers/loveless/20060801.pdf.

Loyd, R. J., & Brolin, D. E. (1997). *Life centered career education: Modified curriculum for individuals with moderate disabilities*. Reston, VA: Council for Exceptional Children.

Lueck, T. J., & Severson, K. (2006, December 6). New York bans most trans fats in restaurants. *New York Times*. Retrieved October 22, 2009, from: http://www.nytimes.com/2006/12/06/nyregion/06fat.html?scp=5&sq=new%20york%20restaurants%20and%20trans%20fats&st=cse.

Luecke, R. (2003). *Managing creativity and innovation*. Boston: Harvard Business School Press.

Lyman, R. (1999, May 23). Bush legacy rides on tax cut and school funds. *New York Times*. Retrieved October 12, 2009, from: http://partners.nytimes.com/library/politics/camp/052399wh-gop-bush.html.

Macdonald, N. (2001). *The graffiti subculture: Youth, masculinity, and identity in London and New York*. New York: Palgrave-Macmillan.

Machin, M. A., & De Souza, J. M. D. (2004). Predicting health outcomes and safety behaviour [sic] in taxi drivers. *Transportation Research*, 7F (4 & 5), 257–70.

Magisos, J. H. (Ed.). (1973). *Career education*. Washington, DC: American Vocational Association.

Manco, T. (2002). *Stencil graffiti*. New York: Thames & Hudson.

Manco, T., & Neelon, C. (2005). *Graffiti Brasil* [sic]. London, UK: Thames & Hudson.

Mani, B. G. (2007). *Women, power, and political change*. Lanham, MD: Lexington.

Manna, L. (2005). *Digital food photography*. Clifton Park, NY: Thomson/Delmar.

Maranci, C. (2005). *A survival guide for art history students*. Upper Saddle River, NJ: Pearson/Prentice Hall.

Marks Beale, A., & Mullan, P. (2008). *The complete idiot's guide to speed reading*. New York: Penguin.

Marland, S. P., McClure, L., & Buan, C. (1973). *Essays on career education*. Portland, OR: Northwest Regional Educational Laboratory/United States Government Printing Office.

Marshall, R. (2007, April 12). The dark legacy of Carlos Castaneda. Salon.com. Retrieved October 30, 2009, from: http://www.salon.com/books/feature/2007/04/12/castaneda/.

Martin, H. (2001, October 23). Behind the wheel: The Botts dot's future may hit a bump in the road. *Los Angeles Times* [Los Angeles edition], B2. Retrieved October 6, 2009, from: http://pqasb.pqarchiver.com/latimes/access/85590220.html?dids=85590220:85590220&FMT=ABS&FMTS=ABS:FT&type=current&date=Oct+23%2C+2001&author=HUGO+MARTIN&pub=Los+Angeles+Times&edition=&startpage=B.2&desc=Behind+the+Wheel%3B+The+Botts+Dot%27s+Future+May+Hit+a+Bump+in+the+Road%3B+The+safety+device%2C+a+simple+ceramic+mound+that+helps+divide+lanes%2C+is+crumbling+under+the+weight+of+increasingly+heavy+truck+traffic.

Martinez, H. (2006). *Graffiti NYC*. New York: Prestel.

Martínez-Alemán, A. M., & Wartman, K. L. (2008). *Online social networking on campus: Understanding what matters in student culture*. New York: Routledge.

Marzano, R. J., Waters, T., & McNulty, B. A. (2005). *School leadership that works: From research to results*. Alexandria, VA: Association for Supervision and Curriculum Development.

Mason, P. (2009). *Meltdown: The end of the age of greed*. London: Verso.

Mason-Whitehead, E., & Mason, T. (2003). *Study skills for nurses*. London: Sage.

Masterman, G. (2007). *Sponsorship: For a return on investment*. Oxford, UK: Butterworth-Heinemann.

Mattila, A. S., Apostolopoulos, Y., Sonmez, S., Yu, L., & Sasidharan, V. (2001). The impact of gender and religion on college students' spring break behavior. *Journal of Travel Research*, 40, 193–200.

Mattson, K. (2006). *Upton Sinclair and the other American century*. Hoboken, NJ: Wiley.

Mayo Clinic. (2009, October 22). Dietary fats: Know which types to choose. Mayoclinic.com. Retrieved October 22, 2009, from: http://www.mayoclinic.com/health/fat/NU00262.

Mayo, A. J., & Nohria, N. (2005). *In their time: The greatest business leaders of the twentieth century*. Boston: Harvard Business School Press.

Mazur, J. (2007). *Zeno's paradox: Unraveling the ancient mystery behind the science of space and time*. New York: Penguin.

McAllister, R. (2007, May 26). Physicians identify obesity as nation's greatest health risk. *Epocrates.com*. Retrieved August 13, 2010, from: http://www.epocrates.com/company/news/10301.html.

McAndrew, W. (1878). Education review: Matters of moment. *School and Society*, 28, 551–58.

McBride, J. (2006). *Whatever happened to Orson Welles?: A portrait of an independent career*. Lexington: University Press of Kentucky.

McCaffrey, P. (2008). *U.S. national debate topic 2008–2009: Alternative energy*. New York: Wilson.

McCarthy, J. (2007). *Louder than words: A mother's journey in healing autism*. New York: Dutton.

McCarthy, J. (2008). *Mother warriors: A nation of parents healing autism against all odds*. New York: Dutton.

McEnteer, J. (2006). *Shooting the truth: The rise of American political documentaries*. Westport, CT: Praeger.

McEvilley, T. (2005). *The triumph of anti-art: Conceptual and performance art in the formation of post-modernism*. Kingston, NY: McPherson.

McGrath, D. (2005). *The collaborative advantage: Lessons from K–16 educational reform*. Lanham, MD: Rowman & Littlefield Education.

McGrath, R. V. (2002). *Managing young adult services: A self-help manual*. New York: Neal-Schuman.

McGraw, P. C. (1999). *Life strategies: Doing what works, doing what matters*. New York: Hyperion.

McGraw, P. C. (2003). *The ultimate weight solution: The 7 keys to weight loss freedom*. New York: Free Press.

McGreal, C. (2009, July 22). Christian right aims to change history lessons in Texas schools. Guardian.com. Retrieved November 4, 2009, from: http://www.guardian.co.uk/world/2009/jul/22/christianity-religion-texas-history-education.

McGuinn, P. J. (2006). *No Child Left Behind and the transformation of federal education policy, 1965–2005*. Lawrence, KS: University Press of Kansas.

McKay, B. (2009, October 5). Public faces long wait to get new flu vaccine. *Wall Street Journal* [national edition], A1, A2. Retrieved October 5, 2009, from: http://online.wsj.com/article/SB125469946745562945.html.

McKay, B. (2010, March 2). The flu season that fizzled. *Wall Street Journal* [national edition], D1, D2. Retrieved March 2, 2010, from: http://online.wsj.com/article/SB10001424052748703429304575095743102260012.html.

McKinley, J. (2010, April 26). Citing obesity of children, county bans fast-food toys. *New York Times* [New York edition], B6. Retrieved May 2, 2010, from: http://www.nytimes.com/2010/04/28/business/28mcdonalds.html.

McKinley, J. C. (2010a, March 10). Texas conservatives seek deeper stamp on texts. *New York Times* [New York edition], A18. Retrieved March 12, 2010, from: http://www.nytimes.com/2010/03/11/us/politics/11texas.html.

McKinley, J. C. (2010b, March 12). Texas conservatives win curriculum change. *New York Times* [New York edition], A10. Retrieved March 13, 2010, from: http://www.nytimes.com/2010/03/13/education/13texas.html.

McKinnon, J. D., & Crittenden, M. R. (2010a, January 14). Panel rips Wall Street titans. *Wall Street Journal* [national edition], A1, A4. Retrieved January 14, 2010, from: http://online.wsj.com/article/SB100014240527487043620045750007527 56113586.html.

McKinnon, J. D., & Crittenden, M. R. (2010b, January 15). Financial inquiry widens to include past regulators. *Wall Street Journal* [national edition], A4. Retrieved January 15, 2010, from: http://online.wsj.com/article/SB10001424052748704281204575002783839802528.html?mod=europe_home.

McKinnon, J. D., & Smith, R. (2010, April 8). Greenspan grilled over role in financial crisis. *Wall Street Journal*. Retrieved April 12, 2010, from: http://online.wsj.com/article/SB10001424052702303720604575169650914317956.html.

McKnight-Trontz, J. (2000). *Yes you can: Timeless advice from self-help experts*. San Francisco: Chronicle.

McNeal, B., & Oxholm, T. (2009). *A school district's journey to excellence: Lessons from business and education*. Thousand Oaks, CA: Corwin Press.

McWhorter, K. T. (2007). *College reading & study skills*. New York: Pearson/Longman.

Meagher, S. (2009, November 25). The sky is not falling: Emails expose the global warming conspiracy. Inquirer.com. Retrieved November 25, 2009, from: http://www.theinquirer.net/inquirer/opinion/1563419/emails-expose-global-warming-conspiracy/.

Media influence on consumer choice: Diet and weight loss. (2009, June 23). Statistica.com. Retrieved October 16, 2009, from: http://de.statista.com/statistik/studiendetail/studie/2406359/q/di%C3%A4t/p/0/.

Meinwald, C. C. (1991). *Plato's Parmenides*. New York: Oxford University Press.

Memorization software reviewed. (2009, December 11). University of Murcia. Retrieved December 11, 2009, from: http://www.quingle.com/softarea/flash.htm.

Mentoring, coaching, and collaboration. (2008). Thousand Oaks, CA: Corwin Press.

Mercola, J., & Killeen, P. (2006). *The great bird flu hoax: The truth they don't want you to know about the "next big pandemic."* New York: Nelson.

Merriam, S. B., Courtenay, B. C., & Cervero, R. M. (2006). *Global issues and adult education: Perspectives from Latin America, Southern Africa, and the United States.* San Francisco: Jossey-Bass.

Merriner, J. L. (2004). *Grafters and goo goos: Corruption and reform in Chicago, 1833–2003.* Carbondale, IL: Southern Illinois University Press.

Merry, K. (2009, April 9). Do former athletes make the best coaches? Katharine Merry's Blog. BBC.com. Retrieved August 23, 2009, from: http://www.bbc.co.uk/blogs/katharinemerry/2009/04/do_those_who_have_been.html.

Meyer, E. J. (2009). *Gender, bullying, and harassment: Strategies to end sexism and homophobia in schools.* New York: Teachers College Press.

Michaels, P. J. (1992). *Sound and fury: The science and politics of global warming.* Washington, DC: Cato Institute.

Middleton, D. (2009, September 16). The top MBA programs if you're in a hurry. *Wall Street Journal*, A11, A13.

Middleton, J., Ziderman, A., & Van Adams, A. (1993). *Skills for productivity: Vocational education and training in developing countries.* Washington, DC: World Bank/Oxford University Press.

Mieczkowski, Y. (2005). *Gerald Ford and the challenges of the 1970s.* Lexington: University Press of Kentucky.

Miller, D. L. (1996). *City of the century: The epic of Chicago and the making of America.* New York: Simon & Schuster.

Miller, E. C., Schulz, M. R., Bibeau, D. L., Galka, A. M., Spann, L. I., Martin, L., Aronson, R., & Chase, C. M. (2008). Factors associated with misperception of weight in the stroke belt. *Journal of General Internal Medicine*, 23, 323–28.

Miller, P., & Buchanan, P. (2009). *Campus voices: A student-to-student guide to college life.* Ventura, CA: Regal.

Miller, R. H., & Bissell, D. M. (2006). *Med school confidential: A complete guide to the medical school experience, by students, for students.* New York: St. Martin's Griffin/Thomas Dunne.

Miller, T. E. (2005). *Promoting reasonable expectations: Aligning student and institutional views of the college experience.* San Francisco: Jossey-Bass.

Miller-Bernal, L. (2000). *Separate by degree: Women students' experiences in single-sex and coeducational colleges.* New York: Peter Lang.

Mintzberg, H. (2009, November 30). No more executive bonuses! *Wall Street Journal* [national edition], R3, R6. Retrieved November 30, 2009, from: http://online.wsj.com/article/SB100014240527487032940045745112234945365 70.html.

Modern methods in navigation and nautical astronomy. (1876, January–April). *London Quarterly Review* [New York edition], 141, 71–89.

Moeller, S. D. (1999). *Compassion fatigue: How the media sell disease, famine, war, and death.* New York: Routledge.

Moeller, S. D. (2009). *Packaging terrorism: Co-opting the news for politics and profit.* Chichester, UK: Wiley-Blackwell.

Moidel, S. (1998). *Speed reading for business.* Hauppauge, NY: Barron's.

Molina, N. (2006). *Fit to be citizens?: Public health and race in Los Angeles, 1879–1939*. Berkeley, CA: University of California Press.

Monroe, K. R., Miller, R. B., & Tobis, J. S. (Eds.). (2008). *Fundamentals of the stem cell debate: The scientific, religious, ethical, and political issues*. Berkeley, CA: University of California Press.

Moody, S. (2007). *Dyslexia: Surviving and succeeding at college*. London: Routledge.

Moore, D. A. (2005). *Conflicts of interest: Challenges and solutions in business, law, medicine, and public policy*. Cambridge, UK: Cambridge University Press.

Moore, M., Baker, J. A., Gore, A., Daschle, T., Bush, G. W., Rice, C., Desjarlais, M., & Gibbs, J. (2004). *Fahrenheit 9/11* [Film]. Culver City, CA: Columbia/TriStar.

Moore, M., Glynn, K. R., Czarnecki, J., Bishop, C., Donovan, M., Heston, C., Danitz, B., McDonough, M., Engfehr, K., & Gibbs, J. (2003). *Bowling for Columbine* [Film]. Los Angeles, CA: MGM.

Moore, M., Moore, A., Birleson, R., Hardesty, J., & Gibbs, J., Paramount Vantage, Overture Films, Weinstein Company, Dog Eat Dog Films, Anchor Bay Entertainment. (2010). *Capitalism: A love story* [Film]. Beverly Hills, CA: Anchor Bay Entertainment.

Moore, R. (2006). *Knowledge, power and educational reform: Applying the sociology of Basil Bernstein*. New York: Routledge.

Moore, R. M. (2006). *African Americans and whites: Changing relationships on college campuses*. Lanham, MD: University Press of America.

Morone, J. A., Litman, T. J., & Robins, L. S. (2008). *Health politics and policy*. Albany, NY: Delmar.

Morris, C. R. (2008). *The trillion dollar meltdown: Easy money, high rollers, and the great credit crash*. New York: PublicAffairs.

Morris, E., Ahlberg, J. B., Feinman, J., Denning, S., & King, C. (2008). *Standard operating procedure* [Film]. Culver City, CA: Sony.

Morris, E., Williams, M., Ahlberg, J. B., McNamara, R. S., & Glass, P. (2004). *The fog of war: Eleven lessons from the life of Robert S. McNamara* [Film]. Culver City, CA: Columbia/TriStar.

Morse, A., & Schifter, D. (2009). *Cultivating a math coaching practice: A guide for K–8 math educators*. Thousand Oaks, CA: Corwin.

Mortensen, K. W. (2008). *Persuasion IQ: The 10 skills you need to get exactly what you want*. New York: AMACOM/American Management Association.

Mosley, G. (2006). *New thought, ancient wisdom: The history and future of the new thought movement*. Philadelphia: Templeton.

Moss, F. A., & Thorndike, E. L. (1949). *Comparative psychology*. New York: Prentice Hall.

Moss, M. (2010, May 29). The hard sell on salt. *New York Times* [New York edition], A1. Retrieved May 30, 2010, from: http://www.nytimes.com/2010/05/30/health/30salt.html.

Mountjoy, S., & McNeese, T. (2008). *The women's rights movement: Moving toward equality*. New York: Chelsea House.

Mowry, W. A. (1908). *Recollections of a New England educator, 1838–1908; Reminiscences biographical, pedagogical, historical*. New York: Silver-Burdett.

Mullan, F. (1989). *Plagues and politics: The story of the United States Public Health Service*. New York: Basic Books.

Muolo, P., & Padilla, M. (2008). *Chain of blame: How Wall Street caused the mortgage and credit crisis*. Hoboken, NJ: Wiley.

Murkoff, H. E., & Mazel, S. (2008). *What to expect when you're expecting* (4th ed.). New York: Workman.

Murphy, J., & Meyers, C. V. (2008). *Turning around failing schools: Leadership lessons from the organizational sciences*. Thousand Oaks, CA: Corwin Press.

Murray, C. (2010, May 4). Why charter schools fail the test. *New York Times* [New York edition], A31. Retrieved May 4, 2010, from: http://www.nytimes.com/2010/05/05/opinion/05murray.html.

Murray, C. A. (2008). *Real education: Four simple truths for bringing America's schools back to reality*. New York: Crown Forum.

Murray, J. T., & Murray, K. L. (2009). *Miami graffiti*. Munich: Prestel.

Naar, J. (2007). *The birth of graffiti*. Munich: Prestel.

Nacos, B. L. (2002). *Mass-mediated terrorism: The central role of the media in terrorism and counterterrorism*. Lanham, MD: Rowman & Littlefield.

Nadeau, K. G. (2006). *Survival guide for college students with ADHD or LD*. Washington, DC: Magination Press.

Nakano, Y., Nakamura, S., Hirata, M., Harada, K., Ando, K., Tabuchi, T., Matunaga, I., & Oda, H. (1998). Immune function and lifestyle of taxi drivers in Japan. *Industrial Health*, 36, 32–39. Retrieved July 6, 2009, from: http://www.journalarchive.jst.go.jp/english/jnlabstract_en.php?cdjournal=indhealth1963&cdvol=36&noissue=1&startpage=32.

Nash, L. L. (2006). *Inescapable ecologies: A history of environment, disease, and knowledge*. Berkeley, CA: University of California Press.

Natavi Guides Company. (2005). *Navigating your freshman year: How to make the leap to college life and land on your feet*. New York: Prentice Hall.

Nathan, J. (1996). *Charter schools: Creating hope and opportunity for American education*. San Francisco: Jossey-Bass.

Nathan, R. (2005). *My freshman year: What a professor learned by becoming a student*. Ithaca, NY: Cornell University Press.

National Center for Education Statistics. (Eds.). (2002). *Vocational education offerings in rural high schools*. Washington, DC: United States Department of Education.

National Highway Traffic Safety Administration. (2009, September). An examination of driver distraction as recorded in NHTSA databases. Retrieved October 8, 2009, from: http://www-nrd.nhtsa.dot.gov/Pubs/811216.PDF.

National Soccer Coaches Association of America. (2004). *The soccer coaching bible*. Champaign, IL: Human Kinetics.

Neiburger, E. (2007). *Gamers . . . In the library?!: The why, what, and how of videogame tournaments for all ages*. Chicago: American Library Association.

Neuman, W. (2010, April 20). F.D.A. is urged to set limits for levels of salt in food. *New York Times* [New York edition], A16. Retrieved April 22, 2010, from: http://www.nytimes.com/2010/04/21/us/21salt.html.

Neustadt, R. E., & Fineberg, H. V. (1983). *The epidemic that never was: Policy-making and the swine flu scare* (rev. ed.). New York: Vintage.

New York City Department of Health and Mental Hygiene. (2009, December 17). Cutting salt, improving health. NYC.gov. Retrieved December 17, 2009, from: http://www.nyc.gov/html/doh/html/cardio/cardio-salt-initiative.shtml.

New York City starts push to reduce dietary salt. (2009, January 30). Redorbit.com. Retrieved December 17, 2009, from: http://www.redorbit.com/news/health/1631261/new_york_city_starts_push_to_reduce_dietary_salt/index.html.

New York preps for battle against salt. (2009, April 22). MSNBC.com. Retrieved December 17, 2009, from: http://www.msnbc.msn.com/id/30352252.

Nicholls, C. (2000). Warlpiri graffiti. In J. Docker & G. Fischer (Eds.), *Race, colour, and identity in Australia and New Zealand* (pp. 79–94). Sydney: University of New South Wales Press.

Nicholson, L. J. (1997). *The second wave: A reader in feminist theory*. New York: Routledge.

Noah, T. (2000, February 18). The 1,000-word dash: College-educated people who fret they read too slow should relax. Slate.com. Retrieved September 2, 2009, from: http://www.slate.com/id/74766/.

Noddings, N. (2007). *When school reform goes wrong*. New York: Teachers College Press.

Norris, P., Kern, M., & Just, M. R. (2003). *Framing terrorism: The news media, the government, and the public*. New York: Routledge.

Nuwer, H. (1999). *Wrongs of passage: Fraternities, sororities, hazing, and binge drinking*. Bloomington, IN: Indiana University Press.

NYC mayor declares war on salt. (2009, January 28). Wbztv.com. Retrieved August 13, 2009, from: http://wbztv.com/health/bloomberg.war.on.2.920740.html.

Obama, B. (2009, September 8). Prepared remarks of President Barack Obama: Back to school event. Whitehouse.gov. Retrieved September 8, 2009, from: http://www.whitehouse.gov/MediaResources/PreparedSchoolRemarks/.

Obama declares swine flu national emergency. (2009, October 24). MSNBC.com. Retrieved October 25, 2009, from: http://www.msnbc.msn.com/id/33459423/ns/health-cold_and_flu.

Offit, P. A. (2008). *Autism's false prophets: Bad science, risky medicine, and the search for a cure*. New York: Columbia University Press.

Ogren, C. A. (2005). *The American state normal school: "An instrument of great good."* New York: Palgrave-Macmillan.

Olivier, C., & Bowler, R. F. (1996). *Learning to learn*. New York: Simon & Schuster.

Olson, E. (2010a, March 3). Education on the company's dime. *New York Times* [New York edition], F9. Retrieved April 1, 2010, from: http://www.nytimes.com/2010/03/04/business/retirementspecial/04LEARN.html.

Olson, E. (2010b, March 3). What states and cities are doing to help small businesses. *New York Times*. Retrieved April 1, 2010, from: http://www.nytimes.com/2010/03/04/business/smallbusiness/04help.html.

O'Neil, R. M. (2008). *Academic freedom in the wired world: Political extremism, corporate power, and the university*. Cambridge, MA: Harvard University Press.

O'Reilly, J., & Cahn, S. K. (Eds.). (2007). *Women and sports in the United States: A documentary reader*. Boston: Northeastern University Press.

Orfield, G., & Eaton, S. E. (1996). *Dismantling desegregation: The quiet reversal of* Brown v. Board of Education. New York: New Press.

Orr, T. (2007). *When the mirror lies: Anorexia, bulimia, and other eating disorders*. Danbury, CT: Franklin-Watts.

Orton, J. L., & Money, J. (1966). *The Orton-Gillingham approach*. Baltimore, MD: Orton Dyslexia Society.

Orton, S. T. (1937). *Reading, writing and speech problems in children: A presentation of certain types of disorders in the development of the language faculty*. New York: Norton.

Orton, S. T. (1966). *Word-blindness in school children and other papers on strephosymbolia (specific language disability-dyslexia) 1925–1946*. Pomfret, CT: Orton Society.

Orton, S. T. (1989). *Reading, writing, and speech problems in children and selected papers* (rev. ed.). Austin, TX: PRO-ED. (Original work published in 1937.)

Osborn, J. E., Crosby, A. W., Millar, J. D., & Viseltear, A. J. (1977). *Influenza in America, 1918–1976: History, science, and politics*. New York: Prodist.

Osgood, R. L. (2008). *The history of special education: A struggle for equality in American public schools*. Westport, CT: Praeger.

Oshinsky, D. M. (2005). *Polio: An American story*. Oxford, UK: Oxford University Press.

Owings, W. A., & Kaplan, L. S. (2006). *American public school finance*. Belmont, CA: Thomson/Wadsworth.

Paige, R. (2006). *The war against hope: How teachers' unions hurt children, hinder teachers, and endanger public education*. Nashville, TN: Thomas Nelson.

Painter, F. V. N. (1886). *A history of education*. New York: Appleton.

Painter, L. (2003). *Homework*. Oxford, UK: Oxford University Press.

Palestini, R. H., & Palestini, K. F. (2005). *Law and American education: A case brief approach*. Lanham, MD: Rowman & Littlefield.

Paletta, D., & Hilsenrath, J. (2009, September 18). Bankers face sweeping curbs on pay. *Wall Street Journal* [national edition], A1. Retrieved September 21, 2009, from: http://online.wsj.com/article/SB125324292666522101.html.

Palomaki, M. J. (1981). *Teaching handicapped students vocational education*. Washington, DC: National Education Association.

Park, C. C. (2001). *Exiting nirvana: A daughter's life with autism*. Boston: Little, Brown.

Parmenides, & Tarán, L. (1965). *Parmenides: A text with translation, commentary, and critical essays* [L. Tarán, Trans.]. Princeton, NJ: Princeton University Press.

Pascarella, E. T., & Terenzini, P. T. (1991). *How college affects students: Findings and insights from twenty years of research*. San Francisco: Jossey-Bass.

Patterson, J. T. (2001). Brown v. Board of Education: *A civil rights milestone and its troubled legacy. Pivotal moments in American history*. Oxford, UK: Oxford University Press.

Patterson, W. P., Allen, B. C., & Brinton, D. G. (2008). *The life & teachings of Carlos Castaneda*. Fairfax, CA: Arete Communications.

Paulsen, K. J. (2005). *Living the college life*. Hoboken, NJ: Wiley.

Paulson, A. (2010, February 1). Education reform: Obama budget reboots No Child Left Behind. *Christian Science Monitor*. Retrieved March 15, 2010, from: http://www.csmonitor.com/USA/Education/2010/0201/Education-reform-Obama-budget-reboots-No-Child-Left-Behind.

Peltzer, K. (2003). Prevalence of traumatic events and post-traumatic stress symptoms among taxi drivers and passengers in South Africa. Sabinet.com. Retrieved July 6, 2009, from: http://www.sabinet.co.za/abstracts/crim/crim_v16_n1_a3.html.

Peltzer, K., & Renner, W. (2003). Superstition, risk-taking and risk perception of accidents among South African taxi drivers. *Accident Analysis and Prevention*, 35 (4), 619–23.

Peña, M., & Bacallao, J. (2000). *Obesity and poverty: A new public health challenge*. Washington, DC: Pan American Health Organization.

Perlstein, R. (2001). *Before the storm: Barry Goldwater and the unmaking of the American consensus*. New York: Hill & Wang.

Perlstein, R. (2008). *Nixonland: The rise of a president and the fracturing of America*. New York: Scribner.

Perry, N., & Sherlock, D. (2008). *Quality improvement in adult vocational education and training: Transforming skills for the global economy*. London, UK: Kogan-Page.

Peterson, A., Wright, M., Troxler, L., Gingrich, N., Barone, M., Morris, D., & Coulter, A. (2008). *Hillary: The movie* [Film]. Washington, DC: Citizens United Productions.

Peterson, P. E., & West, M. R. (Eds.). (2003). *No child left behind? The politics and practice of school accountability*. Washington, DC: Brookings Institution Press.

Phillips, H., & Killingray, D. (Eds.). (2003). *The Spanish influenza pandemic of 1918–19: New perspectives*. London, UK: Routledge.

Phillips, K. A. (1996). *The broken mirror: Understanding and treating body dysmorphic disorder*. New York: Oxford University Press.

Phillips, S. A. (1999). *Wallbangin': Graffiti and gangs in LA*. Chicago: University of Chicago Press.

Phillips, S. M. (1999). U.S. psychologists' suicide rates have declined since the 1960s. *Archives of Suicide Research*, 5 (1), 11–26.

Pierangelo, R., & Giuliani, G. A. (2004). *Transition services in special education: A practical approach*. Boston: Allyn & Bacon.

Pirsig, R. M. (1974). *Zen and the art of motorcycle maintenance: An inquiry into values*. New York: Morrow.

Plato. (1983). *Plato's Parmenides* [R. E. Allen, Trans.]. Minneapolis, MN: University of Minnesota Press.

Plimmer, C. (1988). *Food in focus*. New York: Amphoto.

Popham, W. J. (2004). *America's "failing" schools: How parents and teachers can cope with No Child Left Behind*. New York: RoutledgeFalmer.

Porto, B. L. (2003). *A new season: Using Title IX to reform college sports*. Westport, CT: Praeger.

Promislow, S. (1999). *Making the brain/body connection: A playful guide to releasing mental, physical & emotional blocks to success*. West Vancouver, British Columbia, Canada: Kinetic Pub. Corp.

Pruchno, R., & Smyer, M. A. (Eds.). (2007). *Challenges of an aging society: Ethical dilemmas, political issues*. Baltimore, MD: Johns Hopkins University Press.

Pryzwansky, W. B., & Wendt, R. N. (1999). *Professional and ethical issues in psychology: Foundations of practice*. New York: Norton.

Push-back on charter schools. (2010, March 14). *New York Times*. Retrieved March 15, 2010, from: http://roomfordebate.blogs.nytimes.com/2010/03/14/the-push-back-on-charter-schools/.

Rackensperger, T., Krezman, C., McNaughton, D., Williams, M., & D'Silva, K. (2005). "When I first got it, I wanted to throw it off a cliff": The challenges and benefits of learning AAC technologies as described by adults who use AAC. *Augmentative & Alternative Communication*, 2, 16–186.

Radach, R., Kennedy, A., & Rayner, K. (Eds.). (2004). *Eye movements and information processing during reading*. Hove, UK: Psychology Press.

Rahn, J. (2002). *Painting without permission: Hip-hop graffiti subculture*. Westport, CT: Bergin & Garvey.

Raised pavement marker. (2009, October 6). Allexperts.com. Retrieved October 6, 2009, from: http://en.allexperts.com/e/r/ra/raised_pavement_marker.htm.

Rao, S. S. (2006). *Are you ready to succeed?: Unconventional strategies for achieving personal mastery in business and life*. New York: Hyperion.

Raskin, R. (2006). *Parents' guide to college life: 181 straight answers on everything you can expect over the next four years*. New York: Princeton Review.

Ravilious, K. (2009, October 23). How green is your pet? NewScientist.com. Retrieved October 26, 2009, from: http://www.newscientist.com/article/mg20427311.600-how-green-is-your-pet.html.

Ravitch, D. (2003). *The language police: How pressure groups restrict what students learn*. New York: Knopf.

Ravitch, D. (2007, May 18). What do students know about history? Huffington Post.com. Retrieved November 4, 2009, from: http://www.huffingtonpost.com/diane-ravitch/what-do-students-know-abo_b_48795.html.

Ravitch, D. (2010a). *The death and life of the great American school system: How testing and choice are undermining education*. New York: Basic Books.

Ravitch, D. (2010b, March 9). Why I changed my mind about school reform. *Wall Street Journal* [national edition], A21. Retrieved March 10, 2010, from: http://online.wsj.com/article/SB10001424052748704869304575109443305343962.html.

Ravitch, D., & Finn, C. E. (1987). *What do our 17-year-olds know?: A report on the first national assessment of history and literature*. New York: Harper & Row.

Rebell, M. A., & Wolff, J. R. (2008). *Moving every child ahead: From NCLB hype to meaningful educational opportunity*. New York: Teachers College Press.

Record price for Banksy bomb art. (2007, February 8). BBC.com. Retrieved April 16, 2010, from: http://news.bbc.co.uk/2/hi/entertainment/6340109.stm.

Reeves, D. B. (2009). *Leading change in your school: How to conquer myths, build commitment, and get results*. Alexandria, VA: Association for Supervision and Curriculum Development.

Reeves, R. (1993). *President Kennedy: Profile of power*. New York: Simon & Schuster.

Rein, I. J., Kotler, P., & Shields, B. (2006). *The elusive fan: Reinventing sports in a crowded marketplace*. New York: McGraw-Hill.

Reiner, R., Guest, C., McKean, M., Shearer, H., Chadwick, J., Hendra, T., Kirby, B., & Murphy, K. (2000). *This is Spinal Tap: A rockumentary by Martin DiBergi* (special ed.) [Film]. Los Angeles, CA: MGM.

Renn, K. A. (2004). *Mixed race students in college: The ecology of race, identity, and community on campus*. Albany: State University of New York Press.

Reno, T. (2007). *The eat-clean diet: Fast fat loss that lasts forever!* Mississauga, Ontario, Canada: Kennedy.

Repetto, J. B. (1990). *Issues in urban vocational education for special populations*. Berkeley, CA: National Center for Research in Vocational Education/University of California.

Revkin, A. C. (2009, November 20). Hacked e-mail is new fodder for climate dispute. *New York Times*. Retrieved November 30, 2009, from: http://www.nytimes.com/2009/11/21/science/earth/21climate.html.

Rhode, D. L., & Ogletree, C. J. (Eds.). (2004). Brown *at 50: The unfinished legacy, a collection of essays*. Chicago, IL: American Bar Association.

Rice, H. (1973). *Homer Rice on triple option football*. West Nyack, NY: Parker.

Rice, H. (2000). *Lessons for leaders: Building a winning team from the ground up*. Atlanta, GA: Longstreet.

Rice, H. (2004). *Leadership fitness: Developing and reinforcing successful, positive leaders*. Atlanta, GA: Longstreet.

Rice, H., & Moore, S. (1985). *Winning football with the air option passing game*. West Nyack, NY: Parker.

Rice, J. M. (1893). The public schools of Chicago and St. Paul. *Forum*, 15, 200–15.

Richtel, M. (2009, August 28). Driven to distraction: Utah gets tough with texting drivers. *New York Times* [New York edition], A1. Retrieved October 8, 2009, from: http://www.nytimes.com/2009/08/29/technology/29distracted.html.

Richtel, M. (2010a, March 10). Gadgets in emergency vehicles seen as peril. *New York Times* [New York edition], A1, A4. Retrieved March 12, 2010, from: http://www.nytimes.com/2010/03/11/technology/11distracted.html.

Richtel, M. (2010b, March 2). Digital billboards, diversions drivers can't escape. *New York Times* [New York edition], B1–B2. Retrieved March 1, 2010, from: http://www.nytimes.com/2010/03/02/technology/02billboard.html.

Ritchey, J. A. (Ed.). (2008). *Adult education in the rural context: People, place, and change*. San Francisco: Jossey-Bass.

Robbins, C. G. (2008). *Expelling hope: The assault on youth and the militarization of schooling*. Albany, NY: SUNY Press.

Robelen, E. (2010, March 17). Florida measure would mandate civics class and test. *Education Week*. Retrieved March 19, 2010, from: http://blogs.edweek.org/edweek/curriculum/2010/03/florida_measure_would_mandate.html.

Roberto, M. (2006). *Time management: Increase your personal productivity and effectiveness*. Boston: Harvard Business School Press.

Roizen, M. F., & Oz, M. (2006). *You, on a diet: The owner's manual to waist management*. New York: Free Press.

Rolls, B. J. (2007). *The volumetrics eating plan: Techniques and recipes for feeling full on fewer calories*. New York: Harper.

Romm, J. J. (2007). *Hell and high water: Global warming—The solution and the politics—And what we should do*. New York: William Morrow.

Rosenbaum, J. (2007). *Discovering Orson Welles*. Berkeley: University of California Press.

Rothman, W. (2009). *Three documentary filmmakers: Errol Morris, Ross McElwee, Jean Rouch*. Albany, NY: SUNY Press.

Rothschild, B., & Rand, M. L. (2006). *Help for the helper: The psychophysiology of compassion fatigue and vicarious trauma*. New York: Norton.

Rothstein, R. (2004). *Class and schools: Using social, economic, and educational reform to close the black-white achievement gap*. New York: Teachers College Press.

Rotman, S. (2008). *Bay Area graffiti*. New York: Mark Batty.

Rousmaniere, K. (2005). *Citizen teacher: The life and leadership of Margaret Haley*. Albany: State University of New York Press.

Rowse, D. (2007, March 21). Food photography: An introduction. Digitalphotographyschool.com. Retrieved July 12, 2009, from: http://digital-photography-school.com/food-photography-an-introduction.

Rubinstein, R. (2006). *Critical mess: Art critics on the state of their practice*. Lenox, MA: Hard Press Editions.

Ruiz, M. (2009). *Graffiti Argentina*. New York: Thames & Hudson.

Ruokonen, J. (2003). *How to read how-to and self-help books: Getting real results from the advice you get*. London, UK: Rivion.

Ruschmann, P. (2006). *Media bias*. Philadelphia: Chelsea House.

Ryzik, M. (2010, April 13). Riddle? Yes. Enigma? Sure. Documentary? *New York Times* [New York edition], C1–C2. Retrieved April 15, 2010, from: http://www.nytimes.com/2010/04/14/movies/14banksy.html.

Safford, P. L., & Safford, E. J. (2006). *Children with disabilities in America: A historical handbook and guide*. Westport, CT: Greenwood Press.

Salgado, S. (2003). *The end of polio: A global effort to end a disease*. Boston: Bulfinch Press/AOL-Time Warner.

Salkin, P. E. (2008). *Pioneering women lawyers: From Kate Stoneman to the present*. Albany, NY: Albany Law School.

Saltman, K. J. (2000). *Collateral damage: Corporatizing public schools—A threat to democracy*. Lanham, MD: Rowman & Littlefield.

Sammond, N. (Ed.). (2005). *Steel chair to the head: The pleasure and pain of professional wrestling*. Durham, NC: Duke University Press.

Sanlo, R. L., Rankin, S., & Schoenberg, R. (2002). *Our place on campus: Lesbian, gay, bisexual, transgender services and programs in higher education*. Westport, CT: Greenwood Press.

Sarason, S. B. (1990). *The predictable failure of educational reform: Can we change course before it's too late?* San Francisco: Jossey-Bass.

Sarbanes-Oxley on trial. (2009, December 4). *Wall Street Journal*. Retrieved December 5, 2009, from: http://online.wsj.com/article/SB10001424052748704107104574571662869948676.html.

Saul, S. (2008, February 16). Conflict on the menu. *New York Times*. Retrieved October 26, 2009, from: http://www.nytimes.com/2008/02/16/business/16obese.html.

Saunders, D. (2007). *Direct cinema: Observational documentary and the politics of the sixties*. London: Wallflower Press.

Savage, D. G. (2009, August 23). In *Hillary: The Movie* case, Supreme Court considers major shift in election law. *Los Angeles Times*. Retrieved August 30, 2009, from: http://www.latimes.com/news/nationworld/nation/la-na-campaign-finance23-2009aug23,0,7916109.story.

Savage, L. (Ed.). (2008). *Perspectives on diseases and disorders: Eating disorders*. Detroit, MI: Thomson/Gale.

Sawislak, K. (1995). *Smoldering city: Chicagoans and the Great Fire, 1871–1874. Historical studies of urban America*. Chicago: University of Chicago Press.

Schlessinger, B. S., & Karp, R. S. (1995). *The basic business library: Core resources*. Phoenix, AZ: Oryx Press.

Schlosser, R. W. (2003). *The efficacy of augmentative and alternative communication*. Amsterdam, NL: Academic Press.

Schmoker, M. J. (2006). *Results now: How we can achieve unprecedented improvements in teaching and learning*. Alexandria, VA: Association for Supervision and Curriculum Development.

Schrader, P. (1990). *Taxi driver*. London, UK: Faber & Faber.

Schroeder, A. (2008). *The snowball: Warren Buffett and the business of life*. New York: Bantam.

Schulte, B. (2008, February 11). Outlawing text messaging while driving: Legislators in several states respond to safety concerns. USnews.com. Retrieved October 8, 2009, from: http://www.usnews.com/articles/news/national/2008/02/11/outlawing-text-messaging-while-driving.html.

Scullion, P. A., & Guest, D. A. (2007). *Study skills for nursing and midwifery students*. Buckingham: Open University Press.

Scweikart, L., & Allen, M. (2007). *A patriot's history of the United States: From Columbus's great discovery to the war on terror*. New York: Sentinel.

Seaman, B. (2005). *Binge: What your college student won't tell you: Campus life in an age of disconnection and excess*. Hoboken, NJ: Wiley.

Sears, B., & Lawren, B. (1995). *The zone: A dietary road map*. New York, NY: Regan.

SEC going to trial against BofA over bonuses. (2009, September 22). MSNBC.com. Retrieved September 22, 2009, from: http://www.msnbc.msn.com/id/32960212/ns/business-us_business/.

Seib, G. F. (2010, January 12). No seat for Wall Street at tea party. *Wall Street Journal* [national edition], A2. Retrieved January 12, 2010, from: http://online.wsj.com/article/SB126324071300124959.html.

Sergiovanni, T. J. (2009). *The principalship: A reflective practice perspective*. Boston: Pearson.

Severson, K. (2007, June 29). City says 83% of restaurants have curbed trans fat. *New York Times*. Retrieved October 22, 2009, from: http://cityroom.blogs.nytimes.com/2007/06/29/trans-fats-waning-but-can-city-claim-credit/?scp=8&sq=new%20york%20restaurants%20and%20trans%20fats&st=cse.

Severson, K. (2009, July 29). Film food, ready for its "bon appétit." *New York Times* [New York edition], D1. Retrieved July 29, 2009, from: http://www.nytimes.com/2009/07/29/dining/29movie.html.

Sewell, A., & Thorndike, E. L. (1935). *Black beauty*. New York: Appleton-Century.

Shackelford, K. (2010, March 11). Why the Texas textbook wars matter to every American. Foxnews.com. Retrieved March 12, 2010, from: http://www

.foxnews.com/opinion/2010/03/11/kelly-shackelford-texas-textbook-social-studies-standards-american-history/.

Shafii, M., & Shafii, S. L. (Eds.). (2001). *School violence: Assessment, management, prevention*. Washington, DC: American Psychiatric Press.

Shaker, P., & Heilman, E. E. (2008). *Reclaiming education for democracy: Thinking beyond No Child Left Behind*. New York: Routledge.

Shand-Tucci, D. (2003). *The crimson letter: Harvard, homosexuality, and the shaping of American culture*. New York: St. Martin's Press.

Shapiro, B. (2004). *Brainwashed: How universities indoctrinate America's youth*. Nashville, TN: WND.

Shapiro, H. S. (2006). *Losing heart: The moral and spiritual miseducation of America's children*. Mahwah, NJ: Erlbaum.

Sharp, D. J. (2006). *Cases in business ethics*. Thousand Oaks, CA: Sage.

Shatner, W., Nimoy, L., Kelley, D., Doohan, J., Koenig, W., Takei, G., Nichols, N., Winfield, P., Alley, K., Montalbán, R., Meyer, N., Sowards, J. B., Bennett, H., Roddenberry, G., Horner, J. (2002). *Star trek II: The wrath of khan* [Film]. Hollywood, CA: Paramount Pictures. (Original film released in 1982.)

Shepherd, T. A., Campbell, K. A., Renzoni, A. M., & Sloan, N. (2009). Reliability of speech generating devices: A 5-year review. *Augmentative and Alternative Communication*, 25, 145–53.

Sheppard, S. (2008). *The partisan press: A history of media bias in the United States*. Jefferson, NC: McFarland.

Shiffrin, M. A., & Silberschatz, A. (2009, October 4). Thumbs on the wheel. *New York Times* [New York edition], A23. Retrieved October 4, 2009, from: http://www.nytimes.com/2009/10/05/opinion/05silberschatz.html.

Shih, G. (2010, June 4). The Bay citizen educators are opposed to Obama's school plan. *New York Times* [national edition], A27B. Retrieved June 6, 2009, from: http://www.nytimes.com/2010/06/06/education/06bceducation.html.

Shipps, D. (2006). *School reform, corporate style: Chicago, 1880–2000*. Lawrence, KS: University Press of Kansas.

Shoup, K. (2005). *What can you do with a major in business?* Hoboken, NJ: Wiley.

Shoup, W. J. (1891). *The history and science of education*. New York: American Book Company.

Siegel, M. (2006). *Bird flu: Everything you need to know about the next pandemic*. Hoboken, NJ: Wiley.

Silk, M. L., Andrews, D. L., & Cole, C. L. (Eds.). (2005). *Sport and corporate nationalisms: Sport, commerce and culture*. Oxford, UK: Berg.

Silva, J. M., Metzler, J. N., & Lerner, B. (2007). *Training professionals in the practice of sport psychology*. Morgantown, WV: Fitness Information Technology.

Silver, J. K., & Wilson, D. J. (2007). *Polio voices: An oral history from the American polio epidemics and worldwide eradication efforts*. Westport, CT: Praeger.

Simpson, C. G., & Spencer, V. G. (2009). *College success for students with learning disabilities: Strategies and tips to make the most of your college experience*. Waco, TX: Prufrock Press.

Sinclair, U. (1922). *The goose-step: A study of American education by Upton Sinclair*. Pasadena, CA: Author.

Sinclair, U. (1971). *The jungle*. Cambridge, MA: R. Bentley. (Original work published in 1906.)

Singer, M. (2001). *Dark days*. New York, NY: Palm Pictures.

Skorina, J. K., Bissell, L., & De Soto, C. B. (1990). Alcoholic psychologists: Routes to recovery. *Professional Psychology: Research and Practice*, 21 (4), 248–51.

Slingerland, B. H. (1988). *An adaptation of the Orton-Gillingham approach for classroom teaching of reading*. Cambridge, MA: Educators Publishing Service.

Sloan, K. (2008). *Holding schools accountable: A handbook for educators and parents*. Lanham, MD: Rowman & Littlefield.

Sloan, W. D., & Mackay, J. B. (Eds.). (2007). *Media bias: Finding it, fixing it*. Jefferson, NC: McFarland.

Smick, D. M. (2008). *The world is curved: Hidden dangers to the global economy*. New York: Portfolio.

Smilkstein, R. (2003). *We're born to learn: Using the brain's natural learning process to create today's curriculum*. Thousand Oaks, CA: Corwin.

Smith, B. L. R., Mayer, J. D., & Fritschler, A. L. (2008). *Closed minds?: Politics and ideology in American universities*. Washington, DC: Brookings Institution Press.

Smith, I. (2006). *The fat smash diet: The last diet you'll ever need*. New York: St. Martin's Griffin.

Smith, M. (2005). *Literacy and augmentative and alternative communication*. Amsterdam: Elsevier.

Smith, S. L. (1997). The effective use of fear appeals in persuasive immunization: An analysis of national immunization intervention messages. *Journal of Applied Communication Research*, 25, 264–92.

Smith, W. H. (1884). *The evolution of "Dodd": A pedagogical story*. Chicago: Rand, McNally.

Smylie, M. A., & Miretzky, D. (2004). *Developing the teacher workforce*. Chicago: National Society for the Study of Education.

Snodgrass, B. (2006). *The makeover myth: The real story behind cosmetic surgery, injectables, lasers, gimmicks, and hype, and what you need to know to stay safe*. New York: Collins.

Snyderman, N. L. (2009). *Diet myths that keep us fat: And the 101 truths that will save your waistline—And maybe even your life*. New York: Crown.

Somers, S. (2005). *Suzanne Somers' slim and sexy forever: The hormone solution for permanent weight loss and optimal living*. New York: Crown.

Sommers, C. H. (2000). *The war against boys: How misguided feminism is harming our young men*. New York: Simon & Schuster.

Soros, G. (2008). *The new paradigm for financial markets: The credit crisis of 2008 and what it means*. New York: PublicAffairs.

Sosa, E., & Kim, J. (1998). *A companion to metaphysics*. Oxford, UK: Blackwell.

Sousa, D. A. (2001). *How the special needs brain learns*. Thousand Oaks, CA: Corwin.

Sousa, D. A. (2003). *How the gifted brain learns*. Thousand Oaks, CA: Corwin.

Speed reading software review. (2009). TopTenReviews.com. Retrieved September 11, 2009, from: http://speed-reading-software-review.toptenreviews.com/.

Spencer, J., & Wang, S. S. (2010, March 24). Coming to the menu: Calorie counts. *Wall Street Journal* [national edition], A4. Retrieved March 25, 2010, from:

http://online.wsj.com/article/SB10001424052748704211704575140171439748274.html.

Spencer, R. W. (2008). *Climate confusion: How global warming hysteria leads to bad science, pandering politicians, and misguided policies that hurt the poor*. New York: Encounter.

Sperry, L. (2007). *The ethical and professional practice of counseling and psychotherapy*. Boston: Allyn & Bacon.

Spillane, J. P., & Diamond, J. B. (2007). *Distributed leadership in practice*. New York: Teachers College, Columbia University.

Spinney, R. G. (2000). *City of big shoulders: A history of Chicago*. DeKalb, IL: Northern Illinois University Press.

Spitz, H. H. (1997). *Nonconscious movements: From mystical messages to facilitated communication*. Mahwah, NJ: Erlbaum.

Spivey, D. (1978). *Schooling for the new slavery: Black industrial education, 1868–1915*. Westport, CT: Greenwood Press.

Spohn, M. (2008). *What to expect when your child leaves for college: A complete guide for parents only*. Ocala, FL: Atlantic.

Springer, S. P., & Deutsch, G. (1981). *Left brain, right brain*. San Francisco: W. H. Freeman.

Spyri, J., Thorndike, E. L., & Woodward, H. (1935). *Heidi*. New York: Appleton-Century.

Stamm, B. H. (1999). *Secondary traumatic stress: Self-care issues for clinicians, researchers, and educators*. Lutherville, MD: Sidran Press.

Stanger, M. A., & Donohue, E. K. (1937). *Prediction and prevention of reading difficulties*. New York: Oxford University Press.

Stanley, A. (2010, March 18). It's not easy being fat again. *New York Times* [New York edition], C1. Retrieved March 19, 2010, from: http://www.nytimes.com/2010/03/19/arts/television/19big.html?hpw.

Starr, E. G., Deegan, M. J., & Wahl, A. M. (2003). *On art, labor, and religion*. New Brunswick, NJ: Transaction.

Staudohar, P. D., & Mangan, J. A. (Eds.). (1991). *The business of professional sports*. Urbana: University of Illinois Press.

Stead, W. T. (1894). *If Christ came to Chicago!: A plea for the union of all who love in the service of all who suffer*. Chicago: Laird & Lee.

Stefoff, R., & Zinn, H. (2007a). *A young people's history of the United States: Columbus to the Spanish American War* (Vol. 1). New York: Seven Stories Press.

Stefoff, R., & Zinn, H. (2007b). *A young people's history of the United States: Class struggle to the war on terror* (Vol. 2). New York: Seven Stories Press.

Stein, J. (2007). *Parent guide to hassle-free homework*. New York: Scholastic.

Stein, R. (2009, October 4). Vaccine is on its way, but public still wary. *Washington Post*. Retrieved August 13, 2010, from: http://www.washingtonpost.com/wp-dyn/content/article/2009/10/03/AR2009100303041.html.

Steinhauser, G. (2010, March 3). A game of tag breaks out between London's graffiti elite. *Wall Street Journal* [national edition], A1, A14. Retrieved March 2, 2010, from: http://online.wsj.com/article/SB10001424052748703795004575087043622126412.html.

Stephens, B. (2009, October 27). Freaked out over SuperFreakonomics. *Wall Street Journal* [national edition], A19. Retrieved October 27, 2009, from: http://online.wsj.com/article/SB10001424052748704335904574495643459234318.html.

Stevenson, M. (2010, April 23). 1 year after swine flu, Mexicans split on response. Chron.com. Retrieved April 24, 2010, from: http://www.chron.com/disp/story.mpl/health/6972383.html.

Steward, H. L., Andrews, S. S., Bethea, M. C., & Balart, L. A. (1998). *Sugar busters!: Cut sugar to trim fat*. New York: Ballantine.

Stewart, B. (2007). *Sport funding and finance*. Amsterdam: Elsevier.

Stewart, J., & Stewart, R. (2009). *Graffiti kings: New York City mass transit art of the 1970s*. New York: Abrams.

Stobbe, M. (2009, October 9). US, other nations stop counting pandemic flu cases. ABCnews.com. Retrieved October 10, 2009, from: http://abcnews.go.com/Health/wireStory?id=8788209.

Stone, C. N. (Eds.). (1998). *Changing urban education*. Lawrence: University Press of Kansas.

Story, L., & Dash, E. (2010, January 10). Banks prepare for bigger bonuses, and public's wrath. *New York Times* [New York edition], A10. Retrieved January 10, 2010, from: http://www.nytimes.com/2010/01/10/business/10pay.html.

Strada, J. L. (2001). *Eating disorders*. San Diego, CA: Lucent.

Street, P. L. (2005). *Segregated schools: Educational apartheid in post-civil rights America*. New York: Routledge.

Stringer, C. V., & Tucker, L. (2008). *Standing tall: A memoir of tragedy and triumph*. New York: Crown.

Stubbs, L. (2002). *Documentary filmmakers speak*. New York: Allworth.

Suero, O., & Garside, A. (2001). *Camelot at dawn: Jacqueline and John Kennedy in Georgetown, May 1954*. Baltimore: Johns Hopkins University Press.

Summitt, P. H., & Jenkins, S. (1998). *Raise the roof: The inspiring inside story of the Tennessee Lady Vols' undefeated 1997–98 season*. New York: Broadway.

Survey: U.S. students fail history. (2008, February 27). Suite101.com. Retrieved November 4, 2009, from: http://americanaffairs.suite101.com/article.cfm/us_students_get_a_d_in_history.

Sutherland, P., & Revs. (2004). *Autograf: New York City's graffiti writers*. New York: PowerHouse.

Sutz, R., & Weverka, P. (2009). *Speed reading for dummies*. Hoboken, NJ: Wiley.

Swett, J. (1969). *Public education in California*. New York: Arno Press. (Original work published in 1911.)

Sykes, C. J. (1995). *Dumbing down our kids: Why America's children feel good about themselves but can't read, write, or add*. New York: St. Martin's Press.

Sylwester, R. (2003). *A biological brain in a cultural classroom: Enhancing cognitive and social development through collaborative classroom management*. Thousand Oaks, CA: Corwin Press.

Talbott, J. R. (2009). *Contagion: The financial epidemic that is sweeping the global economy . . . And how to protect yourself from it*. Hoboken, NJ: Wiley.

Tan, M. (2010, February 28). How Kirstie Alley lost 20 lbs.—organically. People.com. Retrieved March 16, 2010, from: http://www.people.com/people/article/0,,20347602,00.html.

Tanner, M. (1999). *Schopenhauer*. New York: Routledge.

Taubes, G. (2007). *Good calories, bad calories: Challenging the conventional wisdom on diet, weight control, and disease*. New York: Knopf.

Taylor, J. B. (2009). *Getting off track: How government actions and interventions caused, prolonged, and worsened the financial crisis*. Stanford, CA: Hoover Institution Press.

Teachout, T. (2009, August 9). Can jazz be saved?: The audience for America's great art form is withering away. *Wall Street Journal*. Retrieved August 10, 2009, from: http://online.wsj.com/article/SB100014240529702046190045743203103850572.html.

Television Food Network. (2004). *Iron chef America: Battle of the masters* [DVD]. Author.

Television Food Network. (2009, October 27). *Iron chef America: The series*. Food network.com. Retrieved October 27, 2009, from: http://www.foodnetwork.com/iron-chef-america/index.html.

Tenenbaum, G., & Eklund, R. C. (Eds.). (2007). *Handbook of sport psychology*. Hoboken, NJ: Wiley.

Terman, L. (1943). Foreword. In G. M. Fernald, *Remedial techniques in basic school subjects* (pp. ii–xv). New York: McGraw-Hill.

Terry, K. (2007). *Rx for health care reform*. Nashville, TN: Vanderbilt University Press.

Thomas, R. M. (2007). *God in the classroom: Religion and America's public schools*. Westport, CT: Praeger.

Thomas, R. M. (2008). *What schools ban and why*. Westport, CT: Praeger.

Thorndike, E. L. (1903). *Educational psychology*. New York. Science Press.

Thorndike, E. L. (1912). *A scale for handwriting of children in grades 5–8*. New York: Teachers College Press.

Thorndike, E. L. (1914). *Teachers' estimates of the quality of specimens of handwriting*. New York: Teachers College Press.

Thorndike, E. L. (1921a). *The teacher's word book*. New York: Teachers College Press.

Thorndike, E. L. (1921b). *The Thorndike test of word knowledge: Instructions for giving and scoring, answer keys and norms*. New York: Teachers College Press.

Thorndike, E. L. (1922). *The psychology of arithmetic*. New York: Macmillan.

Thorndike, E. L. (1931). *A teacher's word book of the twenty thousand words found most frequently and widely in general reading for children and young people*. New York: Teachers College Press.

Thorndike, E. L. (1935). *The Thorndike-Century junior dictionary*. Chicago: Scott Foresman.

Thorndike, E. L. (1936). *The Arabian nights*. New York: Appleton-Century.

Thorndike, E. L. (1940). *Human nature and the social order*. New York: Macmillan.

Thorndike, E. L. (1941). *Century senior dictionary*. Chicago: Scott Foresman.

Thorndike, E. L. (1942). *Thorndike-Century junior dictionary*. Chicago: Scott Foresman.

Thorndike, E. L. (1970). *Educational psychology*. New York: Teachers College Press.

Thorndike, E. L., & Barnhart, C. L. (1997). *Thorndike-Barnhart junior dictionary*. New York: HarperCollins.

Thorndike, E. L., & Barnhart, C. L. (1999). *Thorndike-Barnhart children's dictionary.* Glenview, IL: Scott Foresman/Addison-Wesley.

Thorndike, E. L., & Lorge, I. (1944). *The teacher's word book of 30,000 words.* New York: Teachers College Press.

Thorndike, E. L., & Lorge, I. (1968). *The teacher's word book of 30,000 words.* New York: Teachers College Press.

Thorndike, E. L., Palmer, H. E., & Ballard, P. B. (1973). *The Thorndike junior illustrated dictionary.* London: University of London Press.

Thorpe, D. E. (2009). *Sports law.* South Melbourne, Australia: Oxford University Press.

Tiede, T. (2001). *Self-help nation: The long overdue, entirely justified, delightfully hostile guide to the snake-oil peddlers who are sapping our nation's soul.* New York: Atlantic Monthly.

Tiemeyer, M. (2007, January 19). Fashion industry and eating disorders in the news . . . Again. Guide to Eating Disorders. Retrieved October 22, 2009, from: http://eatingdisorders.about.com/b/2007/01/19/fashion-industry-and-eating-disorders-in-the-news-again.htm.

Tierney, J. (2009, April 6). Public policy that makes test subjects of us all. *New York Times* [New York edition], D1. Retrieved February 23, 2010, from: http://www.nytimes.com/2009/04/07/science/07tier.html.

Tierney, J. (2010, February 22). When it comes to salt, no rights or wrongs. Yet. *New York Times* [New York edition], D2. Retrieved February 23, 2010, from: http://www.nytimes.com/2010/02/23/science/23tier.html.

Tobitani, Y. (2006). *Quantum speed-reading: Awakening your child's mind.* Charlottesville, VA: Hampton Roads Publishing.

Toplin, R. B. (2006). *Michael Moore's Fahrenheit 9/11: How one film divided a nation.* Lawrence: University Press of Kansas.

Torr, J. D. (2003). *Professional sports.* San Diego, CA: Greenhaven Press.

Totty, M. (2009, December 6). What global warming? *Wall Street Journal* [national edition], R4. Retrieved December 8, 2009, from: http://online.wsj.com/article/SB10001424052748703819904574551303527570212.html.

Trans fat. (2009, October 22). Center for Science in the Public Interest. Retrieved October 22, 2009, from: http://www.cspinet.org/transfat/index.html.

Trump, D., & Zanker, B. (2007). *Think big and kick ass in business and life.* New York: Collins.

Tse, T. M. (2009, February 14). Congress trumps Obama by cuffing bonuses for CEOs. *Washington Post,* A01. Retrieved September 21, 2009, from: http://www.washingtonpost.com/wp-dyn/content/article/2009/02/13/AR2009021303288.html.

Tuman, J. S. (2010). *Communicating terror: The rhetorical dimensions of terrorism* (2nd ed.) Los Angeles: Sage.

Turan, K. (2009, August 7). Nora Ephron whips up something wonderful in *Julie & Julia. Los Angeles Times.* Retrieved August 9, 2009, from: http://www.latimes.com/entertainment/news/reviews/movies/la-et-julie-julia7-2009aug07,0,1724703.story.

Tushnet, M. V. (1987). *The NAACP's legal strategy against segregated education, 1925–1950.* Chapel Hill: University of North Carolina Press.

Twachtman-Cullen, D. (1997). *A passion to believe: Autism and the facilitated communication phenomenon*. Boulder, CO: Westview Press.

Twyman, J. F. (2008). *The Moses code: The most powerful manifestation tool in the history of the world*. Carlsbad, CA: Hay House.

United States Department of Education. (2004a). *A guide to education and No Child Left Behind*. Washington, DC: Author. Retrieved October 13, 2009, from: http://purl.access.gpo.gov/GPO/LPS57879.

United States Department of Education. (2004b). *National assessment of vocational education: Final report to Congress*. Washington, DC: Author. Retrieved April 1, 2010, from: http://www2.ed.gov/rschstat/eval/sectech/nave/naveexesum.pdf.

United States Department of Education. (2007). *Building on results: A blueprint for strengthening the No Child Left Behind Act*. Washington, DC: Author.

United States Senate Special Committee on Aging. (2001, September 10). *Swindlers, hucksters and snake oil salesman: Hype and hope of marketing anti-aging products to seniors*. Washington, DC: Government Printing Office.

University of Maryland Women, Leadership, & Equality Program. (2009, December 7). *Women faculty and students in legal education—Bibliography*. University of Maryland School of Law. Retrieved December 7, 2009, from: http://www.law.umaryland.edu/programs/wle/resources/biblio.html.

Urban safaris: Graffiti sites considered for heritage protection. (2008, June 24). Tomorrowmuseum.com. Retrieved February 8, 2010, from: http://tomorrowmuseum.com/2008/06/24/urban-safaris-graffiti-sites-considered-for-heritage-protection/.

USA TODAY's best-selling books of last 15 years. (2008, October 30). USAtoday.com. Retrieved October 16, 2009, from: http://www.usatoday.com/life/books/news/2008-10-29-top-150-books_N.htm.

Vagnoni, N. (2006, July 20). Chicago trans fat ban revised. Slashfood.com. Retrieved October 22, 2009, from: http://www.slashfood.com/2006/07/20/chicago-trans-fat-ban-revised/.

Valk, A. M. (2008). *Radical sisters: Second-wave feminism and black liberation in Washington, D.C.* Urbana: University of Illinois Press.

Van Gompel, R. P. G. (Ed.). (2007). *Eye movements: A window on mind and brain*. Amsterdam: Elsevier.

Vance, A., & Richtel, M. (2010, January 6). Despite risks, Internet creeps onto car dashboards. *New York Times* [New York edition], A1. Retrieved March 1, 2010, from: http://www.nytimes.com/2010/01/07/technology/07distracted.html.

Vanden Heuvel, K. (Ed.). (2009). *Meltdown: How greed and corruption shattered our financial system and how we can recover*. New York: Nation Books.

Vander Hook, S. (2001). *Eating disorders*. Mankato, MN: Smart Apple Media.

Vergano, D. (2006, June 5). Celebs turn the spotlight on global warming. *USA Today*. Retrieved January 9, 2010, from: http://www.usatoday.com/weather/climate/2006-06-01-warming-celebs_x.htm.

Villarosa, L. (2008, May 26). Is there a link between vaccines and autism? Root.com. Retrieved August 1, 2009, from: http://www.theroot.com/views/there-link-between-vaccines-and-autism.

Vinovskis, M. (2009). *From a nation at risk to No Child Left Behind: National education goals and the creation of federal education policy.* New York: Teachers College Press.

Vocational Schools Database. (2010). RWM.org. Retrieved April 1, 2010, from: http://www.rwm.org/rwm/.

Vollstadt, E. W. (1999). *Teen eating disorders.* San Diego, CA: Lucent.

Vye, C., Scholljegerdes, K., & Welch, I. D. (2007). *Under pressure and overwhelmed: Coping with anxiety in college.* Westport, CT: Praeger.

Wade, J. (1982). *Portrait photography.* London: Focal Press.

Wagner, T. (2008). *The global achievement gap: Why even our best schools don't teach the new survival skills our children need—And what we can do about it.* New York: Basic Books.

Wagner, T., & Kegan, R. (2006). *Change leadership: A practical guide to transforming our schools.* San Francisco: Jossey-Bass.

Wagner, V. (Ed.). (2007). *Eating disorders.* Detroit, MI: Greenhaven Press.

Wainwright, G. R. (2001). *Read faster, recall more: Use proven techniques for speed reading and maximum recall.* Oxford, UK: How To Books.

Wakefield, A. J., Murch, S. H., Anthony, A., Linnell, J., Casson, D. M., Malik, M., Berelowitz, M., Dhillon, A. P., Thomson, M. A., Harvey, P., Valentine, A., Davies, S. E., & Walker-Smith, J. A. (1998). Ileal-lymphoid-nodular hyperplasia, non-specific colitis, and pervasive developmental disorder in children. *Lancet,* 351, 637–41. [The editorial board retracted this article in 2010.]

Wakefield, K. L. (2007). *Team sports marketing.* Amsterdam: Elsevier/Butterworth-Heinemann.

Walberg, H. J., & Bast, J. L. (2003). *Education and capitalism: How overcoming our fear of markets and economics can improve America's schools.* Stanford, CA: Hoover Institution Press.

Walde, C. (2007). *Sticker city: Paper graffiti art.* London, UK: Thames & Hudson.

Waldheim, C., & Rüedi Ray, K. (2005). *Chicago architecture: Histories, revisions, alternatives.* Chicago: University of Chicago Press.

Walker, B. J. (2010). *Literacy coaching: Learning to collaborate.* Boston: Allyn & Bacon.

Walker, G., & King, D. A. (2008). *The hot topic: What we can do about global warming.* Orlando, FL: Harcourt.

Walker, V. S., & Byas, U. (2009). *Hello professor: A black principal and professional leadership in the segregated south.* Chapel Hill: University of North Carolina Press.

Wallace, A. (2003). *Sorcerer's apprentice: My life with Carlos Castaneda.* Berkeley, CA: Frog.

Wallace, R. (2008). *Principal to principal: Conversations in servant leadership and school transformation.* Lanham, MD: Rowman & Littlefield.

Wang, S. S. (2010, February 3). *Lancet* retracts study tying vaccine to autism. *Wall Street Journal* [national edition], A8. Retrieved February 3, 2010, from: http://online.wsj.com/article/SB10001424052748704022804575041212437364420.html.

Ward, J. W., & Warren, C. (2007). *Silent victories: The history and practice of public health in twentieth-century America.* Oxford, UK: Oxford University Press.

Warner, M. (2005, September 12). Kirstie Alley shows leaner side in ads. *New York Times.* Retrieved October 17, 2009, from: http://www.nytimes.com/2005/09/12/business/media/12adcol.html.

Wasik, B. (2006). My Crowd or, phase 5: A report from the inventor of the flash mob. *Harpers*, 1870, 56–66.

Water fluoridation and cancer risk. (2006, April 7). American Cancer Society. Retrieved August 4, 2009, from: http://www.cancer.org/docroot/PED/content/PED_1_3X_Water_Fluoridation_and_Cancer_Risk.asp.

Watkins, S. C. (2005). *Hip hop matters: Politics, pop culture, and the struggle for the soul of a movement*. Boston: Beacon Press.

Watt, D. C. (2003). *Sports management and administration*. London, UK: Routledge.

Wechsler, H. B., & Bell, A. H. (2006). *Speed reading for professionals*. Hauppauge, NY: Barron's.

Weil, D. K. (2000). *Charter schools: A reference handbook*. Santa Barbara, CA: ABC-CLIO.

Weil, D. K. (2002). *School vouchers and privatization: A reference handbook*. Santa Barbara, CA: ABC-CLIO.

Weintraub, F., Heller, P., Clouse, R., Allin, M., Lee, B., Saxon, J., Capri, A., Wall, B., Shih, K., & Kelly, J. (1973). *Enter the dragon* [Film]. Burbank, CA: Warner Home Video.

Weisberg, R. (2008). *Critical condition*. New York: Docurama.

Weisman, J., Paletta, D., & Sidel, R. (2010, January 21). New bank rules sink stocks. *Wall Street Journal*. Retrieved January 21, 2010, from: http://online.wsj.com/article/SB10001424052748703699204575016983630045768.html.

Weiss, C., & Melling, L. (1988). The legal education of twenty women. *Stanford Law Review*, 40, 1299.

Welcome to brain gym—Educational kinesiology. (2008). Brain Gym International. Retrieved July 25, 2009, from: http://images.google.com/imgres?imgurl=http://www.eduk.org.za/images/eduk_influence.GIF&imgrefurl=http://www.eduk.org.za/&usg=__FTpTwjnmmYj7Fxoz4W6b_h-ZXjw=&h=509&w=520&sz=46&hl=en&start=8&um=1&tbnid=kkSN6LU8d4TcFM:&tbnh=128&tbnw=131&prev=/images%3Fq%3Dbrain%2Bgym%26hl%3Den%26rls%3Dcom.microsoft:en-us%26sa%3DX%26um%3D1.

Werth, B. (2007). *31 days: Gerald Ford, the Nixon pardon, and a government in crisis*. New York: Anchor.

Westheimer, J. (2007). *Pledging allegiance: The politics of patriotism in America's schools*. New York: Teachers College Press.

Westheimer, R. K., & Lehu, P. A. (2000). *Dr. Ruth's guide to college life: The savvy student's handbook*. Lanham, MD: Madison.

What is speed reading software? (2006). 4BoxReviews.com. Retrieved September 11, 2009, from: http://www.4boxreviews.com/speed-reader-review.html?gclid=COzkro_96ZwCFQog2godLy74kQ.

What parents should know about measles-mumps-rubella (mmr) vaccine and autism. (2009). Academy of Pediatrics. Retrieved August 2, 2009, from: http://www.cispimmunize.org/aap/aap_main.html?http&&&www.cispimmunize.org/fam/autism/a_faq.html.

Whitaker, S. (2007). *Advocacy for school leaders: Becoming a strong voice for education*. Lanham, MD: Rowman & Littlefield.

White, J. B. (2010, February 3). When cellphone bans don't curb crashes. *Wall Street Journal*, D2. Retrieved February 3, 2010, from: http://online.wsj.com/article/SB10001424052748704022804575041552234321736.html.

Whitebread, C. H. (1995). *The eight secrets of top exam performance in law school: An easy-to-use, step-by-step program for achieving great grades!* Chicago, IL: Harcourt Brace.

Whitmire, R., & Rotherham, A. J. (2009, October 2). How teachers unions lost the media. *Wall Street Journal*, W13. Retrieved October 4, 2009, from: http://online.wsj.com/article/NA_WSJ_PUB:SB10001424052970204488304574426991456414888.html.

Wilkins, L. (1987). *Shared vulnerability: The media and American perceptions of the Bhopal disaster*. New York: Greenwood Press.

Willis, J. (2007). *Brain-friendly strategies for the inclusion classroom: Insights from a neurologist and classroom teacher*. Alexandria, VA: Association for Supervision and Curriculum Development.

Wilson, A. L., & Hayes, E. (2000). *Handbook of adult and continuing education*. San Francisco: Jossey-Bass.

Wilson, D. J. (2005). *Living with polio: The epidemic and its survivors*. Chicago: University of Chicago Press.

Wilson, R., & Joyce, J. (2008). *Finance for sport and leisure managers: An introduction*. London, UK: Routledge.

Wilson, S. F. (2006). *Learning on the job: When business takes on public schools*. Cambridge, MA: Harvard University Press.

Winston, B. (2000). *Lies, damn lies and documentaries*. London: BFI.

Winzer, M. A. (1993). *The history of special education: From isolation to integration*. Washington, DC: Gallaudet University Press.

Wisker, G. (2008). *The postgraduate research handbook: Succeed with your MA, MPhil, EdD and PhD*. Basingstoke, Hampshire, UK: Palgrave-Macmillan.

Witcover, J. (2007). *Very strange bedfellows: The short and unhappy marriage of Richard Nixon and Spiro Agnew*. New York: PublicAffairs.

Wonder, J., & Donovan, P. (1984). *Whole-brain thinking: Working from both sides of the brain to achieve peak job performance*. New York: Morrow.

Wong, G. M. (2002). *Essentials of sports law*. Westport, CT: Praeger.

Wong, K. K. (2007). *The education mayor: Improving America's schools*. Washington, DC: Georgetown University Press.

Woodacre, M. E. B., & Bane, S. (2006). *I'll miss you too: What will change, what will not and how we'll stay connected*. Naperville, IL: Sourcebooks.

Worthless, I. M., Competent, U. R., Lemonde-Terrible, O. (2002). Cognitive therapy training stress disorder: A cognitive perspective. *Behavioural and Cognitive Psychotherapy*, 30, 365–74.

Would-be jumper gets "helping" hand. (2009, April 23). China Daily.com. Retrieved April 23, 2009, from: http://www.chinadaily.com.cn/china/2009-05/23/content_7935489.htm.

Wright, C. D., Mather, W., & Swaysland, E. (1906). *Report of the Commission on Industrial and Technical Education*. New York: Teachers College Press.

Wright, R. O. (2005). *Chronology of public health in the United States*. Jefferson, NC: McFarland.

Yorinks, A., & Egielski, R. (2009). *Homework*. New York: Walker.

Yukich, J., Schaetzle, B., Falk, J., Shatner, W., Burger, M., Dias Blue, A., Biggers, S., English, T., Méteigner, J. F., Stratta, A., Yamaguchi, R., Simon, K., Samuelsson, M., Ferguson, J., Terebijon, F., & Kaisha, K. (2002). *Iron chef USA* [DVD]. Santa Monica, CA: Lions Gate Home Entertainment.

Zeleny, J. (2010, March 1). Obama backs rewarding districts that police failing schools. *New York Times*. Retrieved March 1, 2010, from: http://www.nytimes.com/2010/03/02/us/02obama.html.

Zimbalist, A. S. (2006). *The bottom line: Observations and arguments on the sports business*. Philadelphia, PA: Temple University Press.

Zinn, H. (2005). *A people's history of the United States: 1492–present*. New York: HarperPerennial.

Zuckerbrot, T. (2006). *The F-factor diet: Discover the secret to permanent weight loss*. New York: Putnam's Sons.

Zukowsky, J., & Thorne, M. (2004). *Masterpieces of Chicago architecture*. New York: Rizzoli.

About the Author

Gerard Giordano is a professor at the University of North Florida. He has written numerous works, including ten previous books. His most recent books were *Solving Education's Problems Effectively: A Guide to Using the Case Method* (2009) and *Cockeyed Education: A Case Method Primer* (2010). Both were published by Rowman & Littlefield.

Breinigsville, PA USA
23 November 2010

249879BV00001B/5/P